Migration and Urbanization

World Anthropology

General Editor

SOL TAX

Patrons

CLAUDE LÉVI-STRAUSS
MARGARET MEAD
LAILA SHUKRY EL HAMAMSY
M. N. SRINIVAS

MOUTON PUBLISHERS · THE HAGUE · PARIS
DISTRIBUTED IN THE USA AND CANADA BY ALDINE, CHICAGO

Migration and Urbanization

Models and Adaptive Strategies

Editors

BRIAN M. DU TOIT
HELEN I. SAFA

MOUTON PUBLISHERS · THE HAGUE · PARIS
DISTRIBUTED IN THE USA AND CANADA BY ALDINE, CHICAGO

General Editor's Preface

In all of anthropological history no set of phenomena have interested us more than the migrations of peoples, the interplay among their cultures, and the transformation of smaller societies into larger urban and national agglomerations. Yet is was appropriate to await a major International Congress for a full review of our knowledge from a post-colonial point of view. This is one of two complementary volumes which look at modern migrations as they relate to ethnicity. The other — *Migration and development*, edited primarily by Helen I. Safa — deals particularly with problems of group identity and of inequality and power. The two together bring to the social sciences a new and very rich corpus of case material from every continent, synthesized in a series of essays by editors and commentators.

Like most contemporary sciences, anthropology is a product of the European tradition. Some argue that it is a product of colonialism, with one small and self-interested part of the species dominating the study of the whole. If we are to understand the species, our science needs substantial input from scholars who represent a variety of the world's cultures. It was a deliberate purpose of the IXth International Congress of Anthropological and Ethnological Sciences to provide impetus in this direction. The *World Anthropology* volumes, therefore, offer a first glimpse of a human science in which members from all societies have played an active role. Each of the books is designed to be self-contained; each is an attempt to update its particular sector of scientific knowledge and is written by specialists from all parts of the world. Each volume should be read and reviewed individually as a separate volume on its own given subject. The set as a whole will indicate what changes are in store for anthropology as scholars from the developing countries join in studying the species of which we are all a part.

The IXth Congress was planned from the beginning not only to include as many of the scholars from every part of the world as possible, but also with a view toward the eventual publication of the papers in high-quality volumes. At previous Congresses scholars were invited to bring papers which were then read out loud. They were necessarily limited in length; many were only summarized; there was little time for discussion; and the sparse discussion could only be in one language. The IXth Congress was an experiment aimed at changing this. Papers were written with the intention of exchanging them before the Congress, particularly in extensive pre-Congress sessions; they were not intended to be read aloud at the Congress, that time being devoted to discussions — discussions which were simultaneously and professionally translated into five languages. The method for eliciting the papers was structured to make as representative a sample as was allowable when scholarly creativity — hence self-selection — was critically important. Scholars were asked both to propose papers of their own and to suggest topics for sessions of the Congress which they might edit into volumes. All were then informed of the suggestions and encouraged to re-think their own papers and the topics. The process, therefore, was a continuous one of feedback and exchange and it has continued to be so even after the Congress. The some two thousand papers comprising *World Anthropology* certainly then offer a substantial sample of world anthropology. It has been said that anthropology is at a turning point; if this is so, these volumes will be the historical direction-markers.

As might have been foreseen in the first post-colonial generation, the large majority of the Congress papers (82 percent) are the work of scholars indentified with the industrialized world which fathered our traditional discipline and the institution of the Congress itself: Eastern Europe (15 percent); Western Europe (16 percent); North America (47 percent); Japan, South Africa, Australia, and New Zealand (4 percent). Only 18 percent of the papers are from developing areas: Africa (4 percent); Asia-Oceania (9 percent); Latin America (5 percent). Aside from the substantial representation from the U.S.S.R. and the nations of Eastern Europe, a significant difference between this corpus of written material and that of other Congresses is the addition of the large proportion of contributions from Africa, Asia, and Latin America. "Only 18 percent" is two to four times as great a proportion as that of other Congresses; moreover, 18 percent of 2,000 papers is 360 papers, 10 times the number of "Third World" papers presented at previous Congresses. In fact, these 360 papers are more than the total of ALL papers published after the last International Congress of Anthropological and Ethnological Sciences which was held in the United States (Philadelphia, 1956). Even in the beautifully organized Tokyo Congress in 1968 less than a third as many members from developing nations, including those of Asia, participated.

The significance of the increase is not simply quantitative. The input of scholars from areas which have until recently been no more than subject matter for anthropology represents both feedback and also long-awaited theoretical contributions from the perspectives of very different cultural, social, and historical traditions. Many who attended the IXth Congress were convinced that anthropology would not be the same in the future. The fact that the next Congress (India, 1978) will be our first in the "Third World" may be symbolic of the change. Meanwhile, sober consideration of the present set of books will show how much, and just where and how, our discipline is being revolutionized.

This book (and its companion volume) profited from conferences held in Oshkosh, Wisconsin, immediately before the Congress. Many of the authors could attend, and the presentations to the Congress itself could be prepared. The participants could also take advantage there of similar conferences leading to other books on related subjects in this series on *World Anthropology*. Readers of this book will also be interested in the equally rich material the other volumes provide on such subjects as ethnicity, urbanization, population, class competition, and historic developments in all parts of the world.

Chicago, Illinois   SOL TAX
July 11, 1975

Preface

The papers contained in this volume were presented and discussed during a conference on Migration and Ethnicity, held in Oshkosh, Wisconsin, during late August, 1973. This was one of a number of conferences which preceded the IXth International Congress of Anthropological and Ethnological Sciences which convened under the presidency of Sol Tax in Chicago. The conference had a dual aim, to bring together scholars from as many countries as possible and for these persons to contribute theoretical and empirical essays dealing with the study of migration. A secondary theme was the significance of ethnic consciousness and the importance of ethnicity in studies of migration. This latter subject is treated in greater detail in a companion volume to the present study, *Migration and development: implications for ethnic identity and political conflict,* edited by Helen I. Safa and Brian M. du Toit.

In our selection of participants to whom invitations were sent, the organizers attempted to cover as wide a geographical distribution as possible. This does not imply that we included all persons who are conducting significant research on migration, nor did we necessarily include the best-known persons in this field. Due to the time and venue of the conference a number of persons were not able to prepare papers. When during the final weeks it became clear that travel funds were not forthcoming, a number of scholars were forced to withdraw. We are extremely grateful to those persons who could attend the conference on their own funds or with local funding and to those persons who submitted their papers in spite of the fact that they could not be present. This latter group included a number of foreign academicians. Those persons who did attend the session in Oshkosh produced a most stimulating and critical forum in which to present papers and share ideas.

A volume of this nature results in more than simply an editorial relation-ship. It follows almost two years of talking and planning, and took shape during a week when participants and discussants met in formal sessions, talked informally, argued, agreed, and shared ideas and field experiences.

We appreciate the contributions of participants and discussants who combined to make this volume possible.

We would also express our gratitude to Jim Riddell and his team of student assistants from the University of Wisconsin-Oshkosh who oper-ated on less than half a shoestring budget in handling local arrangements. Numerous residents of Oshkosh offered accommodation to conference participants or participated in the "ritual" meal when visitors were entertained by local families. We owe a debt to Karen Tkach who acted as liaison person between conference participants and the publisher's office in The Hague and saw this volume through the press. Lastly I have to express my sincere appreciation to Helen I. Safa who was co-organizer and co-chairperson of this conference.

Durban, South Africa   BRIAN M. DU TOIT
December, 1973

Table of Contents

PART TWO: ADAPTIVE PATTERNS

Introduction
Migration and Population Mobility

BRIAN M. DU TOIT

One of the distinguishing characteristics of *Homo sapiens* is his tendency to migrate, and the frequency and distance of these movements mark him alone. This feature is due in part to the cultural adaptability which allows man to adjust to major ecological changes by employing his mental abilities and technological skills. These same tendencies and abilities may result in the mobility of a total social group, the migration of single families, or of single individuals. A combination of his animal tendency for self-preservation and his culturally defined tendency for self-improvement has resulted in the distribution of *Homo sapiens* to every part of the earth. It has also resulted in population concentrations where man's technological know-how has produced complex machines, mechanical as well as sociopolitical. Each of these situations has its own attractions and its own adaptive requirements.

1.   The concept of MIGRATION, as will be discussed below, may apply to various forms of population movement. It may also imply a smaller or larger degree of volition on the part of the migrant.

While not attempting here any kind of a compendium of migration, it would be useful to point to some of the major forms human migration takes. First and foremost we should distinguish between FORCED and VOLUNTARY migration. In the case of the former, the person who is migrating has either no decision or hardly any say about the decision to migrate. We may distinguish between cases where persons are physically removed from one place to another (as happened during conditions of slavery, in times of war, and in some of the African relocation programs in South Africa) and cases with a degree of volition, even if it implies the choice between life and likely death (these would include the flight of persons during the anti-Semitic legal crackdown in Nazi-Germany or the escape from an endangered area such as followed the eruption of Mt. Lamington).

Not all persons, for instance, who are classified by the United Nations as DISPLACED PERSONS or REFUGEES would fall in this first category. A refugee is defined as "a person who has left, or who is outside of, his country of nationality or of formal habitual residence." This is particularly true of victims of Nazi or fascist regimes, and persons who are unable or unwilling to avail themselves of the protection of their governments. There is in many cases, then, a degree of choice which would remove such persons from the category of forced migrants. This may not be true of a person strictly defined as a displaced person. Here we have to include anybody who "has been deported from or has been obliged to leave his country of nationality or of former habitual residence." Included here are persons who are compelled to leave for racial, religious, or political reasons (United Nations 1947: 816).

Most persons who migrate do so for a variety of voluntary reasons. The decision to move is based on choice. We could include here the migration of total communities, e.g. the seasonal migration of hunters and gatherers, riverine agriculturalists, or nomads. The movement of such cattle, camel, or reindeer herders has been well-documented in anthropological literature.

To a major degree, persons in both the involuntary migration and the voluntary seasonal migration have little to say about the migration. It is forced on them either by sociopolitical or by ecological conditions. In recent years social scientists have increasingly turned their attention to population movements within the same country and between different countries. They have looked at movements of people between different regions: between rural and urban areas as well as intercity and intracity migration. In all of these cases the decision to move followed an evaluation and weighing of factors but the migrant was frequently not conscious of the factors that prompted his move. As research gained in volume it was possible to construct various migration selectivity differentials such as age, sex, or intelligence.

It was frequently suggested that more men than women migrate, that the younger adults are more likely to move than older people, or that the more intelligent members of a community tend towards migration. Thus Petersen suggests that either the less or the more intelligent tend to leave their traditional homes. "In the competition to achieve satisfactory living conditions, by and large, the more intelligent will succeed more often and the less so will thus be forced 'to seek their fortunes elsewhere.'" But the other side of the coin suggests that "in any population it will be the MORE ADAPTABLE, that is to say, the MORE INTELLIGENT, who will respond first to an impetus to emigrate, and the DULLER who will remain behind (1969: 271; emphasis added). As a social anthropologist I have some difficulty in equating intelligence *per se* with adaptability. I also wonder why the sociocultural aspects are almost completely ignored. To return to the possibility of biological or physiological selectivity differentials, the international evidence seems negative. At the International Population Conference in 1961, Donald Bogue suggested that apart from age "...further differentials do not exist and should not be expected to exist" (Jansen 1969: 63). With reference to particular situations and countries, researchers have with justification continued to use such differentials in their hypotheses and models. Even if we agree with Bogue that age is the only significant differential in migration, the effects of the age, sex, etc. of migrants are important. They touch not only the migrant and those closest to him but also the sending and the receiving communities. If he is a unit of labor to the latter he is also a unit lost to the former community. The migration may affect the economy, housing, population density, schooling, and other aspects of both communities. Research should ideally look at both ends of the continuum, partly due to the contact migrants may retain and partly because some migrants, ultimately, return.

In the previous paragraph I suggested that more attention should be given to sociocultural aspects which might allow for an understanding of migration. Migration in any intensity is unlikely to occur in a small isolated community. The larger the community and the more varied its external contacts the greater the diversity of choices. As choice increases so does cultural diversity and the likelihood of cultural marginality. It is exactly this point, I would suggest, which should be kept in mind as we study causes of and stimuli for migration. This does not suggest that only culturally marginal persons will migrate or that all persons who find themselves in such a marginal position will move away. It does, however, suggest that persons who are marginal due to exposure, experiences, and knowledge or who are dissatisfied and frustrated with their conditions will tend to migrate. Cultural marginality does not posit the criteria of intelligence, age, or sex; it may require a person to have seen or heard that the grass is greener on the other side. It does suggest that the likely migrant will be a person not completely satisfied with his conditions and a person who knows that his community permits something to be done about these conditions. Migration may be a form of escape or the following of a star; it may produce a reduction in fear or frustration or it may result in aiming for new hopes and ideals.

2.   Ever since Ravenstein (1885) started looking for the "laws" of human migration, scientists have attempted to discern regularity and predictability in population movements. Some of the earliest studies were concerned with European population movements and particularly the migration waves which brought Europeans to the United States (e.g. Thomas and Znaniecki 1927). As the movement of people continued and the city became the major destination for both immigrants from other countries and large numbers of the American rural population, academicians started to search for ways of understanding such urban migration. The urban sociologists who flourished at Chicago during the second and third decades of this century developed the now famous concentric theory of urban structure. In the transitional zone of old structures and older homes, small industry was taking over and the immigrants were finding a temporary footing (Park, Burgess, and McKenzie 1925).

Stimulated by the growing interest in subgroups and migrant groups, the Social Science Research Council financed a study on migration, and Dorothy Thomas, the author of the report, placed emphasis on a methodology for the study of migration. In her view, case studies are needed to understand fully the persons under study, as well as statistical data to be sure of the research sample. Both the case material and statistical analyses must be seen against the ecological setting to understand points of origin and points of destination (D. Thomas 1938: 162–67).

Relatively few migration studies have attempted to meet this combined methodological requirement. Perhaps due to the fact that anthropologists, with their disciplinary preoccupation with the total person, have only recently started to conduct migration studies, one finds that such earlier works are usually statistical analyses which lack detailed case studies. One of the exceptions to this must be the carefully planned Beech Creek Study dealing with migrants who leave the Kentucky mountains. The research team in this case (see Brown, Schwarzweller, and Mangalam 1963 for an initial statement) assured the inclusion of a large number of structured interviews which produced empirical material for statistical analysis and participant observation of family groups. These case studies provided the material for well-documented case history analysis.

An increasing number of studies have been conducted which deal with the mobility theme in a variety of contexts such as intercontinental migration, intercountry migration, migration between states in the same country, and especially rural-urban migration. This emphasis resulted from the supposed contrasting life styles. The emphasis in rural-urban migration is usually with wage laborers, age groups, the depopulation of the farm, or similar categories. Recent studies have appeared which look specifically at urbanization and at intercity or intracity migration. All of these studies qualify under the general term of migration studies.

The concept of migration, however, should be clearly understood. Meyer Fortes has distinguished between MOBILITY, which represents movement within boundaries, and MIGRATION, in which persons cross boundaries (1971:1). Such boundaries may be geographical, structural, ethnic, or some other division which is recognized by the actor as setting him apart. Thus, when a person migrates to the city he is faced with the challenge of mobility within the new setting. This mobility may require a new life style, new attitudes, and new behavioral forms. Just as the migrant has been socialized into his rural life ways, so he now must learn the new social structure of the city (Hanson and Simmons 1968). This PROCESS (Mayer 1970: xviii) of socialization allows the migration of a person to become a mobility process. It allows the researcher then to record behavioral changes in individuals as these persons are trying new roles in adjusting to the changed setting. Most writers who define migration tend to speak only of the physical transition from one geographical area to another. Thus Beijer distinguished between migrations which are based on choice and those which are involuntary (1969:13) but accepts for his definition simply the "movement of a person or persons involving a permanent change of residence." Eisenstadt goes one step further in pointing out that "this transition usually involves abandoning one social setting and entering another and different one" (1955:1). It is infrequently that one finds in the definition a recognition of the fact that such a move is based on a weighing of advantages and disadvantages, and also that the interaction pattern of the migrant changes. For the theme of this discussion the following definition will be accepted:

Migration is a relatively permanent moving away of a collectivity, called migrants, from one geographical location to another, preceded by decision-making on the part of the migrants on the basis of a hierarchically ordered set of values or valued ends and resulting in changes in the interactional system of the migrants (Mangalam 1968:8).

For a long time there has been a tendency to see migration as resulting basically from the weighing of various economic factors (B. Thomas 1954) and the decision to move as being triggered by priority in the "push-pull" of economics. A number of studies have looked at migration and specifically asked the question regarding incentives and reasons for migration. In many cases, and this may be a product of the theoretical approach and the methodology the researcher employed, an emphasis on non-economic factors is found along with a disclaimer that migration was caused primarily by economic reasons (Bogue 1959; Petersen 1955; Tarver 1961). These latter studies in fact emphasize reasons already discussed many years ago for the migration of Polish peasants, among whom a combination of social and individual phenomena was influential. Here Thomas and Znaniecki recognized the mutual influence of values and attitudes which combine to become a forceful stimulus to move. If these factors are important in the stimulus to move, they are even more important in the adjustment of the migrant when he gets to the destination. Eisenstadt (1955) found that the migrant's basic motivation and his role expectations were the critical factors in triggering the move and in fostering the absorption of the migrant into the new community.

Perhaps due to the fact that urban migration studies were based almost exclusively on Western European cases, numerous misconceptions resulted. One of the most serious was the idea that *anomie* resulted because, it was said, people who moved to the city lost their kinship bonds and became individualistic. The extended family was thought to be dysfunctional for an industrial society:[1] one could not have both a healthy dynamic industrial society and persons who maintain and employ kinship relations. As cross-cultural studies appeared and as anthropologists and sociologists turned to study urbanization outside Western Europe and the United States, this misconception was first questioned and then rectified.

People tend to migrate to places where they already have kinsmen. An Australian aboriginal may go 200 miles to a place where he is "known" rather than 10 miles to a place where he is not. "Usually being KNOWN means having kinsfolk who will receive him and act as his sponsors..." (Beckett 1965:9). Such support and direction in migration is also found among people of the Middle East (Knowlton 1955) and in Africa, as will be discussed below. Soon researchers were finding that kinsmen determine the direction of individual migration among young people in Canada (Kohl and Bennett 1965; Piddington 1965:148–49) and even among white Americans in Buffalo (Litwak 1960) and Indianapolis (Smith 1956). This, of course, had always been the case, but it had not been recognized before the gradual change in theory in urban research.

Many social scientists in the United States had also held that the great mobility and the kind of living conditions which resulted from urban residence would naturally lead to a breakdown in kinship ties and an isolated nuclear family with an individual household arrangement (Davis 1949:422; Mead 1948; Parsons 1954; Wirth 1938). It was argued

---

[1] One of the earliest statements to this effect may be that of Max Weber (1950:111) though sociologists generally tended to accept it for a long time.

that even though kinship ties might retain their significance for non-Westerners under urban conditions, this was normal since these people had usually had stronger lineal and clan bonds and been exposed to urban conditions much more recently. However, studies by Axelrod (1956), Bell and Boat (1957), Rose and Warshay (1957), and others have emphasized the fact that rural kinship ties are maintained by Americans after settling in the city, and that urban kinship ties can serve as an important primary group in assisting the migrants' adjustment to the city. Southerners, in the United States of America, in fact, strive to reinforce kin ties or to create pseudo-kin relationships in the city (Blumberg and Bell 1959) in much the same way as the Batak in Sumatra extends his kinship system in the city (Bruner 1961; 1963:6–8). These kin relationships, within the city or between persons in the city and their rural kinsmen, retain their significance and are drawn on in time of need.

In spite of the fact that Latin America represents different traditions and forces of change we find much the same information for migrants to cities.[2] Lewis, discussing Tepoztecans who migrated to Mexico City, explains that "in all cases during this period, the migrants came to live with relatives or *compadres* [ritual kinsmen]" (1965:428). One finds then that the *barrios marginales* or *villas miserias* [urban slums] of Buenos Aires and the Spanish speaking world, as well as the *favelas* [urban slums] of Rio de Janeiro, are in fact occupied by rural migrants who either had prior kinship relations, or have created such in the city. One finds, too, that *compadrazgo* [ritual kinship] and friendship from the rural area or town is carried over to the city (Mangin 1965:315).

In the same way, migrants to Mexico City go to "the doorstep of a relative or *compadre*" (Butterworth 1970:102). Much the same picture emerges from Morse's historical survey of urbanization (1965) and especially his earlier study of function and structure in Latin American cities. Referring to various UNESCO reports, he states:

In the *favelas* of Rio de Janeiro, to be sure, Pearse found only 17 "nuclear families with accretions" in a total of 279 families studied. He also found, however, that migrants to the city came as links in a chain of kin groups "both preceded and followed by kin in persistent movement citywards." City dwellers

---

[2] In contrast to Africa and other extensive regions, Latin America, when considered superficially, represents a fair degree of uniformity with Spanish and Portuguese language and cultural influences; Roman Catholicism as standard religion; the *indigena* constituting a social category rather than racial group (Mörner [1967:145] sees them as forming a subculture of *Lumpenproletariat* — *Lumpen* meaning 'scum' or 'riff-raff' — a term since used by van den Berghe [1970] to refer to the Africans in South Africa); and large landed estates in the hands of a small oligarchy. This latter characteristic is the process of modification due to programs of land reform.

give every assistance to in-migrants belonging to their kin group. New groups are created within the city by marriages, and the appointment of godparents may either reinforce existing groups or extend them by incorporation of non-kin. Visiting tends to occur among kin-groups, families of the same or different *favelas* rather than among neighbors. Little sentiment attaches to the geographic neighborhood, and attendance at general gatherings for the public is not well looked upon. The kin group serves as "the dominant and almost exclusive sanction group" for the behavior, protection and collective action of its members (1962:478).

Much the same information is available for London, where urban dwellers maintain ties with kinsmen in the country and visit them regularly (Hubert 1965:65). [3] This "going home" sounds a great deal like the African who is going *ekhaya* [home], or the Indian who maintains contact and returns to his rural family in times of crisis (Crane 1955; Eames 1954; Ishwaran 1965). In the city we also find the cushion effect of kinsmen to whom the migrant goes and among whom he finds comforting cultural similarities to the ruralness of his origin. These kin-based associations are common in Cairo (Abu-Lughod 1961), and India (Gould 1965:15–46; Sovani 1966: 72), and form the major basis for informal groupings among the urbanized Maori (Metge 1964).

This very concise survey of literature on migration, both in Western European countries and further afield, throws a sharp question mark behind the old idea that one could not have industrialization (*cum* urbanization) and the effectively functioning extended family. In the appendix to a volume dealing with kinship geographical mobility, Christopher (1965:184) concludes that: the extended family is not necessarily a hindrance to industrialization; the extended family may well be a positive force in making industrialization speedier than it otherwise could be; social policies inimical to the extended family should be seriously reconsidered; and prognostications based on the assumption that with industrialization will come the weakening and perhaps disappearance of the extended family should be supplemented by forecasts based on the contrary assumption.

3.   Eighteen months before the IXth International Congress of Anthropological and Ethnological Sciences, the idea of a session on migration was discussed. Safa and du Toit at that stage contacted an international body of social scientists, inviting them to participate in a pre-Congress conference. At a slightly later stage it was decided to use the theme of

---

[3] While not speaking of rural-urban ties, Young and Willmott (1962:114–118) show convincingly the great importance of kinship for people moving to or living in Bethnal Green.

ETHNICITY as a qualifier for the session. The initial response was very good but as summer turned to winter, or winter to summer in the northern hemisphere, participation declined. This was due, no doubt, to the lack of funds for travel support. The resultant conference was a lively session, but one in which only six of the authors in this volume were in attendance.

The first two papers of the present volume, by Cardona and Simmons and by du Toit, aim at developing models for the study and understanding of migration. While they deal specifically with Latin America and southern Africa respectively, they have wider applicability. Models, of course, are useful but they should not form ends in themselves. The model is simply a tool, a device for collecting the kind of information the researcher sees as important, or a device which guides the organization and analysis of the information. The model is related to the theoretical approach of the researcher; it may be presented visually or schematically, and it may be a relatively simple outline or consist of a complex system with subsystems. Both papers present a variation of the evaluation of the aspects model schematically presented by positive and negative symbols. Both papers also treat the wider (sociocultural rather than single-cause) factors. Thus Cardona and Simmons concentrate on migration directly to cities due to acculturative forces which allow for the recognition of certain similarities between rural and urban conditions. They postulate, then, that as the similarity in cultural terms between two areas increases, the migratory movement between them will also increase. The first two papers, while studying different geographical regions, are actually complementary. Together they set the stage for the detailed studies which follow.

Methodologically McGee's study of Malays in Kuala Lumpur should be set apart. The author uses twenty-eight indices to measure the URBAN ADAPTABILITY of this subject and these indices, divided into seven major sectors, are then presented in a hologram. In addition to these measures, the author presents a brief ethnography of each of his key subjects. As he states, the attempt is to see each individual in the context of his urban situation. The attempt is most satisfying. Whiteford and Adams present material collected by the senior author dealing with Bolivian migrants in Argentina. Halpern and Lattes, writing about Yugoslavia and Argentina respectively, are dealing at the macro-level with national and even international patterns. The use of census data to analyze macro-demography is well illustrated by the last of the two authors.

The second section contains a number of field studies of migrants. Gonzalez presents an in-depth study of migration based largely on one group of Dominican siblings. Kemper describes the urban social adaptation of Tzintzuntzan peasants in Mexico City while Schreiber illuminates the marginal position of southern Italians who go north as migrant laborers. Schildkrout looks at the ethnic complexity that is Kumasi and singles out the Mossi for detailed scrutiny, while Southall roams the African scene as he points at the structural and cultural variables which produce similar ethnic relations and linkages.

Without attempting in any way to summarize the excellent papers which follow, I would like to deal briefly with a few themes which seem to emerge from these sudies. It is significant that whereas the conference organizers spoke merely of MIGRATION, almost every paper deals with URBAN MIGRATION. This may in fact be a reflection of current anthropological preoccupation with urban studies. But the emphasis was more on urban adaptation than on the question of the kind of persons who migrate to cities or elsewhere. Cardona and Simmons suggest that age and education are variables which affect the frequency (and perhaps predictability) of migration, and that women migrate with greater frequency. Lattes, in his analysis of census data, finds that foreign immigration is also marked by age and literacy, but that males predominate, as was found by Schreiber in her study of southern Italians. The criterion of education is also mentioned by González who suggests that pigmentation, or "the racial factor," emerged as a second variable in her study of Dominicans.

As regards the actual migration, Halpern states that in Yugoslavia the KIN NETWORK forms a kind of bridge which operates between villages and city in both directions. It is often through kin or fellow villagers that initial educational and employment opportunities are perceived and activated. The same is true for the Dominican situation. But migration may also intensify identification both between fellow migrants in a strange setting and between the migrant and his natal community. Thus Schreiber states that migration increased the ethnic consciousness of southern Italians and made them feel more consciously members of their home community.

The migratory path and the initial adaptation in the new setting repeatedly involve kinsmen, home boys, or joking group members – thus ethnicity. Whiteford and Adams explain the significance of "contacts" who smooth over the initial period of urban adjustment and job hunting for Bolivians. This is also true for Tzintzuntzan migrants who utilize ties with those who have preceded them to Mexico City. Schreiber makes an important point in her statement that Sicilian villagers feel closer to New York City and Boston, where they have kinsmen, than to Rome. The significance of home boy ties and associations in Africa is once again emphasized by Southall with reference to Zambia where such ties form the basis for labor organizations and also for the United National Independence Party.

In the second part of this Introduction it was stated that frequently urban kinship ties serve as an important basis for migrant adjustment in the city and in some cases pseudo-kin relationships are created. Schildkrout states that the rural-born Mossi migrants to Kumasi often voluntarily contract kinship relationships by the metaphorical use of kinship terms and the performance of kinship roles. She also illustrates how joking (both in address and behavior) is used between individuals who do not know each other, as a way of placing each other in familiar categories.

It is a well-documented fact that ethnicity frequently underlies the formation of voluntary associations, especially among recent arrivals in a strange setting. This topic has been well-illustrated in anthropological literature. The papers in this volume do not specifically treat voluntary associations but a number of authors remark on the significance of their absence. Kemper has shown that in the absence of such associations the Tzintzuntzanos' social organization must rest solely on kinship, friendship, or *compadrazgo* ties. Whiteford and Adams mention the presence of voluntary associations among Bolivian peasant migrants but many urban proletarians participate in a form of voluntary associations – the *fiesta* complex. The complex is an adaptive institution, supporting the Bolivians' self-identity as Bolivians in a foreign country.

A topic about which much has been written is the degree to which the city constitutes a strange and novel type of milieu, requiring new adaptations and foreign institutions. Many authors have written on the subject as though the city represents a completely strange and uniquely organized phenomenon. Increasingly, anthropologists have shown that the life in any city can best be understood with reference to the total setting within which it operates. This has called for the acceptance of two concepts, namely cultural continuity and situational behavior. Neither of those presuppose or require the acceptance of primeval, tribal, or primitive behavioral patterns, but demand ethnic and cultural variables and values which may be held and acted out in diverse physical and social settings.

McGee speaks to the point when he states that we tend to underestimate the capacity of a person to hold seemingly antithetical attitudes at the same time and the range of choice such persons have in deciding on certain actions. He goes on to suggest that the longer a person has resided in Kuala Lampur, the more capable he is of adapting to the urban pitfalls of "urbanized" or "urban commitment," but he speaks of the ability to adapt, thus the person's familiarity with varying choices and alternate modes of behavior. He concludes that the majority of his Malay subjects are rural people and urban people at the same time. Both González and Halpern speak of migrants who retain a rural foothold while they are in the city or even abroad. Since they have this frame of reference they may also retain some of the attitudes and behavior patterns of the traditional culture. And so we find that the social patterns of Dominican migrants to Santiago and to New York City tend to resemble those in the country areas from which they came more than they resemble those of each other after migration has taken place.

While we certainly agree with Cardona and Simmons who state that migrants change as they adapt to the city, we must also recognize that the city ultimately reflects the life ways and values of its residents. Thus González states that being in the city, *per se*, is not a sufficiently strong socializing force to create homogeneity. McGee concludes that ultimately the individual is the product of his society, not of his city.

REFERENCES

ABU-LUGHOD, J.
> 1961 Migrant adjustment to city life. *The American Journal of Sociology* 67:22-32.

AXELROD, MORRIS
> 1956 Urban structures and social participation. *American Sociological Review* 21:13-18.

BECKETT, JEREMY R.
> 1965 "Kinship, mobility and community among part-Aborigines in rural Australia," in *Kinship and geographical mobility*. Edited by Ralph Piddington. Leiden: E. J. Brill.

BEIJER, G.
> 1969 "Modern patterns of international migratory movements," in *Migration*. Edited by J. A. Jackson, 11-59. Cambridge: Cambridge University Press.

BELL, WENDELL, MARION D. BOAT
> 1957 Urban neighborhoods and informal social relations. *The American Journal of Sociology* 62:391-398.

BLUMBERG, LEONARD, ROBERT R. BELL
> 1959 Urban migration and kinship ties. *Social Problems* 6:328-333.

BOGUE, DONALD J.
> 1959 "Internal Migration," in *The study of population*. Edited by Philip Hauser and Otis Dudley Duncan. Chicago: University of Chicago Press.

BROWN, JAMES S., HARRY K. SCHWARZWELLER, JOSEPH G. MANGALAM
> 1963 Initial statement in Kentucky mountain migration and the Stem family. An American variation on a theme by Le Play. *Rural Sociology* 28:48-69.

BRUNER, EDWARD M.
> 1961 Urbanization and ethnic identity in North Sumatra. *American Anthropologist* 63:508-521.

1963 "The role of kinship in an Indonesian city," in *Pacific port towns and cities.* Edited by Alexander Spoehr. Honolulu: B. P. Bishop Museum Press.

BUTTERWORTH, DOUGLAS S.
1970 "A study of the urbanization process among Mixtec migrants from Tilantongo in Mexico City," in *Peasants and cities.* Edited by William Mangin. Boston: Houghton Mifflin.

CHRISTOPHER, S. C.
1965 "A note on research relevant to the extended family and geographical mobility," in *Kinship and geographical mobility.* Edited by Ralph Piddington. Leiden: E. J. Brill.

CRANE, ROBERT I.
1955 Urbanism in India. *The American Journal of Sociology* 60: 463-470.

DAVIS, KINGSLEY
1949 *Human society.* New York: MacMillan.

EAMES, E.
1954 Some aspects of urban migration from a village in north central India. *Eastern Anthropology* 8:13-26.

EISENSTADT, S. N.
1955 *The Absorption of Immigrants.* Glencoe, Ill.: The Free Press.

FORTES, MEYER
1971 Some aspects of migration and mobility in Ghana. *Journal of Asian and African Studies.*

GOULD, HAROLD A.
1965 "Lucknow Rickshawallas: the social organisation of an occupational category," in *Kinship and geographical mobility.* Edited by Ralf Piddington. Leiden: E. J. Brill.

HANSON, R. C., O. G. SIMMONS
1968 The role of Path. A concept and procedure for studying migration to urban communities. *Human Organization* 27:152-158.

HUBERT, JANE
1965 "Kinship and geographical mobility in a sample from a London middle-class area," in *Kinship and geographical mobility.* Edited by Ralph Piddington. Leiden: E. J. Brill.

HUTTON, CAROLINE
1970 "Rates of labour migration," in *Urban growth in Subsahara Africa.* Edited by Josef Gugler. Nkanga Editions 6, Makerere Institute of Social Research.

ISHWARAN, K.
1965 "Kinship and distance in rural India," in *Kinship and geographical mobility.* Edited by Ralph Piddington. Leiden: E. J. Brill.

JANSEN, C.
1969 "Some sociological aspects of migration," in *Migration.* Edited by J. A. Jackson, 60-73. Cambridge: Cambridge University Press.

KNOWLTON, CLARK S.
1955 "Spatial and social mobility of Syrians and Lebanese: in the city of Sao Paulo, Brazil." Unpublished Ph. D. dissertation, Vanderbilt University.

KOHL, SEENA, JOHN W. BENNETT
  1965   "Kinship, succession, and the migration of young people in a Canadian agricultural community," in *Kinship and geographical mobility*. Edited by Ralph Piddington. Leiden: E. J. Brill.
LEWIS, OSCAR
  1965   "Urbanization without breakdown: a case study," in *Contemporary cultures and societies of Latin America*. Edited by Dwight B. Heath and Richard N. Adams. New York: Random House.
LITWAK, EUGENE
  1960   Geographic mobility and extended family cohesion. *American Sociological Review* 25:385-394.
MANGALAM, J.
  1968   *Human migration*. Lexington: University of Kentucky Press.
MANGIN, WILLIAM P.
  1965   "The role of regional associations in the adaptation of rural migrants to cities in Peru," in *Contemporary cultures and societies of Latin America*. Edited by Dwight B. Heath and Richard N. Adams. New York: Random House.
MAYER, P.
  1970   "Introduction," in *Socialization: the approach from social anthropology*. Edited by P. Mayer. London: Tavistock Publications.
MEAD, MARGARET
  1948   The contemporary American family as an anthropologist sees it. *The American Journal of Sociology* 53:453-459
METGE, JOAN
  1964   *A new Maorie migration*. London School of Economics Monographs on Social Anthropology 27. London: Athlone Press.
MÖRNER, MAGNUS
  1967   *Race mixture in the history of Latin America*. Boston: Little, Brown.
MORSE, RICHARD M.
  1962   Latin American cities: aspects of function and structure. *Comparative Studies in Society and History* 4 (4).
  1965   Recent research on Latin American urbanization: a selective survey with commentary. *Latin American Research Review* 1 (1):35-74.
PARK, R. E., E. W. BURGESS, R. D. MC KENZIE
  1925   *The city*. Chicago.
PARSONS, TALCOTT
  1954   "The kinship system of the contemporary United States," in *Essays in sociological thought*. Edited by Talcott Parsons. Glencoe, Ill.: The Free Press.
PETERSEN, WILLIAM
  1955   *Planned migration: the social determinants of the Dutch-Canadian movement*. Berkeley: University of California Press.
  1969   *Population* (second edition). London: Macmillan.
PIDDINGTON, RALPH
  1965   "The kinship network among French Canadians," in *Kinship and geographical mobility*. Leiden: E. J. Brill.
RAVENSTEIN, E. G.
  1885   The laws of migration. *Journal of the Royal Statistical Society* 48.

ROSE, ARNOLD M., LEON WARSHAY
1957   The adjustment of migrants to cities. *Social Forces* 36:72-76.
SMITH, ELDON D.
1956   Non-farm employment information for rural people. *Journal of Farm Economics* 38:813-827.
SOVANI, N.V.
1966   *Urbanization and urban India.* New York: Asia Publishing House.
TARVER, JAMES D.
1961   Predicting migration. *Social Forces* 39:207-213.
THOMAS, BRINLEY
1954   *Migration and economic growth.* Cambridge: Cambridge University Press.
THOMAS, DOROTHY SWAINE
1938   *Research memorandum on migration differentials.* New York: Social Science Research Council.
THOMAS, W. I., FLORIAN ZNANIECKI
1927   *Polish peasant in Europe and America,* two volumes. New York: Alfred Knopf.
UNITED NATIONS
1947   *Yearbook of the United Nations, 1946-1947.* New York.
VAN DEN BERGHE, PIERRE L.
1970   "Race, class and ethnicity in South Africa," in *Social stratification in Africa.* Edited by Arthur Tuden and Leonard Plotnicov. New York: The Free Press.
WEBER, MAX
1950   *General economic history.* Translated by F. H. Knight. New York: The Free Press.
WIRTH, LOUIS
1938   Urbanism as a way of life. *The American Journal of Sociology* 44:1-24.
YOUNG, MICHAEL, PETER WILLMOTT
1962   *Family and kinship in East London.* Pelican Books.

PART ONE

Models

Toward a Model of Migration
in Latin America

RAMIRO CARDONA, ALAN SIMMONS

It continues to be a paradox that such an important fact as the accelerated urbanization of Latin America remains unknown. The conclusions drawn from studies on the patterns of internal migration in various parts of the world are no more advanced than those done more than a hundred years ago by the English historian Ravenstein (1889).[1]

As long ago as 1940 there existed four cities in Latin America with more than 1,000,000 inhabitants, four with populations between 500,000 and 950,000, and eight with populations between 125,000 and 500,000. In 1960, twenty years later, Latin America had ten cities with more than 1,000,000 inhabitants. (Map 1 shows the increase of the urban population in Latin America during several periods.) Perhaps what best characterizes this migratory process is that it has been an important cause of the economic, social, and ecological transformations that these countries experience today. In effect, we know that migration has been selective, that a substantial proportion of the migrants are young and innovative, and that their economic resources and their education are greater than those of persons who have remained in their place of origin. We know also that of these young people, it is the women who tend to move in greater numbers to the large cities.[2]

It is clear that this selectivity affects the places where migration originates as much as the places where it ends. The standards of masculinity[3] and the structure by age are altered in both places equally. Nevertheless,

---

[1] There is a recent and valuable review of Ravenstein in Lee (1966).
[2] As will be seen later, some countries, for example Peru, show the opposite tendency: the men form the larger portion of the migration to the large cities. See Note 9.
[3] Proportion of men in relation to women.

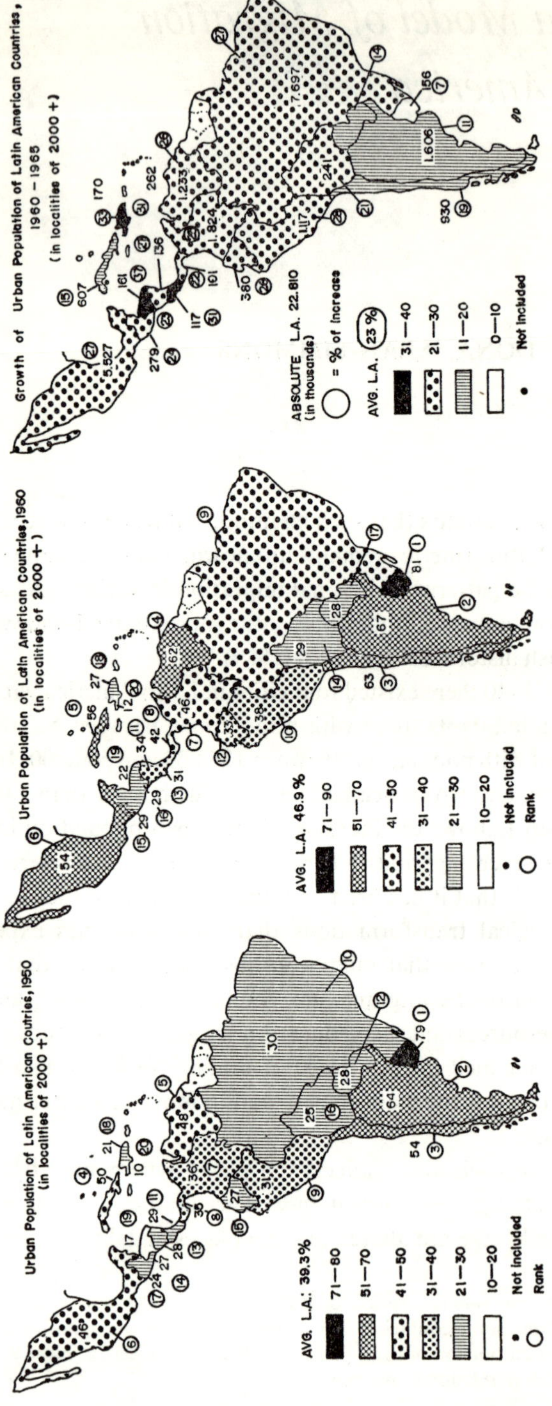

SOURCE: Walter D. Harris The growth of Latin American Cities, (Ohio University Press, 1971). pp 48-50.

Map 1.   Urban population growth in Latin America, 1950-1965

what is even more important is the impact that selectivity by education, intelligence, and the capacity for planning has on the different regions in time. It is also clear that the return migration,[4] given its characteristics, plays a significant role in the areas that generate it.

Analyses of these phenomena have not sustained the most well-known and vehement positions on the migration: generally they emphasize its "negative sign" in the major cities, claiming that these cities are incapable of absorbing the additional demands. They also claim that there remains an important sign in the migrants and their families, attributing to them a high proportion of delinquency, prostitution, alcoholism, and domestic disintegration.

Some investigators are certain that the complexity of urban life itself produces a cultural shock that the migrants will not be able to overcome, and that, on the other hand, will produce a series of incompatibilities that will be translated into one or another form of erratic behavior. This in turn is reinforced by the frustration of not finding employment and by the realization that the tools that allow the migrants to compete with the urban natives are not available to them. Certainly they also are frustrated when they find that the characteristics and opportunities of the urban world are very different from what they initially thought when they made the decision to migrate.

Policies consistent with this view have been formulated with the clear, though partial, objective of stopping migration to the city.[5] Paradoxically, such policies are impelling agents for migration, in that they offer difficult alternatives, as, for example, cooperative systems of working and living which, without adequate programs for education and participation, become a stimulus for leaving, not as a result of the project but as a result of perceiving an unstructured situation for which migrating is seen as the most adequate solution.

We will delineate a preliminary model of migratory patterns in Latin America and, on the basis of this model, will establish some hypotheses with respect to the possible consequences. The model is based principally on a study conducted by the authors in Bogotá, Colombia, and sponsored by the Colombian Association of the School of Medicine and the "Population Council" (Appendix 1 lists the details of the experiment).

---

4   See notes 18 and 21.
5   There are two exceptions to the lack of focus on rural problems and agrarian reform as causes of migration in Colombia and in Peru: Martínez (1966) and Duràn and Jameson (1965).

TOWARD A MODEL OF INTERNAL MIGRATION IN LATIN AMERICA

Figure 1 schematizes some of the basic aspects related to the migratory process: the opportunities for work and the obstacles to migration.[6]

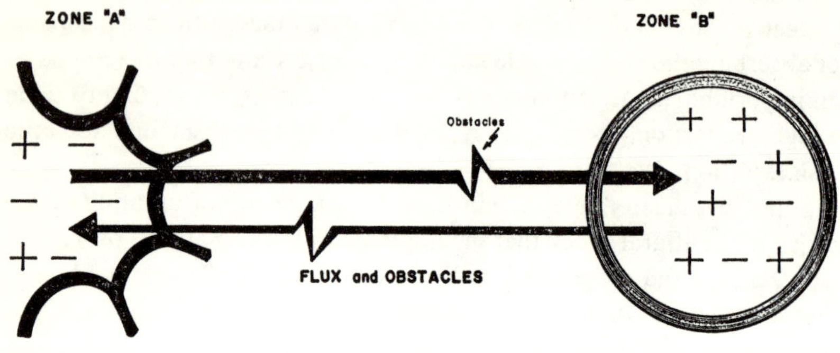

Figure 1

Opportunities for Work

At the time of the decision to migrate, each area of residence has advantages and disadvantages with respect to another area. These advantages and disadvantages are conceived in terms of social environment, political environment, and especially the different opportunities for work which they offer at the time of making the decision. The individuals motivated to migrate have distinct capabilities and ideas concerning the type of occupation they will be able to perform; it is for this reason that their migration is directed toward those places where they believe they will be able to find the best opportunities for work. Therefore some areas will experience migration but also receive migrants coming from other areas, thereby establishing movement in two directions, but of a very different intensity.

Obstacles to Migration

The obstacles to migration are basically of two types: physical, for example, distance and lack of transportation; and psychocultural, for example,

---

[6] A detailed inquiry into the different studies that have led to the effects related to the migratory process, with particular emphasis on Latin America, is presented in Appendix 2.

the lack of information and the fear of different cultural patterns and languages. In addition, there are other obstacles that intervene, principally the tendency for migration to be positively selective.[7] Another important barrier is the lack of correct information about the opportunities in other places. For example, it is possible for better opportunities to exist in nearby areas — opportunities about which the migrant is unaware. In this manner the migratory process is determined basically by the diffusion of information concerning opportunities in specific areas.

Figure 1 stresses the fact that obstacles to migration in one direction are not the same as obstacles in another; for example, the diffusion of information can be of greater intensity in one direction than in another.

Let us sum up the preceding with two general hypotheses:

1.   Changes in the structure of opportunities for work at a given moment, associated with the economic process, constitute the principal cause of migration between regions and determine the selective characteristics and patterns of acculturation of the migrants. An increase in the rural population areas where the number of opportunities is limited generates migration in toward other areas, especially by young men who are trying to incorporate themselves into the work force.

2.   The existence of physical and psychocultural obstacles to migration determines that the relationship between relative opportunities in two areas and the migration from one area to another are always different.

The two hypotheses of orientation established above now permit us to derive a group of working hypotheses with respect to: (a) the magnitude and direction of migration, (b) the selectivity of the migrants, (c) the process of migration, and (d) the psychological aspects of migration.

MAGNITUDE AND DIRECTION OF MIGRATION

The magnitude of total migration increases with the general diversification of the economy because the growth and change of the economic structure permits a growth in the division of labor and therefore an increase in opportunities.

In an area where the rate of immigration is higher, the corresponding rate of emigration will be lower; therefore, the migration from city to

---

[7]   With respect to the impact of migration on economic development, Ravenstein was emphatic in considering it positive: "The process of migration moved human resources from regions with few economic opportunities toward places where they could contribute more to the development of the Industrial Society" (1889:225, 286).

country is lower when compared with the movement from rural areas and from small- and medium-sized urban centers to cities, where better opportunities for work and, therefore, higher salaries and the possibility for social advancement already exist.

As the number of obstacles between two areas increases, the migratory movement between them decreases. Let us distinguish between physical obstacles and psychocultural obstacles. Physical obstacles can be defined basically in terms of the cost and duration of the journey. Because the cost and the duration of a journey increase with the distance, as the distance between two areas increases, the migratory movement between them decreases. The distance factor is understood here not only as a mathematical one, but as one which encompasses such factors as the inconvenience and the difficulty of displacement.

The psychocultural obstacles refer to the difficulties which an individual will encounter in migrating to a place in which there are different cultural and economic patterns. As the similarity in cultural terms between two areas increases, the migratory movement between them increases. Persons prefer to live in zones that have cultural characteristics similar to those of their place of origin. The principal reason for this phenomenon is a desire to live in a place about which one has sufficient information in relation to possibilities for work, living, and services. Generally, those places that are better known are within the same "network" of communication, that is to say, within the same cultural area. But when economic opportunities in the cultural area of origin are not satisfactory, a movement toward the best-known places among the more economically active areas begins. Generally, the people of the more separated areas have more information about large cities, and as a result they go there.

It should be emphasized that although the information obtained through mass communication is important, personal communication from families and friends who live in the city is more relevant for the potential migrant when it is a matter of making the decision to migrate. Contrary to what is often thought, this information is very widespread, so that the migrants generally find in the place of destination an environment similar to what they thought they would find when they left their place of origin.

Because the information about different places is provided principally by personal contracts, the migration movements tend to reflect the "chains" of those contacts. This fact is more clearly seen when the migrants go to culturally different places.

SELECTIVITY OF THE MIGRANTS

Selectivity by Age

The more economically active a youth is, the less will be his integration into the work force, the fewer his familial obligations, and the smaller the probability that he will migrate to other places seeking new opportunities. It is for this reason that the highest rates of migration are found in groups of ages fifteen to twenty-five.

It is to be expected that those migrants who arrive at metropolitan areas directly from their place of origin are younger than those who have journeyed with one or two stops. Therefore a greater proportion of bachelors can be expected in this group. It is also to be expected that a significant group of men and women who range from forty-five to fifty years of age will move to the city; this group would correspond to the parents of those migrants who have already been established in the city for several years.[8]

The fact that it is the young who migrate can be interpreted as a result, first, of a clear perception by the parents of the different and greater opportunities for their children in urban areas; second, of the existence of greater generation barriers between parents and children than those found in the cities; and third, the lack of integration of the youths into the sociocultural context of the rural and less urbanized areas.

Selectivity by Sex

Although a large number of men generally move into the large cities, the phenomenon tends to occur in the areas of colonization and in the border areas. Women migrate more toward neighboring cities; however, in some cases, such as that of Peru, where large cities are far from inhabited zones, more women tend to migrate to distant places than men.[9]

---

[8] This tendency, which involves a considerable group of migrants between the ages of forty and fifty, has also been observed in Chile. See Elizaga (1970).

[9] The proportion of women who migrate over longer distances and in greater numbers, whatever the distance, varies considerably from one region to another in time. The period of migration can be especially important. In families, the men can migrate first (for work) and the women later, creating in this way a predominance of men in the first wave and a predominance of women in the second wave. See Alers and Applebaum (1968) for a review of other points in Peru, where in the last few years the number of women between fifteen and fifty-nine years of age migrating to Lima has surpassed the number of men.

According to Bogue (1963:405–411, cited by Brigg 1971) migration has historically tended to follow a series of stages. The initial invasion involves more men than women. The risks and hazards are greatest during this period. Finally, the process becomes routine and institutionalized, and the number of migrating women equals or exceeds that of men.

Capability

Because the diversification of the economy implies specialization of work, the most capable (specialized) persons in any expanding economic group will present the highest rate of migration. This results possibly from the fact that, in the city, there are fewer opportunities for illiterate people; therefore, the migration of illiterates toward these centers is small. Another reason is that illiterates are less informed about opportunities in other areas. The larger the city of the migrant's origin, the greater is the probability of his having high qualifications and the greater the probability that his migration will be oriented toward the larger metropolitan areas.

Concentration of the Capable Population

Clearly the most capable population lives in the cities, where there are more schools and greater opportunities for specialized persons. Therefore, the migration of this population occurs principally between cities, even when they are not close. The greatest proportion of migration involving long distances is between cities.

In order to overcome obstacles of distance and cultural differences it is necessary to have resources like information, economic support, and occupational abilities; therefore, the more resources a person has, the greater will be the probability of his migration. Migrants are better qualified as to occupation, education, information, and economic resources than the nonmigrants in the place of origin. The more qualified a person is, the less important will be the DISTANCE barrier. This is one of the reasons why those immigrants who cross long distances are generally the most capable.

Economic, cultural, and social obstacles that are presented to the city dweller who desires to go back to the country or a town are greater than the obstacles presented to a person from a town who desires to migrate to a city. Therefore, those who migrate from a city to a town will be more qualified than those who leave the country or town for a city. In other words, the greater opportunities in the country are for capable persons, such as technicians specialized in agriculture and businessmen who offer new or professional services (such as doctors and lawyers). These migrants to places less economically developed are "pioneer" individuals,[10] characterized by a wider vision about the possibilities offered by unknown areas and by a perspective toward a better future different from those who do not emigrate.

Changes of Selectivity in Time[11]

It was emphasized that migration is selective in two aspects: the greater education and economic resources of the migrant. It was stated that there are young adults, especially women, who tend to move to the city with greater frequency, that there are bachelors who migrate alone, that distance plays a role in the selection, that there are men who tend largely to move across long distances, and likewise women who tend to move across short distances. Finally, with respect to the size of the last residence of the migrant before he moves to the large city, it has been observed that the greater this locality in terms of population, the greater also will be the possibility that the migrant has relatively high qualifications in what is referred to as his education and his income.

The point that should be emphasized is that this selectivity is gradually weakened; likewise, changes in the characteristics of the migrants become changes in their incorporation into the economic and social structure of the city. In fact, several studies, from which we have selected those of Brasilia, Monterrey, Buenos Aires, and Bogotá, have observed this phenomenon. In Brasilia: "The first migrants tend to have more resources and tend to establish themselves and to remain permanent, while the more recent ones tend to be less established" (Wilkening 1968). In Buenos Aires: "The family income of recent migrants is less than that of the preceding ones and of the natives... The level of general education is higher among the first migrants than among the more recent migrants" (Brigg 1971, based on Germani 1959).

Some of the data for Monterrey and Bogotá allows us to maintain that the positive selectivity of migrants with respect to socioeconomic variables

---

[10] This concept has been developed initially by Browning and Feindt (1969a). See also Cardona (1968).

[11] For more information on the instruments of measurement that were used in relation to this and other aspects presented in this work, see: Cardona, Simmons, and Rodrígues-Espada (1972).

diminishes in time. In the study of Monterrey (Browning and Feindt 1969b), one reaches the conclusion that generally the migrants are positively selective with respect to the towns where they originated, but that this type of selectivity experiences a certain decline owing to the greater contribution which the more rural and backward zones have contributed to migration in recent times. The authors look for an explanation of this phenomenon in the large increase of jobs in the city at the end of World War II and in the massive growth in the means of communication that awakened interest in moving to urban zones.

Another fact which, according to the authors, is associated with this phenomenon is that the number of migrants multiplied considerably during the last decades, implying that the tendency toward selectivity decreases as the number of migrants increases. As Browning and Feindt state, the smaller selectivity is only found among those migrants who originate in the more backward socioeconomic zones; those who originate in the more advanced zones show an increase in selectivity, although the increase is smaller than the diminution in the selectivity of the migrants who come from less developed zones.

In Bogotá (Simmons and Cardona 1970), it was found that the migrants, both from small towns and from large cities, are a select group in relation to their communities of origin in terms of the status of their fathers, of their own education, and of their own status. It is claimed that even when the characteristics of the migrants do not appear to have changed systematically in the last forty years, in terms of their social origins and their education, the general progress in the educational level of their places of origin suggests that the migrant population of recent years has a smaller positive selectivity than the migrant population of former years (Múñoz et al. 1972:17, 18).

The decrease in selectivity will continue and selectivity will possibly become negative. This hypothesis is based on the following statements:
1. Selectivity decreases proportionally as migration increases and information spreads about the actual opportunities which the larger urban areas offer compared with the smaller and rural areas. This information originates substantially with friends and relatives of the potential migrants, who in turn are receiving agents and orienters in the city; thus it is they who help stimulate, but this time not necessarily selectively.
2. The necessary transformations in the agrarian sector can lead to a series of official measures in this sector, which, in introducing changes, will start an exodus toward other localities by that portion of the population that does not accept or participate in the said changes. In turn, however, these changes will motivate the most capable and ambitious to remain.

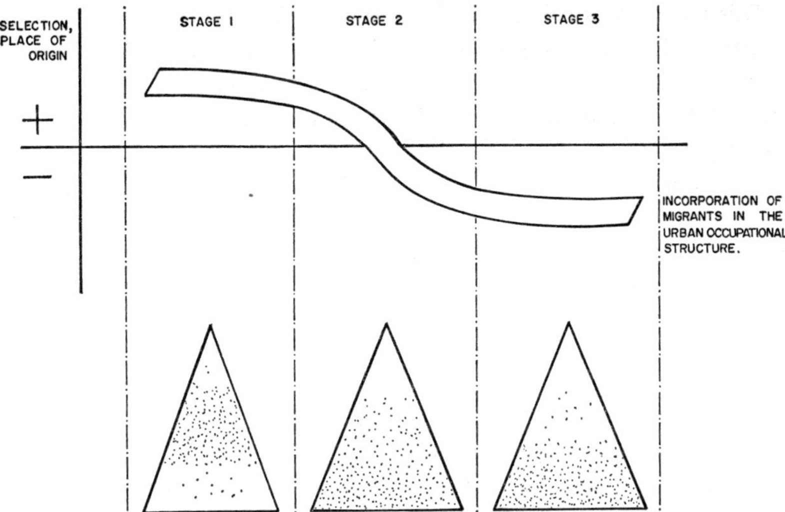

Figure 2.   Illustration of decrease in selectivity hypothesis

3.   The process of urbanization in Latin America has been accompanied by an increase in the TERTIARY SECTOR of the urban economy. A substantial part of the increase in this sector involves persons in individual occupations not institutionalized or clearly accepted (bootblacks, walking vendors, caretakers of carts, prostitutes). The "tertiarization," besides being possibly increased by the migrants, contributes in turn to motivating migration, providing opportunity for groups without any specialization. Figure 2 illustrates and sums up the hypothesis.

THE PROCESS OF MIGRATION

Migration by Stages

The fact that urban culture has rather different features than rural culture explains in some way what the migratory process has already realized principally by stages: the exit from the rural area is directed toward the nearby towns, and from these, toward the cities. It seems that in most cases this process has occurred in intergenerational stages. The destination points of migrants from rural areas have been towns and small cities, while the population that leaves the latter is oriented toward the large cities.

This tendency is being modified, however. The impact of "agents of modernization" on the rural sector, for example, on the coexistence of characteristic cultural patterns of the rural area within urban areas, lessens more and more the "cultural shock" which the migrants experience when they try to incorporate themselves into the urban world. This process gradually makes migration by stages less necessary as a mechanism of acculturation and makes direct migration more frequent. When the migration occurs over long distances it is more probable that the destination is a large city.

Residence in the City

Many investigators have observed a strong tendency among a large part of the migrant population to locate themselves in the central areas of the city during the first years of residency. They live in habitations which they rent in the so-called "tenant houses" or "little convents." It is here that a substantial part of the process of acculturation occurs. The Worldwide Congress of Turgurios clearly defined the role that these places play in the process of incorporation of migrants into the city, emphasizing that in the majority of countries where urbanization is rapid, these "tenant houses" are the only existing elements of reception and orientation.

After several years, once the migrant has incorporated himself into the city (possibly he is married and has some source of income), he will seek a more definitive location, either in the dwellings offered by government programs or in popular quarters consisting principally of clandestine places, those that are "pirated" and occupied by invasion.

These facts have been well-confirmed in other studies.[12] Recent studies conducted in Bogotá[13] suggest that the tendency of initial location in central areas is diminishing and that reception, in an ever-increasing pattern, now occurs in the popular quarters which are not located in the central areas of the city. This new fact is linked to the lack of tenant houses, which have not increased in proportion to the demand made for this type of habitation, and to the fact that in the majority of cases the houses do not fulfill the existing legal requirements.[14] This situation has encouraged the renting of habitations in the popular quarters.

[12]   A bibliography on the particulars is offered in Cardona (1969).
[13]   There were two investigations. The first was directed by Cardona and Simmons. Appendix 1 illustrates some of its characteristics. Partial analyses have been published by Cardona (1972). The second investigation was an analysis of five popular quarters in Bogotá; see Anonymous (1972).
[14]   Nevertheless, housing policies are beginning to take into account these dwellings.

Another explanation may be the existence of relatives and friends, or at least of preceding individuals from the same region, in these quarters (the first migrants did not encounter this favorable situation) who constitute a source of information and orientation, making it less necessary that the first location be in the tenant houses. The observed tendency that the popular quarters are formed, in large measure, by homogeneous groups from the same place of origin supports this hypothesis.

SOCIOLOGICAL ASPECTS OF MIGRATION

Urbanization and internal migration are clearly social processes, because their causes and consequences can be sought in terms of the society as a whole. Urbanization and internal migration are also PSYCHOLOGICAL processes, because both affect the attitudes and decisions of the migrants and are influenced by them. Thus, the causes and consequences of migration can be discussed on a social level, in terms of such factors as the distribution of opportunities of work, and on a psychological level, in terms of the migrants' attitudes and aspirations.

Often the two perspectives, social and psychological, have to be considered together in order to understand several implications of urbanization in their totality. For example, in order to analyze the effect of migration on the political events in a nation, one must take into account not only the number of inhabitants who live in the city, but also the influence of urban life on participation and political attitudes of the immigrants.

Psychological Causes of Migration

Sometimes social and psychological factors are so closely tied together in a given process that it is difficult to separate them. Studies have been made on the social characteristics (age, education, occupation, etc.) of the migrant, and in accordance with the general pattern of the results of these studies, it was concluded (in the previous section) that male migrants are RELATIVELY well-educated and occupationally prepared,

---

In Colombia, as part of the National Plan of Development, a joint program has been proposed by the Institute of Territorial Credit (the official agency of popular housing) and PROVICOP (an agency that stimulates cooperative living) for stimulating and financing the subdivision of large under-used dwellings. This program is expected to satisfy the demand for this form of habitation in transition.

in that they have a more elevated status within the family and have more resources (in money and in advantageous opportunities) for overcoming the barriers they encounter, such as finding work and establishing a new home, when they move from one place to another. This explanation is on a SOCIAL level, because it refers to the distribution of opportunities and resources among members of a society.

Nevertheless, we also know that not everyone from the same social level in semirural areas or in small towns migrates to the city; some remain and others go. It is worthwhile at this point to ask if migrants and nonmigrants from the same social level differ as to information about the opportunities, aspirations, and other psychological characteristics. It has been argued that migrants having higher aspirations are more energetic and more active. The facts which support this hypothesis, however, are extremely limited. Very few studies have compared migrants with non-migrants at the place of origin, and when such comparisons have been made, the differences in aspirations have been so related to differences in occupational status and education that it is difficult to say which is the key to the understanding of selective migration.

We can conclude tentatively that the selective migration of people belonging to a more elevated status originates in greater occupational opportunity, in greater economic resources, and in greater skills and more favorable attitudes toward changes and progress. It is presumed that migrants will probably be somewhat more "modern" in their attitudes and aspirations than non-migrants with the same education and the same occupational skills.

Psychological Consequences of Migration

A considerable number of studies have been made on the psychological and economic consequences of urban life on individuals born in rural areas.[15] In Latin America these studies have taken the form of an analysis of the skills, attitudes, and patterns of social participation (membership in an association, reading habits, voting, etc.) of individuals born in rural areas and belonging to a low social class, insofar as these migrants have adapted to urban life. These studies typically show that when migrants born in rural areas or small towns arrive for the first time in the city, they are relatively "traditional" in terms of skill, attitude, and social partici-

---

[15]   There are a great number of studies in this area, each one of which emphasizes different aspects of the process of adaption. One of the first studies, the conclusions of which have been supported by subsequent studies, is that of Germani (1959).

pation, but with time (particularly after the first ten years) they become more modern in each of these dimensions.[16]

The principal studies in the area of migrant adaptation generally compare the recent arrivals with the migrants who came to the city first and who have spent some time there. It is presumed that the differences in skill, attitudes, and social participation between the two groups result from the apprenticeship that has taken place among those who have spent more time in the city. Nevertheless, it is possible that the first migrants were different. This could have happened in one or two ways. On the one hand, the first migrants might have been the more select members of the communities of origin (i.e. the most capable individuals belonging to the higher social classes were historically the first to begin the exodus from the small towns).[17] On the other hand, those first migrants who arrived in the city, the least adapted to city life (i.e. the most traditional, the ignorant migrants, the ones from a lower social environment), could have been "rejected" by the city and have had to return to the rural area.[18]

The hypothesis here set forth is that the migrants change through time as they adapt to the city, but that selective migration toward the center and toward the outside helps to explain the differences in skills and attitudes between the first and most recent migrants.

Inkeles and others have maintained that industral employment is what motivates the changes in the migrants' skills and attitudes while adapting to the city. According to this argument, the requisites for employment in a mechanical and routine job tend to accentuate a change of communication, planning, and efficiency. The work in such an atmosphere, therefore, tends to produce an "industrial man" who shares a common mass of attitudes favorable for planning and interchange with other industrial workers.

Although it is certain that industrial work operates in this way, it is also certain that studies of residents in urban suburbs from the lower

---

[16]   Appendix 2 provides an ample bibliography on this.

[17]   This may be the case in countries such as Colombia, where the initial urbanization was not characterized by rapid industrial expansion and new opportunities for manual labor (unskilled or semi-skilled). In the greater part of Latin America, including Colombia, the initial opportunities in urban areas were for men, in professional financing and administrative positions. Balan (1969) proposes that the less developed countries in Latin America, where the process of urbanization was begun recently, are characterized, even today, by heavy migrations of elites from the rural area and small towns toward the capital city and by (proportionally) light migration of farmers and rural workers.

[18]   For example, Alers and Applebaum (1969:14) propose: "The return migration is explained by a variety of economic and social factors, often related to the failure of the migrant to adapt himself to the surroundings in the objective locality."

classes in Latin America, very few of whom have industrial jobs, show rather notorious changes directed toward "modern" attitudes and toward social participation (Inkeles 1960, 1969). In this way, it is presumed that the complexity of work is not without an element of urban environment which directs the migrant toward new attitudes. Other factors, such as contact with mass communication and informal social communication (with friends, neighbors), play an important role in this direction.

The speed with which personal aspirations (greater economic incomes, better housing, education for the children, etc.) are awakened among the poor people has been largely recognized as the "revolution of the emergence of growing expectations." One common interpretation of this process is that the ever-widening vision of social progress and material wealth (that often comes directly from more advanced nations) has a "demonstrative effect" on "traditional" individuals. It has been argued that this process is one of the basic sources of revolutionary political attitudes among the less privileged people.

Nevertheless, the "revolution of growing expectations" is a somewhat more complicated process. First, the "demonstrative effects" of social change and of material progress do not always have an impact on personal expectations, that is, on what people think concerns them directly. Thus, an individual in the city from a low social class can be aware of the advantages of a better education for his children and can desire that his children have this education. However, he may not believe that they will ever have it, much less believe that a good education is his natural "right." The migrants may realize that their aspirations for progress itself and for the education of their children are exaggerated in relation to the real possibilities which the reigning social and political system offers them.

Second, this discrepancy between aspiration and realization does not always produce frustration, much less political discontent or revolutionary attitudes. One has to specify carefully the circumstances under which unsatisfied aspirations lead to frustration and political discontent because the migrants tend to assimilate the values and attitudes that often maintain the status quo. Although a proportion of migrants who have spent several years in the city will probably vote and take positions on political and economic events, some studies now indicate that a considerable length of residency in the city and greater political consciousness do not seem to produce "radical" political points of view.[19] This is, never-

---

[19]   For a broad résumé of studies on migrant adaption and political adjustment in Latin American cities, see Wayne (1970).

theless, a rather unexplored field in which one cannot make very concrete assertions.

CONCLUSION

The lack of sufficient information as well as the limited theoretical explanations concerning migrants in Latin America do not offer a basis for a clear understanding of the situation. Nevertheless, recent serious studies indicate a positive influence which stimulates economic and social development.[20]

Some authors claim that the migratory process tends to equalize the economic situation of the various regions, diminishing their differences in terms of the ability each one has in meeting the needs of its people. This will be true insofar as the movements of people cause an increase in the incomes in the places from which people emigrate by reducing the supply of manual labor and by lowering the incomes in the receiving areas (Okun and Richardson 1961, cited by Brigg 1971:15). But one shouldn't ignore other factors. The trends of internal migration in Latin America, as in any other place, have two principal characteristics: first, the more numerous movements are from the poorer and less developed regions toward the richer and more urbanized areas; and second, although the movements include migrants from all social classes, the men at least have higher levels of education.

As a consequence of the combined influence of these two tendencies, the capable individuals of a nation manage to concentrate themselves in small and powerful urban centers. A great number of poor areas are not developed because of the loss of young, well-trained workers. Although the richer regions which attract migrants are generally large cities, the process of regional polarization is also a process of urban-rural polarization in which economic differences between small cities and the rest of the nation increase at an accelerated rate. Figure 3 illustrates some of the characteristics of the migratory process in Colombia.

Whatever the economic consequences of migration at the regional level (insofar as the migratory process is a function of the perceived differences in terms of the meeting of actual needs, and given its apparent rationality), it seems probable that if migration becomes strongly dysfunctional and the patterns of urban unemployment increase sharply, the process will be more or less self-corrective (Schultz 1969, cited by Brigg 1971:26).

[20]   See Miracle and Berry (1970); also, Okun and Richardson (1961, cited by Brigg 1971:13). A recent and very interesting work can be found in Singer (1972).

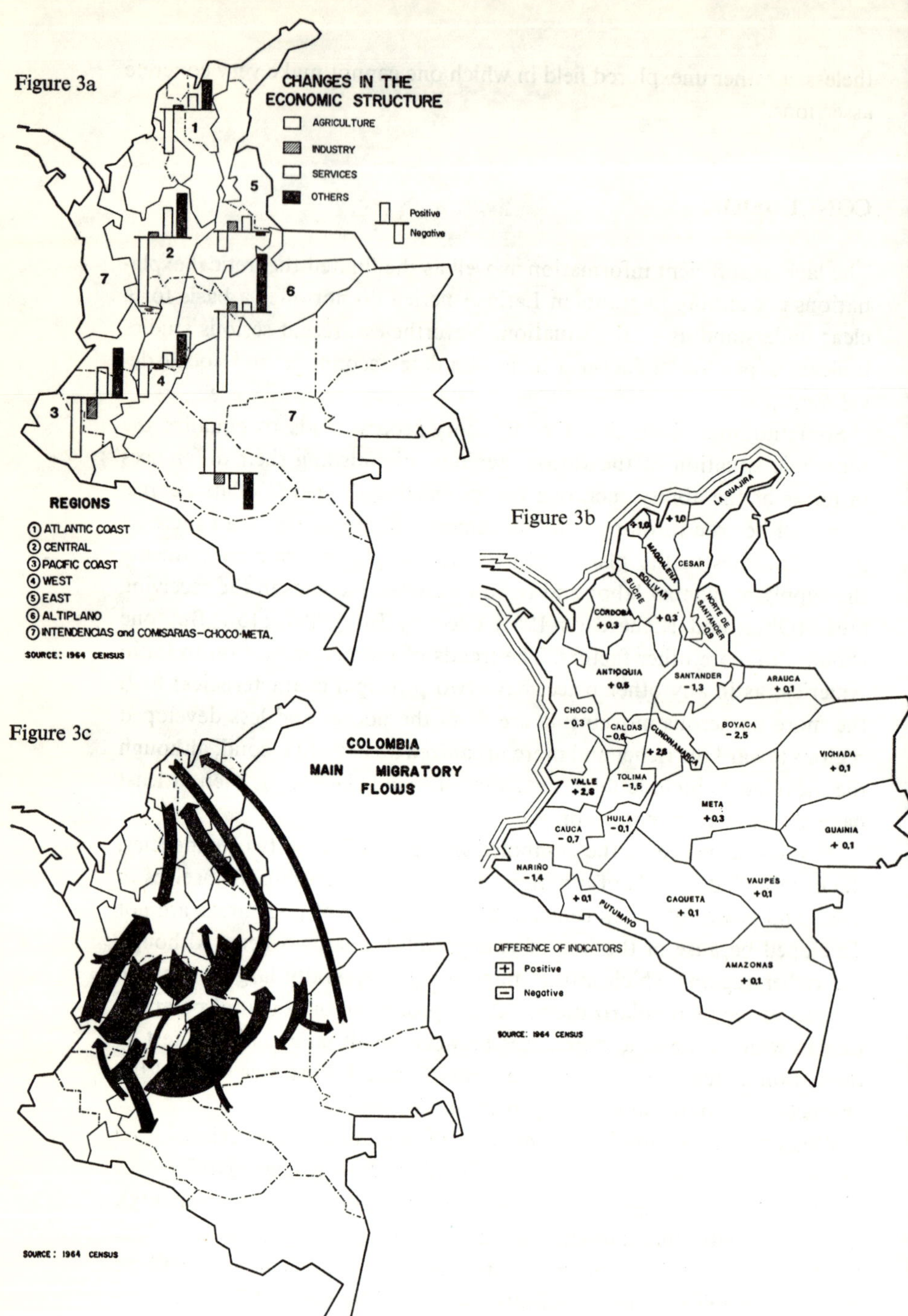

Figure 3.   Characteristics of the migratory process in Colombia

Figure 3d

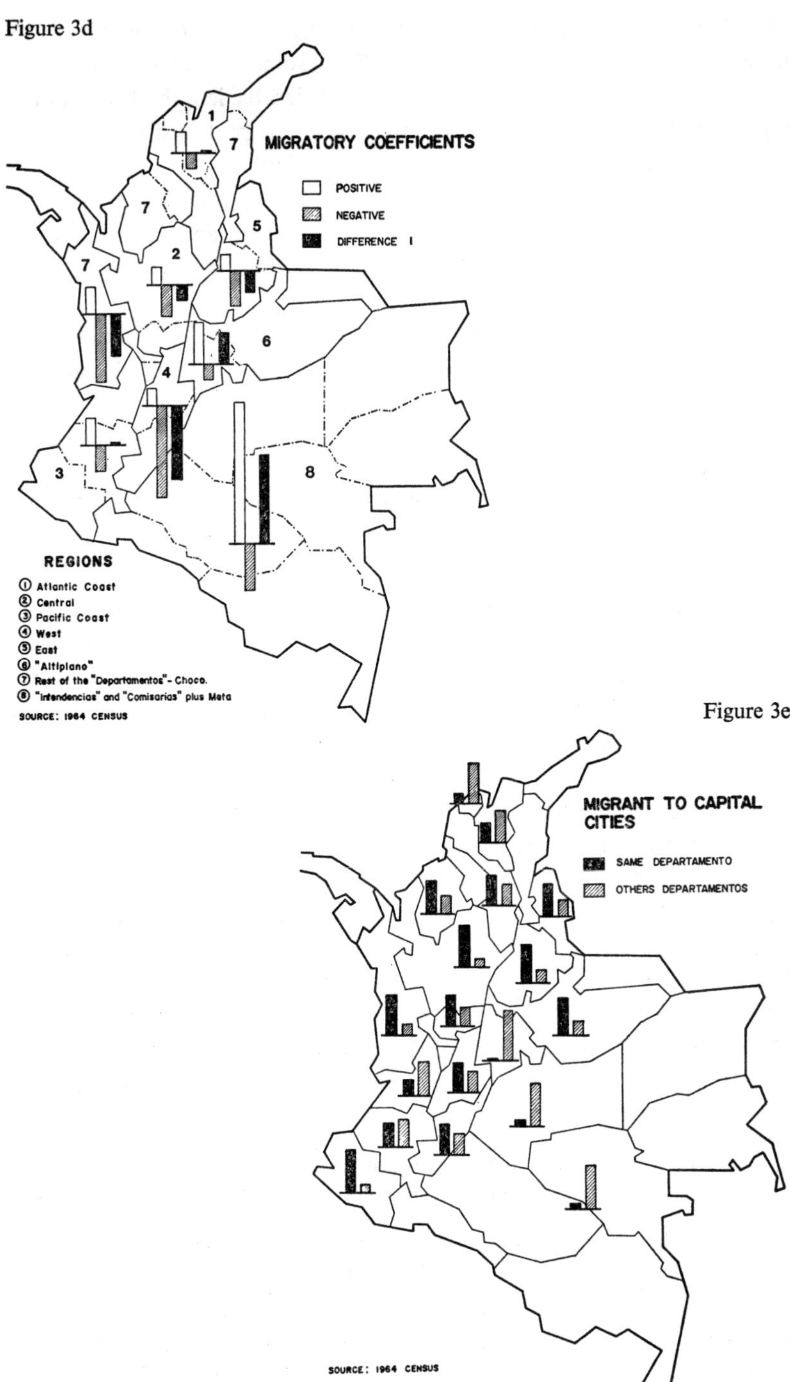

Figure 3e

On the other hand, one mechanism which compensates for the effects of selectivity is return migration. In effect, some studies conclude that many of the migrants who have spent a considerable length of time in the city return to their place of origin; they return as part of a plan and not as a result of their success or failure to assimilate in the city.[21] This return migration, which in Colombia seems to be on the order of 20 percent, is made up principally of young adults with an education which is better on the average than those who do not migrate from the same region.

Another compensatory factor for selectivity is offered by certain government programs in the agrarian sector, which, given their characteristics and their complexity, motivate the most capable to remain and the least capable to leave.[22] Likewise, they motivate capable individuals in the city to move to those areas.

Another relevant consequence of migration is the pressure applied by a population on the political system. Although one cannot claim that the rural inhabitants and those from less urbanized areas are passive, or that migrants become radical and active with residency in the city, it is expected that the numerous direct contacts which the city offers individuals who share the same needs and who are vigorously exposed to the same effects of city life should be converted into real demands. One cannot fail to recognize the existence of large and well-organized informal groups motivated by a search to meet their own needs.[23]

The success with which these demands have been met in Latin America in the construction of dwellings on urban land is unquestionable. In fact, the quarters of invasion and other forms of clandestine housing constitute a considerable part of the larger cities,[24] and it is clear that the housing policies in several countries now accept these dwellings as irreversible facts and are attempting to cope with these trends.[25]

One interesting point has been the impact of migration on the structure of the population by age and sex. Given its selective character, migration alters the standards of masculinity and the age structure of the emitting

---

[21]   The study on migration to Bogotá (Cardona, Simmons, and Rodrígues-Espada 1972) supports this claim concerning the impact of the return migration; see also Miracle and Berry (1970).

[22]   This is an hypothesis as yet unproven, which is consistent with the general findings on the factors that have motivated diverse forms of selectivity in immigration.

[23]   One discussion in this respect is offered by Cardona (1971).

[24]   In some Latin American cities these dwellings take up about 50 percent of the space.

[25]   Peru has been pointed out as an example with its programs of "Young Quarters," and also Colombia, with its new program of "Minimal Norms" of urbanization and community services.

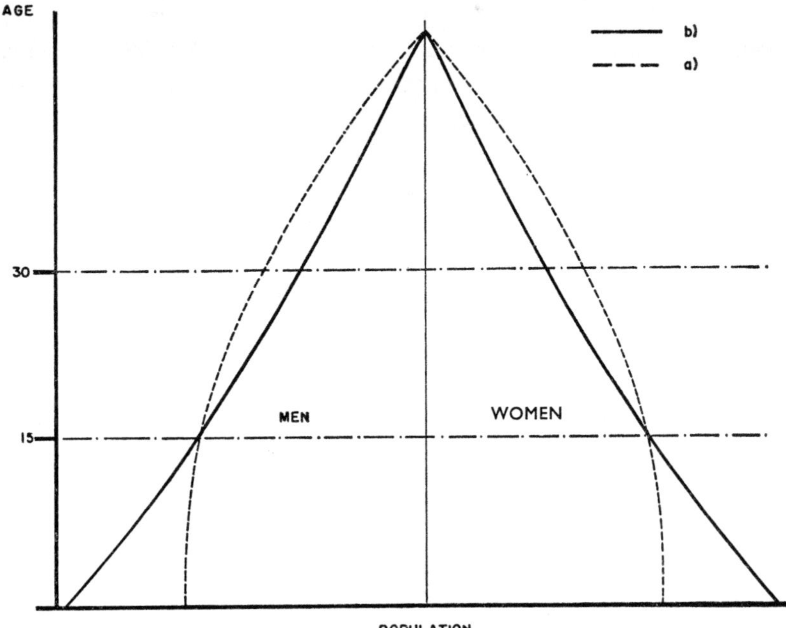

Figure 4. Impact of migration on the structure of the population by age and sex.

and receiving areas.[26] Because the migrating population which goes to the major cities is made up of young adults, an enlargement of the pyramid for the ages between fifteen and twenty-five (curve a in Figure 4) is to be expected. This young population (predominantly female) surpasses the reproductive potential which the city had in its initial situation; in time, there will be repercussions in the form of an increase in the rates of fecundity. This fact again modifies the structure by age of the population, which acquires a form similar to what it had before the process began (curve b).

One last point which deserves to be mentioned and which requires more information and analysis is the impact of migration on the family structure. As noted at the beginning, there are frequent assertions with respect to how migration works in a negative way toward the disintegration of the family; however, the limited available evidence also allows for a very different argument:

1. A considerable number of families emigrate totally, that is, the parents go with the children. In the case of Santiago, for example, 50

---

[26] One analysis of the structure by age and sex of the four primary Colombian cities during the periods 1938–1951 and 1964 clearly shows this tendency.

percent of male and female immigrants arrive alone, while in Monterrey the proportion of men who arrive alone is 20 percent. For this same city, it is shown that approximately 40 percent of the men migrate in a "separated" form, and, in these cases, a considerable amount of time passes before the migratory group is reunited in the city. Also, one can observe a clear tendency for the migratory group to consist of married couples and their children. In the period 1961–1965, 51 percent of the migrants were in this category (Elizaga 1964; Browning and Feindt 1969).

2. On the other hand, because the children plan this separated migration together with their parents (Múñoz and de Oliveira 1972), there is noreason to think that there has been a conflict or a break in the family.

3. A substantial portion of the children who have migrated provide economic help to their families and maintain a certain degree of communication with them; thus, the migrating child constitutes an agent of familial modernization.

4. A significant number of parents whose children have migrated come later as a result of their familial contacts.[27]

5. There is evidence that there are more altered rates of industrialization and legitimization of the family in urban zones. It is expected that, as part of the process of acculturation, the migrant assimilates these norms which lead him to conform to a type of stable institutionalized family directed by a wide perspective in time.[28]

We have tried to offer with this work a quick view of the migratory process and some of its consequences in Latin America. The model presented is based on a study conducted by the authors in Colombia, and on the findings of other investigators in other regions.

Appendix 1 presents some details of the Colombian study. Appendix 2 offers an annotated bibliography of various points which conform to the model.

[27] This finding predates that of the "National Inquiry of Fecundity" (i.p.). See Note 8.
[28] The study in Bogotá conducted by the authors revealed that urban residency was clearly related to positive individual orientations toward planning.

APPENDIX 1: THE SAMPLE

The Design

The design of the theoretical sample was planned so that it would correspond to various fundamental criteria that define a highly qualified sample.

The criteria observed were the following:

a. The obtaining of a group of migrants and nonmigrant residents in the city of Bogotá.

b. The individuals or units of the sample were not to be less than twenty years old nor more than fifty years.

c. Sex: male.

d. Civil state: married.

e. There would have to be a group of migrants that included individuals who had been in the city for a short period (one to five years and six to ten years) and individuals who had been in the city for a long period (eleven or more years).

f. The geographic origin of the group of migrants was limited to the rural area of Cundinamarca and Boyacá. This criterion was established later, based on an analysis of the waybills.

The frame of reference for the sample was worked out using a special list provided by the National Administrative Department of Statistics. It was based on the male population between the ages of twenty to fifty-four and was arranged by the sectors, neighborhoods, and city blocks in the city of Bogotá that were used in the national census of 1964. The study was done in 1968 and it was necessary to update this list in view of the increase in Bogotá's population at that time. For this reason, the list was made to reflect the increase in population resulting from newly urbanized areas of the city, new invasions, and the projected male population (twenty to fifty-four years of age) for 1968.

For the effects of stratification on the sample, we used a list of the existing neighborhoods of Bogotá in 1968. This list was prepared for the studies on "Induced Abortions and the Use of Contraceptives in Latin America." With respect to this stratification we took into account the factors of residential segregation in the city of Bogotá from a purely ecological point of view, which included 43 percent of the neighborhoods of high socioeconomic status. This stratification was corrected once the inquiry was begun.

In accord with the criteria of the study, with respect to the comparative analysis of distinct strata and the internal analysis of the subgroups in each strata, we drew a minimal sample of 900 units, which was equally divided in groups of 300 units per strata. The latter was another criterion used for controlling the sample even more. (See Table 1.)

Table 1.   Final sample

Strata	Number of Inquiries Made	Percentage
High	284	32
Middle	274	31
Low	323	37
Total Inquiries	881	100

Control Groups

In order to compare the differences and similarities that might exist among different qualified groups of the sample and to verify the implications of certain assumptions, several control groups were needed: one group of rural inhabitants, one group of resident tenants, one group of urban workers, one group of women, wives of the men studied, and one group for the administration of an intelligence test.

GROUP OF RURAL INHABITANTS.   For the rural control group, we tabulated the waybills so that we could compare the representativeness of the sample and select a series of representative rural localities for the migrants in question. For this selection, any locality whose district capital had more than 10,000 inhabitants was not taken into account because it was thought that it did not typify the rural area. The following localities in Cundinamarca were chosen: Guanchetá, Tausa, Sutatausa, and Ubaté; in Boyacá: Tenza, Sutatenza, Garagoa, Chinavita, and Somondoco.

The rural sample of migrants who had returned to the country and natives who had not migrated was taken in eleven towns of a size between 2,000 and 6,300 inhabitants. Five of the towns were located to the north of Cundinamarca (area of Ubaté) and six to the south of Boyacá (area of Miraflores). The two areas of Ubaté and Miraflores are highly populated and contribute strongly to the migration toward Bogotá. These towns were selected for their size and locality, because they represented a "cross section" of the places of orgin of the majority of rural migrants who go to Bogotá.

APPENDIX 2: FURTHER READING

Various theoretical models have been developed in order to explain the causes of migration; see: Dudley Kirk, 1946, *Europe's population in the interwar years* (Princeton: Princeton University Press); D. J. Bogue and Margaret Hagood, 1953, *Subregional migration in the United States, 1935–1940* (Miami, Ohio: Scripps Foundation), pages 124–128; Juan C. Elizaga, 1970, *Migrations to metropolitan areas of Latin America* (Santiago: Latin American Center of Demography).

In relation to the distribution between international migrations and internal migrations, see: "A general typology of migration," in *Population*. Edited by William Peterson, 606–618 (New York: Macmillan, 1961).

On personal motivations for migrating, see: Wolpert, "Behavioral aspects of the decision to migrate," in *Papers and Proceedings of Regional Science Association*, volume fifteen, 1965.

Migration has been associated with distance and has been explained in mathematical terms; see: Samuel Sauffer, 1950, "Intervening opportunities: a theory relating mobility and distance," *American Sociological Review*, 5:845–847; and Samuel Sauffer, 1960, "Intervening opportunities and competing migrants," *Journal of Regional Science* 2:1–26.

In relation to the selectivity of migrations, there exists ample evidence that persons with professional and administrative occupations have the highest rates of migration in industrialized countries. For example: J. Tarver, 1964, "Occupational migrational differentials," *Social Forces*, 43:231–241. Evidence about industrialized countries in Latin America suggests that, with some modifications, this may be a rather universal phenomenon. For example: B. Hutchinson, 1963, "The migrant population of urban Brazil," *América Latina* 6:41–71. Also, Elizaga (1970), earlier citation; Harley Browning and Waltraut Feindt, 1969, "Selectivity of migrants to a metropolis in a developing country," *Demography* 6:347–358; and A. Simmons and Ramiro Cardona, 1970, "The selectivity of migration in an historical perspective: the case of Bogotá," *Paraguay Review of Sociology*.

See: S. Goldstein, 1955, "Migration and occupational mobility in Norristown," *American Sociological Review* 20:401–408, for a discussion of factors related to the greater migration of less capable persons. A more recent study on this matter can be seen in: Dorothy Swaine Thomas, 1938, *Research memorandum of migration differentials* (New York Social Science Research Council Bulletin 43).

In relation to migration and stages of the family cycle (especially the marriage age and the age when children leave home), see: Gerald Leslie and Arthur Richardson, 1961, "Life-cycle, career patterns and the decision to move," *American Sociological Review*, 26:894–902.

On the adaptation of migrants to the new urban world, a classical study on Latin America is: Gino Germani, 1959, "Inquiry into the social effects of urbanization in a working class sector of greater Buenos Aires," in *Urbanization in Latin America*. Edited by Philip Hauser, 206–233 (Paris: UNESCO).

On the process of the social mobility of migrants in the city, see: Otis Durant Duncan, 1956, "The theory and consequences of mobility of farm population," in *Population theory and policy*. Edited by J. Spengler and O. Dudley Duncan, 417–434 (Glencoe, Illinois: Free Press).

In relation to the impact of migration on economic and social structures in the place of origin and in the place of destination, one can find an excellent discussion of these points with respect to Latin America in: Bruce Herrick, 1965, *Urban migration and economic development in Chile* (Cambridge, Massachusetts: MIT Press). A summary of several related points on Colombia is at the Center of Studies on Economic Development (CEDE), University of the Andes.

Latin America

Studies of this type in Latin America have concentrated above all on migration to large cities such as Santiago, Chile (Elizaga [1970], earlier citation and Herrick [1965], earlier citation), Río de Janeiro (Hutchinson [1963], earlier citation) and Monterrey, Mexico (Browning and Feindt [1969], earlier citation). These studies suggest that the occupational characteristics of rural-urban migrants can vary substantially according to the size of the city and that it is almost certain that they reflect the general structural pattern of socioeconomic development within the country in question (J. Balan, 1969, "Migrant-native socio-economic differences in Latin American cities," *Latin American Research Review* 4:3–29). Nevertheless, a cursory examination of the characteristics of age, sex, and occupation of migrants to cities of different sizes in Colombia did not reveal any strong relation between the size of the city and the characteristics of the migrants in this country, although it was more probable that the men migrating to the larger cities (principally Bogotá) were bachelors, had migrated directly to the city, and had more education than men migrating to small cities (Carlos García, 1970, *Characteristics of immigrants in five Colombian cities* [Bogotá: CEDE, University of the Andes]).

Questions such as "Why did you leave the place where you lived before?" are the norm in most questionnaires administered to migrants. A very high proportion of adult male migrants respond to these questions with answers which reflect their search for better jobs, although sometimes they also present other reasons that migrants give for migrating in Colombia and Peru; see: William P. McGreevy, 1968, "Causes of internal migration in Colombia," in *Employment and unemployment in Colombia* (Bogotá: CEDE, University of the Andes). In contrast, relatively few studies have asked about the equally important "causes" of migration, such as the number and intensity of friendships and other personal contacts in the city which the migrants were able to have before leaving the rural area. Many men have relatively poor job opportunities in rural areas, but only some of these individuals go to the city. It is possible that an important factor which distinguishes between those who migrate and those who remain has to do with their contact with friends and relatives in the city.

With respect to migrant assimilation to the socioeconomic and political structures in cities and in areas around large cities, see: M. Morse, 1965, "Recent research on Latin American urbanization: a selective survey with commentary" (Recent study on urbanization in Latin America: a selective inquiry with commentary), *Latin American Research Review* 1 (Fall) for a review of several of these myths and the empirical evidence that refutes them. Nevertheless, the tendency for migration studies on Latin America to focus basically on lower class migrants has considerably limited the ability to generalize the findings. We know relatively little about the characteristics of middle and upper class migrants who, in spite of their relatively small numbers, have had a considerable impact on the class structure of the cities.

On the contribution of migration to the increase of urban population, see: E. Arriaga, "Components of city growth in selected cities in Latin American countries," *Milbank Memorial Fund Quarterly* 46:237–252.

On the contribution of migration to the work force, see: Bruce Herrick, (1965), earlier citation.

On the characteristics of migrants compared with those of nonmigrants, three studies which have focused on this aspect of selective migration are: Browning and Feindt (1969), earlier citation; Simmons and Cardona (1971), earlier citation; and Rafael Prieto Durán and Bill Jameson, 1965, *Agricultural study of river basin of the Suárez River* (Bogotá: CEDE, University of the Andes).

On the migration to towns and to intermediate cities, one can find some information in: Carlos Garcia (1970), earlier citation; and Carlos

García, 1968, *Employment and unemployment in Colombia* (Bogotá: University of the Andes).

REFERENCES

ALERS, OSCAR, RICHARD P. APPLEBAUM
  1968   Migration in Peru — an inventory of propositions. *Studies of Population and Development* 1 (4):28–29.
ANONYMOUS
  i.p.   "National inquiry of fecundity." Colombian Association of Faculties of Medicine, Division of Population Studies. Bogotá.
ANONYMOUS
  1972   *Minimal norms of urbanization and community services.* Bogotá: Institute of Territorial Credit, Administrative Department of District Planning, and National Department of Planning.
BALAN, J.
  1969   Migrant-native socio-economic differences in Latin American cities. *Latin American Research Review* 4:3–29.
BOGUE, DONALD J.
  1963   "Techniques and hypotheses for the study of differential migration: some notes from an experiment with U.S. data." International Population Conference, New York, 1961. London: UNESCO.
BRIGG, PAMELA
  1971   "A survey of case studies in migration to urban areas." Economics of Urbanization Division, Economics Department, World Bank.
BROWNING, H., W. FEINDT
  1969a Selectivity of migrants to a metropolis in a developing country: study of a Mexican case. *Demography and Economy* 2:186–200.
  1969b Selectivity of migrants to a metropolis in a developing country: study of a Mexican case (revised version). *Demography and Economy* 3:8.
CARDONA, R.
  1969   *The invasions of urban terrains – elements for a diagnosis.* Bogotá: Third World.
  1971   *Savage urbanization in Colombia.* Space and Society International Critical Review of the Management of Architecture in Urbanization 15F. Paris: Editions Anthropos.
CARDONA, R., *editor*
  1968   *Urbanization and marginality.* Bogotá: Third World.
  1972   *Internal migrations.* Bogotá: Editorial Andes.
CARDONA, R., A. SIMMONS, E. RODRÍGUES-ESPADA
  1972   "Migration to Bogotá," in *Internal migrations.* Edited by R. Cardona, 135–161. Bogotá: Editorial Andes.
DURÁN, RAFAEL PRIETO, BILL JAMESON
  1965   *Agricultural study of the river basin of the Suárez River.* Bogotá: Center for Studies on Economic Development, University of the Andes.

ELIZAGA, J. C.
1964 *Inquiry on the immigration to Greater Santiago*. Santiago de Chile: Celade.
1970 *The migrations*. Santiago de Chile: Latin American Center of Demography.

GERMANI, GINO
1959 "Inquiry into the social effects of urbanization in a working class sector of greater Buenos Aires," in *Urbanization in Latin America*. Edited by Philip Hauser, 206–233. Paris: UNESCO.

HARRIS, WALTER O.
1971 *The growth of Latinoamerican cities*. Columbus: Ohio University Press

INKELES, ALEX
1960 Industrial man: the relation of status to experience, perception and value. *American Journal of Sociology* 66:1–31.
1969 Making men modern: on the causes and consequences of individual change in six developing countries. *American Journal of Sociology* 72: 209–255.

MARTÍNEZ, HECTOR
1966 *The high plateau migrations and the colonization of Tambopata*. Lima: Center of Population and Development Studies.

MIRACLE, M. P., S. S. BERRY
1970 Migrant labour and economic development. *Oxford Economic Papers* (March).

MÚÑOZ, H., O. DE OLIVEIRA
1972 "Internal migrations in Latin America: exposition and criticism of some analyses," in *Migration and Development*. Latin American Council of Social Sciences Report of Investigation Series (Population). Buenos Aires.

MÚÑOZ, H., O. DE OLIVEIRA, P. SINGER, C. STERN
1972 *Migration and urban development, theoretical considerations*. Buenos Aires: Latin American Council on Social Sciences.

OKUN, BERNARD, RICHARD W. RICHARDSON
1961 Regional income inequality and internal population migration. *Economic Development and Cultural Change* (June).

RAVENSTEIN, E. G.
1889 The laws of migration. *Journal of the Royal Statistical Society* 52: 241–301.

SCHULTZ, T. PAUL
1969 "Internal migration: a quantitative study of rural-urban migration in Colombia." Rand Corporation.

SIMMONS, A., R. CARDONA
1970 "The selectivity of migration in an historical perspective: the case of Bogotá, Colombia, 1929–1968." Paper presented to the First Regional Latin American Conference on Population, Mexico, August, 1970.

SINGER, PAUL
1972 "Internal migrations, theoretical considerations on their study," in *Migration and development*. Latin American Council of Social Sciences Report of Investigation Series (population). Buenos Aires.

WAYNE, CORNELIUS, JR.
   1970   "The political sociology of city-ward migration in Latin America," in
          Latin American urban annual, volume two. Edited by Francine Rabi-
          novitz and Felicity Trueblood. Beverly Hills: Sage.
WILKENING, E. A.
   1968   Role of the extended family in migration and adaption in Brazil.
          Journal of Marriage and the Family 30 (4).

A Decision-Making Model for the Study of Migration

BRIAN M. DU TOIT

The continuous movement of peoples has been one of the main characteristics of African society. As far back as we know, hunters have been following game, herders accompanying their cattle to greener pastures or avoiding tsetse infestations, and horticulturalists abandoning old and eroded gardens. The Bantu expansion and establishment of kingdoms in West Africa resulted in internal pressures. Contact with Arabs and Europeans increased the population pressure as slavery became valued and firearms came to be associated with political aggression. East and central Africa were devastated by Arabs and slave-trading chiefs and in what is presently Malawi these unsettling forces were not stopped before 1896. By this time colonial powers had introduced a variety of new pressures.

In a large percentage of cases, then, the decision to move from one place to another was forced upon the migrant. He had very little to say about the pros and cons of the impending migration. More recently, however, we are observing the same high incidence of population movement, not only within the same geographical region but also to neighboring countries or to towns and cities. In these cases the decision to move is made after a process of evaluation and weighing of factors.

The aim of this paper is to introduce the factor of migration, and by extension also of urban migration, on a general scale and then to apply it more specifically to the southern African scene. In developing a social model for migration a multi-causal nexus must supersede the trait listing of factors so common in earlier studies. But such a nexus of causes is, in the last analysis, arrived at after the study of numerous factors and large numbers of individuals. The model, furthermore, is based on choices and decisions and thus represents the decision-making model of which Howard

(1963) speaks. The ultimate aim of social research is to understand human behavior and to plan for such behavior. The model discussed here is an attempt in that direction.

It should be emphasized at the outset that as I am arguing for a nexus of causes which influence any decision, I am also arguing for an integration of research methodologies. Just as the uni-causal explanation for migration must be discarded, so must the researcher beware of uni-methodological research. Such a decision-making model is influenced by, and should always be considered in the context of, social institutions and a variety of networks, associations, and other interactional and organizational aspects of a people's life. We should recognize the presence of individual and societal determinants – that is, we should be conscious of psychological and sociological factors. Used contextually the decision-making model integrates a variety of methods and subjects.

AFRICAN MIGRATION

Migration as a specific aspect of human mobility has become more pronounced as modern industrial and mining centers have arisen, and as old population concentrations have been modernizing. Since industrial urban concentrations are relatively new to Africa and their membership is still largely being drawn from a rural and village reservoir, the kinds of migrations and the motives for the migration which bring Africans to the cities should be analyzed.

Many people see the city as a place where needed cash can be earned but also as a place which can offer only temporary residence. They work there but do not live there; the city offers a house, not a home. Theirs is a temporary migration as they return to peri-urban or rural conditions weekly, seasonally, or at least periodically. In this category of temporary migrants there are three distinct groups.

The first is comprised of those people who work in the city — even in industries — but live on the borders of the city proper. They travel to and from their work during the week, spending their weekends in non-urban conditions while planting a field or tending a flock which is otherwise cared for by a wife or relatives (see Mayer 1962, regarding the Xhosa in East London). The migrant in this category is exposed to urban influences but not permanently. He may even be in regular contact with kinsmen or fellow tribal members who are urbanized. He is one of the links in an important chain of communication to be elaborated on in a later section of this discussion. While it is not the same kind of influence, the degrees of intensity which are present in the distinction between Gulliver's "low-wage, rural employment" and "higher-wage, industrial employment" (1960:159), are important in understanding this type of migrant. Both rural and industrial employment remove the men from their homes for periods of time; both are major factors in cultural change even though the former does not take the men to a city, or at least not right away. In this regard, we must speak of step migration (originally Ravenstein 1885; and more recently Caldwell 1969:21). The migrant moves from the rural home to a small town and then to a larger town while continuously improving his position, until he finally arrives in the city. In such cases he may finally end up in a city where he does not have kinsmen, but more often than not kinship ties facilitated his step-by-step migration.[1]

A second important group of migrants are those adult males who go to the city for five or six months when rural agricultural undertakings do not require their presence. This seasonal migration (Prothero 1957, 1962, 1965) does not disrupt the rural or village economy and allows the family to earn additional income. This is principally a male activity, and while women may migrate for short periods, Caldwell recorded "more than twice as many male seasonal migrants as females" (1969:39, 45). This kind of migration differs only slightly from the first in that we may now speak of temporary urban residents. Many persons in this second group of migrants return to the city every year, establishing a regular channel of communication between kinsmen or tribal group members who reside in the city and those in rural areas. These regular seasonal migrants who are very common in West Africa are even recognized terminologically in certain cases. Berg notes, for example, that throughout northern Nigeria seasonal migrants are apparently referred to in the local language as "men who while (eat?) away the dry season," and R. C. Abraham's *Dictionary of the Hausa language* gives a definition of "migrant" as follows: "In order to eke his corn out, he has gone to spend the hot season elsewhere in exercise of his trade" (1965:166).

The third group of temporary migrants into the urban areas includes all those persons who come from the rural setting to work for periods up to two years. This type of temporary migrant is found in most of Africa, but especially in south and central Africa where the city has come to be identified with a preponderance of adult males, bachelors' hostels,

---

[1] The step-migration theory has frequently been mentioned for Latin America. Flinn, in his study of the migration of persons between rural barrios and Bogotá', Colombia, states: "In both cases reported here, the majority of migrants moved directly to Bogotá without intermediary steps" (1971:83–84).

mining compounds, and typically urban situations of time clocks and machines. The males who make these migrations become temporary urban residents, but their orientation is rural; they live and work in the city, but they are not committed to it. They may become urbanites in due course, but for the time being they are migrants and contemplate their return to the village. Watson (1967) speaks of this as OSCILLATORY MIGRATION. In some cases, such a man may return home even after twelve years of absence (Fortes 1965: 76). Loyalties to the home region and kin group are maintained and migrants frequently retire to the village after a lifetime in the city (van Velsen 1961).

The three types of migrants noted above are only general types which apply to all of Africa. Different parts of the continent — and even different countries — exhibit these types in varying intensities. The urban migration in West Africa differs from that in southern Africa, and while the cities in both cases are industrial centers, the stimuli which initially prompt migration cause exposure in varying degrees of intensity and duration to urban conditions. It should furthermore be kept in mind that large and complex population concentrations are not new to Africa. The West African peoples have long been characterized by urban centers and large villages, and Herskovits points out that urbanization represents a far more radical departure from traditional living patterns in south and east Africa than is the case in West Africa (1957:21).

In addition to the temporary kinds of migration already outlined, there is a type of migration which brings people to the city on a more or less permanent basis. This may be termed URBANIZATION or at least the establishment of the necessary condition for this process to take place. Prothero (1965:2) speaks of DEFINITE MOVEMENTS in which "people sever completely their links with rural areas and settle permanently in towns." While one may agree in principle with people relocating themselves more or less permanently, links with rural areas are seldom severed and even when they lapse due to minimal communication they are still present and may be reactivated by persons in both directions. Although temporary migrants constitute an important group in urban centers, it is important to realize that for urbanization to occur, there must be permanent migrants to the city.

The more or less permanent migration of people to the cities is primarily responsible for the growth of African urban centers, and while natural increase soon takes over as a contributing factor to a permanent urban population, it is the population movements in urban migration which are of great social interest. Due to the enduring influence of kinship ties, the nature of African cities with their locations as proximate to rural tribal areas, and the small number of cities per country, one would expect to find a relatively smaller percentage of intercity migration in comparison with Europe, the United States, and Great Britain where, according to the 1961 census, more than 60 percent of all migrants were intercity migrants. This becomes even more true as a result of the influx controls and legislation which have been more severe in colonial and neocolonial eastern and central Africa and especially South Africa. On the other hand, we should keep in mind that controlled migration is not unique to these parts of Africa. Beijer states that "every government has means at its disposal to encourage or to discourage certain forms of migration" (1969:37) and this applies both to movements within political boundaries as well as across them (see also Caldwell and Okonjo 1968:370). Both of these may be rural-urban migration and both may in fact result in long-term urban residence. We must then look at both of the major kinds of population movement, namely, migration into the city on a temporary basis, and migration by persons who say that they are migrating permanently.

It is essential that research focus on the kinds of persons who leave their village homes to move to a large town or a city and their reasons for leaving. Current research must analyze the sources of such urban migration, and this would entail a study of rural-urban as well as urban-urban migration. In addition there is a factor which has generally been ignored in urban studies and that is the urban-rural migration. This latter subject should become a definite topic in research dealing with the dissemination of urban influences and an urban life style. It forms one part of the process which leads us to study the ruralization of the urban setting as well as the urbanization of the rural setting. Both of these settings are defined by life styles rather than population size. Both are parts of a wider social complex which includes ethnic, linguistic, interactional, cognitive, and structural components.

TOWARD A SOCIAL MODEL OF MIGRATION

Urban migration in southern Africa is a relatively recent phenomenon as compared with Europe and the United States, but its impact on traditional life styles has been far reaching. The early development of urban centers was all coastal and, especially in the case of Cape Town, represented only slight influences on the indigenous communities. Even when the northward expansion took whites into the interior and established towns and farming communities, the sociocultural influences were sporadic. "The Voortrekkers had become 'free and independent,' but they were poor, scattered, disunited, politically inexperienced, and virtually surrounded by Africans" (Thompson 1969:424).

The discovery of diamonds in 1866, and especially the major strike in June, 1871, at Kimberley, as well as the discovery of gold in 1886, caused a population explosion and concentration in the interior which had dramatic consequences. It created markets and opportunities for employment on a large scale and produced industrial centers surrounded by vast farming and rural areas. To these urban centers came whites, especially Afrikaners, as natural disaster, population pressure, and the Anglo-Boer War led to conditions of indigence and landlessness.[2] Grosskopf (1932) has discussed the conditions under which whites either explored the more arid regions of southern Africa or moved directly to the growing urban centers. In both cases the migration involved large families and frequently resulted from already existing links of kinship, language, or church membership.

The South African Asians, brought in originally from India to work as indentured laborers on the sugar plantations, have remained a relatively immobile group (Kuper, Watts, and Davies 1958:74). Settling originally in Natal, they have remained a coastal population group, partially due to strong kinship and religious solidarity and partially due to social and legal restrictions in the Orange Free State and Transvaal. While the legal restrictions on segregated residential areas have curtailed the mobility of most Indians, they have not created ethnic or kinship concentrations which were not already present among these people.

The population group, however, which has been influenced to the greatest degree by geographical population mobility, and especially labor migration and urban migrations, is the indigenous African peoples. While this discussion will focus on the urban migration of the African, we must keep in mind that the city in southern Africa is an ethnic, linguistic, and cultural melange — a factor which influences and affects the process of

[2]   Holzner and Hart discuss the growth of South African cities in terms of the poor, whites and Africans, who immigrated to the city. They state: "South African cities have been industrializing rather late. Until 1937 more than twenty-five per cent of all urban whites lived below the bread line and posed a serious poor-white problem to the government. At the same time, the poor-black problem was even more critical with 1.2 million in the cities making up no less than thirty-eight per cent of the total urban population. The way of life and qualifications possessed by these two groups of under-privileged people made them entirely unsuited to their new environment, and inevitably the poor-whites posed a serious threat to white supremacy, for they were unable to compete with Africans in some sectors of the labor market. It was the combination of these factors: the poor-white problem coupled with the poor-black problem in the cities; the "push" and "pull" factors; the lack of secondary industry and the general state of unpreparedness of the cities and towns which provoked the discriminatory legislation which has been a part of the traditional scene ever since (1970: 69–70).

urbanization and the structure of urbanism. Today more than 85 percent of the Asians and whites, 70 percent of the coloreds, and 35 percent of the Africans in the Republic of South Africa are urban residents. The factors which have influenced and are influencing this migration are thus a fitting subject for inquiry.[3]

Researchers in the past have frequently fallen into the trap of ascribing urban migration to unicausal factors. The cause most often mentioned was economic, which resulted in labor migration and finally in urban migration. Others have tended to describe the "push-pull" factors which at best sound mechanical, and at worst, super-organic. It will be more rewarding, I think, to consider the people who are the actors, who weigh gains against sacrifices, advantages against disadvantages, and then decide on a plan of action. We always find various factors entering into the consideration and a certain set of advantages outweighing a set of disadvantages. This nodal approach may finally tend in the direction of economic or some other considerations but this is a long way removed from the unicausal explanation.

The factors that have been found to enter this consideration are varied, but can be categorized roughly under five headings. These are, of course, the factors on which choices and decisions are made and the factors, therefore, which must constitute our decision-making model.

1. *Taxes and the Need for Money*

Any country that is being developed and industrialized depends on money and know-how balanced by workers who can make the wheels turn. Early South Africa leaders felt that the first were present, even if they were brought in by *Uitlanders* [foreigners], but that the workers were too slow in presenting themselves. As the lush green bush and rolling pastures of Natal were used to grow sugarcane the Zulu men, a proud pastoral people, looked on in disgust as employers wanted them to work in the fields like women. The result was that Natal imported 6,000 indentured Indians between 1860 and 1866. With the wheels turning and the Witwatersrand mining shafts increasing in depth, Milner brought in 51,000 indentured Chinese workers after the Anglo-Boer War. Most of these

---

[3] Akin Mabogunje (1970) has recently proposed a systems approach to a theory of rural-urban migration. He sees a system as "a complex of interacting elements, together with their attributes and relationships." I still have trouble conceiving of a thinking, valuing, acting human being as an "element," and while the systems approach has proven valuable in analyzing and understanding the city or a wider cosmos, it must represent the system within which or into which PEOPLE migrate.

were repatriated after 1906, but they had held jobs which now needed to be filled. The local white leaders had been bothered by the fact that Africans were not more fully involved in the labor, and so the Rhodes government in 1894 inserted in the Glen Grey Act a labor tax. This taxation method for forcing laborers to present themselves was also used in French Equatorial Africa, the former Belgian Congo (Rotberg 1965: 288, 299) and Nyasaland (Mitchell 1956:20). The effect of this and other forms of taxation was to force healthy young people to offer their services in various forms of employment. For males the mines and growing industries offered a variety of jobs, but commercial and domestic services were also important. Thus in 1904 there were already 65,146 males and 122,534 females in domestic service in South Africa.

In one of the early studies of migrant labor Margaret Read found large numbers of males leaving Nyasaland for South Africa, or for Rhodesia and thence to South Africa. There was the usual periodic return, the sending of gifts and money, and the later follow-up migration by kinsmen. Even at that date the author already stated that "the material economic changes in the villages... are the most obvious and the most widespread effects of migration" (Read 1942:627). Along with economic changes in traditional villages and the development of felt cash needs, further migration is stimulated and there gradually develops a process where the two subsystems, rural and urban, are mutually dependent upon each other for certain needs. There quickly develops a network of relations and communications which permits the flow of personnel, information, and goods in both directions. While the village economy depends on money and goods returned by migrant laborers, the urban dweller is dependent on visitation and gifts from rural areas and the haven the village offers him to return to on vacation, during critical periods or upon retirement. It is also the place he can send his young children to be cared for by kinsmen or grandparents.

While the labor migrant and the emigrant were frequently guided by real money needs, they were also very often responding to indirectly related pressures. The two most important factors here were population pressure and farmland made infertile by long-term use, lack of fertilizing, and erosion. This was especially true in South Africa where reserves were established and the free movement of Africans curtailed. The Native Economic Commission, after two years of study, in 1932 reported to the Union of South Africa government that the reserves could not provide for the population because they were too small and because they were too underdeveloped and poor (Union of South Africa Parliamentary Papers 1932:274 *passim*).

With the need of earning money, whether this was due to taxation, poor agricultural productivity or population pressure, large numbers of young to middle-aged African males started visiting farming estates, towns, mines, and cities in search of cash earnings. In some cases regular paths and roads took workers to towns or to bus stops; others travelled by train; and more recently still others by airplane. The reciprocal relationship between those seeking work and organizations seeking laborers gave rise to a number of recruiting agencies. These include the Rhodesian government-sponsored Native Labour Bureau (RNLB) in 1904 and its successor, the Native Labour Supply Commission (RNLSC) formed in 1946 (Scott 1954:32). These recruiting organizations covered the whole of southeast Central Africa and must be seen as a critical factor not only in the circulatory labor migration but also in the growing urban centers. Similar organizations served the mines in South Africa, such as the Witwatersrand Native Labour Association (WNLA), the Native Recruiting Corporation (NRC), and more recently the South West Africa Native Labour Association (SWANLA).

The influence and long-term effect of these organizations cannot be overstated. They recruited Africans from field and village, provided free transport to and from the center of employment and also transported their material purchases back with them, and by doing these things irrevocably altered village routine, rural living and the expectations and wants of villagers. Here, often, was the start of a lifetime of migration. Houghton and Walton (1952:120 ff.) explain how people keep returning to labor centers and discuss one case of a fifty-six-year-old man who has made no fewer than fourteen such labor migrations over the past forty years. The history of culture change and urban migration in southern Africa must be seen in terms of taxes which had to be paid and mines which offered jobs where such cash could be earned.[4]

But the need for money to pay taxes is only one of a variety of economic reasons for entering a labor market — especially if we keep in mind that relatively few Africans resident in South Africa entered the mines. Thus, speaking of Botswana, then Bechuanaland, Schapera (1934:49) pointed out that "of the men who go out to work, the great majority find ultimate employment as unskilled industrial labourers in the Witwatersrand and

---

[4] In his very thorough analysis of the development of labor migration in Malawi, Sanderson (1961:268) explains that the African Lakes Corporation (registered in Nyasaland) and the Tanganyika Concessions Ltd. (registered in Northern Rhodesia) recruited Africans as porters in Nyasaland in 1901. These porters transported goods from Karonga (at the northern tip of the lake) and later from Blantyre to the Luapula River and thence to Katanga in the Congo. "This traffic inevitably led to some recruiting of Nyasas for the Katanga copper mines."

other urban areas of the Transvaal... The mines do not attract many of
them." While the Native Labour Regulation Act of 1911 facilitated the
recruitment of mine workers throughout southern Africa, the largest
percentage of African mine laborers have always come from areas outside
South Africa (Table 1).

As increasing numbers of persons were influenced by missionaries,
schools, white residents, and returning workers, the WANTS for money
became more important than the NEEDS for money. Once we have reached
this point, of course, it is increasingly difficult to delineate the primary
reason for migration. While money needs may have caused early migrations, money wants become avenues by which to satisfy secondary and
personal needs.

Table 1.   Geographical sources of black labor employed by the chamber of Mines,
in percent (from F. Wilson 1970:207)

	1896–1898 (n=54,000)	1936 (n=318,000)	1969 (n=371,000)
Transvaal	23.4	7.0	3.8
Natal and Zululand	1.0	4.9	1.9
Swaziland		2.2	1.4
Cape		39.2	23.6
Lesotho	11.1	14.5	17.5
O.F.S.		1.1	2.1
Botswana	3.9	2.3	4.0
Mozambique	60.2	27.8	26.8
North of latitude 22° South	0.5	1.1	18.8

2.   *Man Does Not Live by Bread Alone*

One of the first changes in the pattern of urban migration came with the
rapid influx of African women. This changed both the composition and
nature of the population as an increasing number were migrating to towns
and cities for reasons other than simply to earn the necessary cash. As
women arrived and urban family life took on a new meaning, observers
could record and analyze the new urban life style.

While initial male migration may have begun because of the direct
need for cash, these first migrants opened avenues which led away from
the village. These avenues were used by an increasing number of persons,
male and female, who had other wants which could be satisfied by leaving
the village or by living in the city.

African villages have always been characterized by a certain degree of individual migration. These migrants may be categorized as those who had to leave and those who wanted to leave. In the first category would be persons who, due to social or personal circumstances, find life in the village community less than pleasant. This may include barren or divorced women, persons of a quarrelsome disposition, persons found to be suspect in sorcery accusations, younger sons where birth order gives preference to seniority, and others "who, through accident of birth and personal circumstances, are badly placed to compete for position of authority" (Garbett 1967:312) in the traditional system. In the second category would be persons who have developed wants which cannot be satisfied in the traditional village. One of the major factors here was education, especially for males, which equipped them for urban jobs (Ejiogu 1968: 326), while others might migrate to town because the setting promises better educational facilities for their children. There are also those migrants who see the social structure of the urban center as offering a potential for achieving positions of prestige in a new status system. In the new setting wealth and the ability to use it allow the younger kinsman and the junior lineage member opportunities to gain recognition. Migration might allow the young man an escape from parental or avuncular authority at an age when he resents it. It might also offer a person a place in which to abide while he awaits a time when land will become more easily transferable (Gugler 1969:148) or his status *vis-à-vis* his kinsmen will improve.

We must include here, of course, "repeaters." By this I mean those persons who might have been forced by economic hardship to make their first migration and then, for a variety of reasons, repeat the journey. Here we are dealing with the characteristic group who spend their lives alternating between a period in the industrial center and a period in the rural village. Houghton (1958:42) explains that millions of Africans spend their lives in this way, and Mitchell (1969:179) has constructed a paradigm representing this oscillation. While the length of time in the city or in the country on each visit might vary, Margaret Read calculated that the average length of absence in Nyasaland was three years and seven months (Read 1942:620).

Since the first labor migrants and thus the first returnees from the city were male, it is to be expected that a class of unattached women, many of them prostitutes, would soon follow the same avenues to the mine or city. It should be kept in mind that indentured labor resulted in a higher age of marriage, and that the influence of missionaries and teachers resulted in fewer polygynous marriages, with the result that there were increasing numbers of single girls, unmarried widows, and divorced women. In regard to the early Copper Belt development Godfrey Wilson (1941) has pointed out that prostitutes did not regard their positions as permanent. Many of these relationships between a woman and a man with whom she cohabits for money soon change into a domestic union. Much the same observations have recently been made concerning Hausa women. Cohen observes that such unattached women may be listed in census figures simply as "petty traders" in constrast to "housewives." Such women would be present in every urban Hausa community in Yorubaland, frequently moving from community to community. "The significance of this institution is not that it has supplied migrant men with sexual pleasures in foreign lands, but that it has been perhaps the most important channel for mobilizing potential housewives for the pioneering communities" (1969:61–62).

It would seem that the route from prostitute to concubine to wife was not an unfamiliar one for women urban migrants. Regarding Langa (Levin 1947:84) and Rooiyard (Hellmann 1948:55), we find that marriage stability is affected by sexual licentiousness, while in East London "five minute lovers" are much more prevalent than actual prostitutes (Pauw 1963:135).

The original reason why such women left their natal villages must be our concern. As in the case of males who drift to the city for employment, a variety of personal and social factors might influence the decision.

3.   Domestic Stresses and Strains

The social factor alluded to above may originate in the domestic, kin, or local group. While different strains may apply to males or females, depending on the descent system and the residential pattern in the traditional social structure, such stresses and strains are not new.

It is well known that traditional African village life is marked by strains in social relations and interaction, like all communities, but that these often lead to accusations of witchcraft and sorcery, (e.g. J. Krige 1947; Marwick 1965a, 1965b; Wilson 1951). Such strained relations frequently resulted in segmentation or in the individual removing himself. Labor migration offered a new "out." It also offered an escape for young women who had learned or heard about the town, about marriage for love, and had idealized the new position of women. Thus Mayer mentions a variety reasons why Xhosa migrate to town (1961:237–242); among them is that of young women who revolt against traditional parents who marry them off with little concern for their feelings. Many may in fact drift to town to follow an absent boy friend.

Domestic situations may involve the death of a parent or a provider, leaving the person with little social or material support. They might also involve quarrels with a clan elder or a chief, thus with authority, and the relative anonymity of the urban conditions thus gain in attraction.

4. Social Norms and Networks

These factors are likely not to have been the first causes, but are the out-flow of previous migrations by kinsmen, village members, or fellow tribesmen. These persons had opened an avenue, and it is used by others wishing to travel to a city or by those who are expected to travel to the city.

In this last category are such societies as Tswana, Alur, and others where "migration is considered almost a *rite de passage*, marking the attainment of adulthood" (Mitchell 1970:31). It is thus expected that a man spend time away in the city or in the mines. It is superfluous to point out that such an initial step may result in a repetition of the journey or in permanent migration. In this type of analysis the researcher must re-peatedly refocus his attention from individual to individual as he follows networks and social ties. Such personal relationships, which are at the bottom of evaluations and decisions regarding migration, have been emphasized by Philip Mayer in his research on the Xhosa as townsmen or tribesmen. In this context he states "... a migrant's willingness to stay on in town depends upon how he evaluates the new personal ties he has formed there in relation to the older ties with persons still in the country. If the new ties have sufficient moral content, he will have become personally rooted in town.... If the strong moral content remains solely the attribute of... the extra-town ties, the migrant will expect to go away again..." (1964:24). We are obviously dealing here with an evaluation of ties, an evaluation which each person makes for himself. While he is single this decision and evaluation is an easy one. When he establishes personal ties through friendship, love affairs, marriage, or a family, the evaluation becomes more complex and the decision a more difficult one.

Such migration may also, and usually does, utilize a complex network of social ties, based on either kinship or non-kin based amity. (Meyer Fortes argues that "kinship predicates the axiom of amity" [1969:237].) The rural community then becomes one micro-field in a complex set of social relations and networks in which there is a continuous flow of communications, visitations, gifts, and personnel between the rural micro-field and the urban micro-field. Thus the urban contacts become major acculturative forces in the village community, while the latter acts as a "reservoir of tradition" (Krige 1936:3) influencing behavioral patterns of urban residents.

It becomes possible then for a person to send his children to the rural areas during their younger years, or to send older children to kinsmen in the city for better schooling. The urban resident may also utilize this network to return to the village when he is ill, unemployed, or too old to work. The village ties then take the place of institutions of social security which are largely lacking in most African cities. In her study of urban family structure in London, Elizabeth Bott (1957) differentiates between loose-knit networks and close-knit networks, in which the latter refers to networks in which there are numerous relationships between the component units. These units (people) may be kinsmen, friends, neighbors, co-workers, and similar persons who know each other and interact regularly. The African city is marked by such close-knit social networks which, however, extend beyond the geographical limits of the city (see also Busia 1950:73; Mabogunje 1962:4).

5. *Bright Lights and the Great Unknown*

For a brief period social scientists considered African urban migration in terms of the attractions the city offered. Phillip Gulliver coined and then dismissed the "bright lights theory" (1957:58) while others have emphasized the new urban frontiers to be explored by modern-day African explorers. Most social scientists now agree that while these factors might be involved in the evaluations of a prospective migrant, they will not be the primary considerations. While they may be considered as part of the attraction in the new setting they will seldom be the mechanisms that trigger the migration. This does not deny the fact that persons may mention them as influencing a decision to move. Mayer refers to young Xhosa who migrate to town because of the freedom and anonymity of the city in contrast to the "dull" life in the rural setting (1961:241). It is needless to point out that the city very often turns out to be vastly different from what the migrant had expected it to be. Any research must then include a category which distinguishes beliefs about the city and perceptions upon arrival. (This will be discussed below.)[5]

---

[5]   Mabogunje states that "a major area of research into rural-urban migration thus concerns the flow of information between the urban and the rural areas" (1970:13).

6. *The Multi-causal Nexus*

The way in which this model will operate depends on the region of Africa
we are considering and will also depend on the time under consideration.
There are significant variations between urban migration in Nigeria and
South Africa, or between Ganda and Zulu. There are also significant
differences in the way this phenomenon occurred, say in 1929, in contrast
to the present. While economic or social stimuli may have been of basic
importance at a particular time or for one specific group of people, we will
always find a nexus of advantages and disadvantages which are considered. While we may construct a hierarchy of causes in which one receives
primary rating over another, each forms a part of the multi-causal nexus.
If anthropology is in fact the total study of man, this holistic approach
must carry over to the urban scene. We must see urban man as influenced
by a multi-faceted complex of causes.

APPLYING THE MODEL

Interest in southern African urbanization and such changes in traditional
African culture is somewhat recent, but fortunately it has included observations by Africans. Some of the important early observations were
made by such well-known persons as John L. Dube, D. D. T. Jabavu and
Mrs. Jabavu, Mrs. C. M. Maxeke, S. S. Tema, and R. V. Selope Thema.

Soon, persons trained in the social sciences entered the field of urban
African life. Some of the best known early observers are Ellen Hellmann
(1935, 1937, 1948), Eileen Krige (1936), and J. D. Rheinallt Jones (1934).
The impact of urban conditions also drew the attention of various church
and religious associations. Thus the Christian Council of South Africa
convened a conference in Pretoria in 1940 where papers were read dealing
with "The Disintegration of African Family Life."

From these studies of life in urban conditions and similar studies of
traditional village life a relatively well-documented picture of African
life was constructed.[6] However, except for Schapera early on (1947) and
Mayer more recently (1961), there has been little concern with the

---

[6] In the light of all that is known I find it strange that Berglund still characterizes
the migrant by "the lack of family ties" and "the absence of the shades." These things,
he states, contribute to "the complete lack of responsibility in various ways" amongst
migrants (1970:42). Even more disturbing is Berglund's discussion of the "world-
view" of the migrant and it is refreshing to keep in mind that we have more balanced
and objective studies. See Bernard Magubane's perhaps overly-critical analysis of
ethnocentrism on the part of researchers in southern and central Africa (1971).

process of moving to the city, and back again, with planning or predicting this movement, and with the implications of this movement.[7] To recognize the implication we must study: (a) the person who moves, (b) the village or community from which he moves, and (c) the city or community into which he moves.

The theoretical model which will guide this discussion has been outlined in general terms elsewhere (du Toit 1968). Briefly, the model postulates an effective and continuous link, or series of links, between the rural community and the urban community. Between these two points there is frequent communication and both personnel and goods flow in both directions between village and city. This does not suggest that a person in the village can travel to the city and act there without some adaptation in his behavioral pattern. In fact, both institutions and individual behavior must adapt to new situations:

It should be emphasized that the kind of inter-personal relations and the institutions which are formed in rural villages differ fundamentally from the developments in the urban micro-field. While they differ, they do serve as the prototype from which new institutions and new kinds of associations develop in new situations. Since there is this degree of cultural continuity it is possible to distinguish between micro-fields in the multi-tribal city. Logically, then, the study of the African city will present us with varieties of relationships, types of institutions, and kinds of associations which are distinctively African (du Toit 1968:1969).

This kind of link which is so typical of African urbanization, and which assures cultural continuity is schematically represented in Figure 1.

The question which follows is why particular people leave the rural tribal area for the city, or return from the city to a rural village or farm. For this discussion we will speak simply of the "rural tribal area" in Figure 1 as ORIGIN and the urban area as DESTINATION with the clear understanding that these labels may be reversed when a person moves away from the city.

Following Rossi (1955) we need to establish at the point of origin an index of pros and cons regarding mobility. For our purposes we must adapt his MOBILITY POTENTIAL INDEX (which applies to intracity or inter-city migration in the United States) to a MIGRATION POTENTIAL INDEX (hereafter referred to as MPI) which applies to rural-urban or urban-rural migration in Africa. Figure 2 shows a point of origin in which numerous positive and negative symbols appear. The same is true for the point of

[7] Mabogunje states: "Few studies have concerned themselves with the universe of potential migrants. More often, the tendency has been to study only those who successfully made the move" (1970:5).

1. political unions
2. kinship system — clan and lineage
3. rural based institutions and structure

4. reciprocity based on kinship
5. marriages arranged by family groups
6. village residential pattern

a. marriage intratribal
b. friendship ties
c mutual aid associations
d. class structure and elite
e. wife/a companion in marriage
f. tribal social distance

u. work groups
v. labor unions
w. intertribal marriage
x. schools
y. church groups
z. intertribal friendship

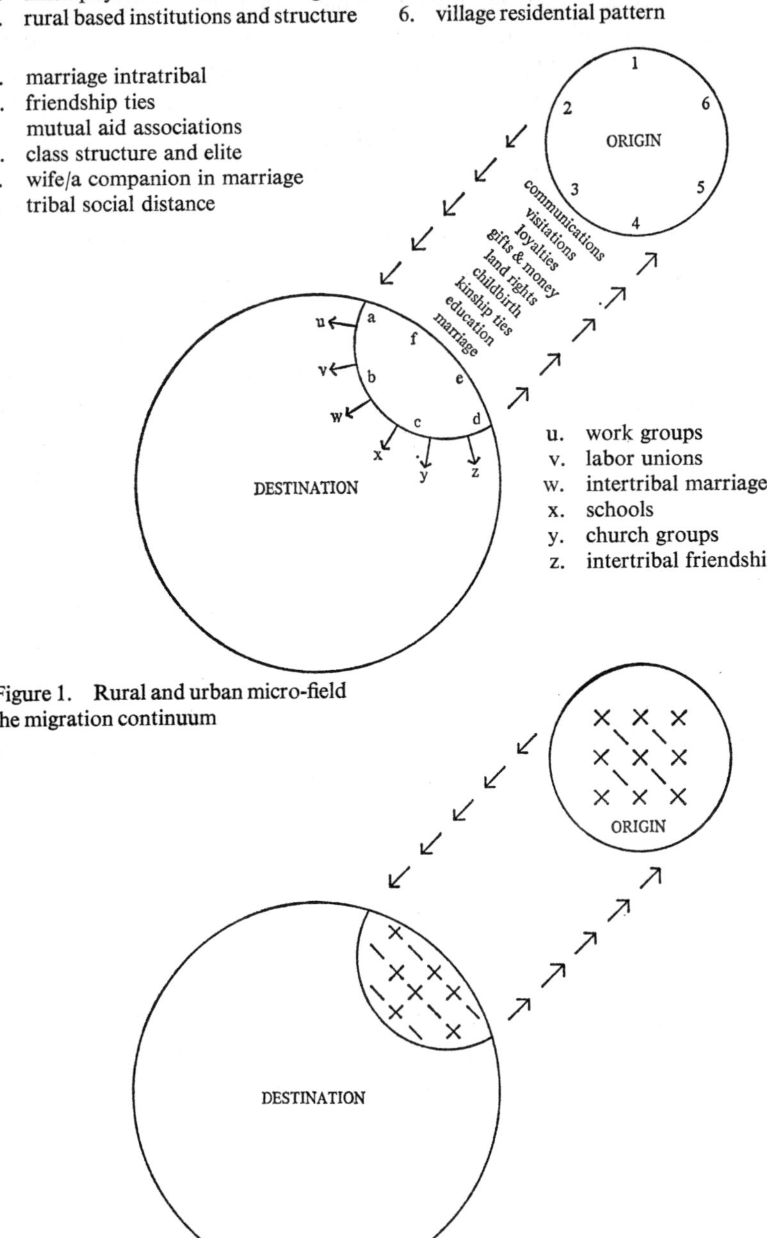

Figure 1.   Rural and urban micro-field
the migration continuum

Figure 2.   Rural and urban micro-fields in the migration continuum, each representative of advantageous and disadvantageous factors

destination. A positive symbol represents an aspect of living in a condition which is desirable, acceptable, or pleasurable to the person making the evaluation while a negative symbol represents aspects or conditions which are undesirable, unacceptable, or unpleasant. Each and every person in whatever situation he finds himself is continuously evaluating his living conditions and surroundings as well as his future and ways of coping with it. In other words, for every aspect of living such as housing, space, income, social relations, schooling, and similar aspects a person is consciously (or perhaps subconsciously) making a positive or negative evaluation. At the same time, each person is the recipient of information about conditions in other places such as other villages, rural areas, towns, or cities. This information is constituted of rumors, suspicions, and factual information about specific conditions elsewhere. Thus the person may know that he can earn more money in the city, that he can therefore purchase more food or clothing (both represented by positive symbols), but on the other hand he would be in unfamiliar surroundings, he would not have the same degree of support of kinsmen, he would have to buy all his clothing and food, while much of the latter is raised in the rural setting. These factors would be represented by negative symbols.

It might be expected that when the positive in the Destination outweighs the negative, or when the negative in the Origin outweighs the positive, or when the positive in the Destination outweighs the positive in the Origin, a person would be ready to migrate. In other words, the MPI indicates a balance in favor of the Destination. But there is much more to such an MPI than simply weighing two situations.

The destination is always surrounded by a certain amount of uncertainty. Can one get a house, will the family be happy, what will be done in a crisis? The tendency then is for a positive evaluation in the Origin to be more weighted than a positive in the Destination.

There are also in the MPI certain PRIMARY CONSIDERATIONS (concerned with the basic needs for staying alive and making a living) and SECONDARY CONSIDERATIONS (which deal with less important needs and wants). A positive evaluation in one case is therefore not necessarily of equal weight to a positive in another case. Every person, furthermore, has his personal background and personality which predispose him toward particular values and choices. These must be kept in mind when a person's migration potential is calculated. It makes a great deal of difference whether a person is married or single, whether a couple is childless or has children, whether the children are pre-schoolers or older, whether they have cordial residential relations or not.

When a pattern is established in a particular society it is much easier to follow a choice which receives normative sanction than to be deviant by "running off to the city." In many cases such a "Road to Work" (Niddrie 1954) exists and the expected and accepted mode of travel is even established. In other cases a person may travel to a more distant urban center and thus innovate and initiate a new migration route. This kind of empirical material is best gathered in terms of individual histories of migration in the way Garbett (1960) has done.

The paradigm which presents itself for south and central African conditions has been drafted by Mitchell and is presented as Figure 3. The "pressures" of which Mitchell speaks are equivalent to my positively or

Age	Pressures operating while in rural areas	Pressures operating while in labor centers
18	Normal expectation to start work. Economic pressures especially to acquire marriage payment. School fees for	
20	younger siblings.	
		Obligation to parents, especially agricultural, and interest in marriage.
25	Pressure from parents-in-law and wife and young family	
		Need to maintain agricultural production and necessity of visiting his wife and children and building a house for them
30	Rising costs of growing family, especially school fees, taxation	
		Kinship obligations to ageing parents and parents-in-law. Responsibilities in connection with sisters; need to repair houses and maintain agriculture.
40	Purchase of cattle and acquisition of farm equipment. Alternatively accumulation of capital for rural enterprises.	
		Greater difficulty of re-employment if job is lost. Loss of housing if means of support disappears. Succession to office and position of authority in rural system — especially if father is dead. Eldest son about to make his first trip to town.
50		
55		

Figure 3. Paradigm of a labor migrant career (from Mitchell 1969:179)

negatively charged evaluation of conditions in a particular Origin versus Destination. When these two are basically equal in evaluation one would tend to find the oscillation represented in the figure, but when one definitely outweighs the other a firmer commitment may be made by remaining in Origin or migrating for a longer period to Destination. There may also be other intervening obstacles such as responsibilities or commitments which prevent migration. These would be built-in negative aspects to migration and thus be scored against Destination.

The discussion above argues for a multi-causal nexus of stimuli which influence urban migration. That nexus needs to be broken down here into different factors which would constitute an MPI and which can in fact be tested in research.

a. Indices which are primarily economic in nature would include such factors as: income in cash, cost of housing, housing facilities, space in housing, cost of food, cost of clothing, cost of transport, support from neighbors and kin not measurable in cash.

b. Indices which are basically individual in nature and relate to the person, are: the person's age (or the stage in the life cycle), sex (biologically and sociologically considered), and position in the family of origin. Also physical and psychological conditions, such as social integration, barrenness of females, and relations with fellow village members.

c. Familial factors which would influence a person's decision to migrate include whether he is married or single, has parental or sibling commitments, the number of children (if married), proximity and relations with kinsmen, and the stage in the household's life cycle (married couple only, small children, older children, old couple, etc.)

d. One would also consider such related factors as marital instability, relations with kinsmen and affines, relations with chief or headman or political leader, relations with neighbors. On this level, too, are desires for prestige, consideration of educational opportunities, entertainment ("brighter lights factor") opportunities, and similar but more subjective and more nebulous considerations.

Once the researcher has constructed such an index (and obviously it will differ for each city or village under study) it can be scored by testing each of the criteria which constitute the final index for a given city or village against statements by the subject and against statements by the other persons who know the subjects. In addition, the researcher may make his own evaluation of the importance of such a criterion as deduced from the statements and reactions he gathered. Each of the criteria can then be scored on a three- or four-point score and a tabular sheet considered.

In his study of the social and psychological influences on urban residential mobility in Philadelphia, Rossi makes a number of points which would seem to place people in the U.S. at variance with Africans. The author states that "the most mobile elements in the two mobile areas studied were families with children" (1955:6), and not childless couples or single persons as one would expect. Along these same lines he found that:

a. The younger the head of a household, the higher its inclination toward mobility,
b. the larger the household, the higher its mobility,
c. age and size are independently related, but age is more strongly related to mobility than household size (Rossi 1955:71).

The importance of age has also been confirmed by other urban workers. Leslie and Richardson (1961:894) explain that "high mobility rates for young persons presumably reflect new marriages, families expanding with the birth of children, and moves associated with the husband's employment. Each of these factors operates with less force at older ages." We would suggest that in Africa we find a new high point in mobility at a later age when retirees and widowed persons return to the rural area.

If this model is used and the great complexity of variables analyzed, all of which are then constructed as indices in a Migration Potential Index, the researcher should arrive at data regarding: (1) THE DESIRE TO MOVE. This would include reasons for dissatisfaction with the *status quo* and *locus quo* as well as factors which seem especially attractive in Destination. (2) THE DECISION TO MOVE. This gives an indication of the mobility intentions, and a choice of particular factors over others. (3) PREPARATIONS TO MOVE. The person or family starts loosening ties at Origin, establishing contacts at Destination, saving money, and planning. (4) ACTION OR INACTION. At this stage, the individual or family may decide to move either as a family, serially (the husband going ahead), or they may decide not to move. This leaves the researcher then with the actual migrant plus two subcategories: (a) unexpected movers, and (b) unexpected stayers.

Once again, it should be stressed that ORIGIN and DESTINATION denote places which may change depending on whether we deal with rural residents contemplating migration to the city, or urban residents who are attracted to the rural area. We should also keep in mind that there are two kinds of information about Destination, that based on fact or observation in contrast to varying levels of oral accounts, fantasies and perhaps idealization.

The logical continuation of this discussion touches on the next phase of the migration, namely adaptation. We are dealing now with the man (and the family) who have migrated and settled down in Destination — the urban area.

It is generally accepted that when a person has been educated and enculturated into a given culture with its own world view, values, as well as problem-solving methods and personality orientation, special changes are necessary before he can adjust harmoniously into a new cultural setting. It would also be accepted that a person who was enculturated into rural village culture would not be equipped to live and function normally in the city without special adaptation. In the rural setting, he had gradually been given a set of premises which led to rewarded choices and actions. These cultural rules were no doubt arrived at through experimentation and innovation until the "proper" way of doing things was arrived at.[8] Such "proper" action in the village has consensus but it applies to village or rural conditions and is sanctioned by the members of a rural community. The urban migrant who attempts to act according to the traditional "proper" way when he arrives in the city is disillusioned — he fails. And so a number of "smart" ways to act or make choices are arrived at. These are based on innovations when the urban dweller is confronted with novel situations and finds that he must try out a number of empirical guides to action. In the early stages, these actions are usually experimental and speculative but as the new arrival learns from selecting and acting in the new situation and from association with others, his acts and choices become more rational. The culture of the city is therefore an urban variation of the culture in which a person was encultured. "The African city must be seen as one end of a cultural continuum which produces a kind of urban culture which differs from other urban cultures... in that they draw on different reservoirs and grow from different rural bases" (du Toit 1968:69).

CONCLUSION

This paper has dealt with the subject of human migration as it applies to southern Africa. Our point of departure and final discussion dealt with Mangalam's definition of migration (see page 5), which implies: (a) the weighing of a hierarchiacally ordered set of advantages and disadvantages involved in moving, (b) the decision-making process which

---

[8]   I am indebted to Morris Freilich for the concepts "proper" and "smart." He states: "The natives, it is assumed, divide their world into what is proper (traditional) and what is smart (rational and speculative). What is smart is then subdivided into what is probably smart (rational), and what is possibly smart (speculative). What is smart and what is proper are then dichotomized into what is popular (has consensus), and what is not popular (lacks consensus)" (1970:515).

is followed by (c) the relatively permanent move which then results in (d) changes in the interactional system of the migrant. The model suggested would see a continuous interactional system, with different rates and different kinds associated with the rural versus the urban situation. This analysis did not deal with the adjustment of migrants to new situations. Much has in any case been written concerning the urban African and the emergence of an urban life style.

As regards southern Africa, we are dealing with cities which are permanently marked by interaction patterns and social networks which involve whites and Africans. This social setting and these components in the interactional system influence decisions to migrate, and the process of adjustment. The setting is also marked by industrial plants and employment possibilities. A true differentiation cannot be made in the south African system. However, two poles can be posited. These are represented by a rural, agriculturally-based, relatively homogenous peasant village which is in continuous interaction with an urban, heterogeneous, industrial complex. Neither of these exists without the other, and there is a continuous interchange of personnel, goods, and ideas between the urban and the rural area.

Our primary concern in this paper has been the factors which are considered when a person is presented with the possibility of changing his place of residence. This place of residence implies the work situation, the home, friends, relatives, and a host of other factors. *Invariably we find that the migrant evaluates a complex nexus of factors, factors which are given perspective by their social and cognitive context.* While the title of this paper refers to language and ethnicity as factors in migration, we might think of them as CONTEXTUAL FACTORS, or what Philip Mayer called "moral content." The income which can be earned in one situation over another may be important or not, depending on the context within which it can be earned. When we add to this the importance of the ethnic or linguistic group member in opening up avenues for migration, providing information regarding the potential destination of migration and then smoothing over the migration and subsequent adjustment of the migrant, it becomes clear that *we are in fact dealing here with two of the most important contextual qualifiers.*

In and of themselves they may not be critical. A person might not migrate simply because he has ethnic and linguistic contacts (although this sometimes allows the migrant to move and then to consider the implications), but given a certain amount of information and a decision-making situation, the choice is invariably made in terms of these factors. While these factors decrease in significance as persons become urban oriented or as they are better able to travel, they must be considered of primary importance for persons making the initial migration from their natal family and social setting.

If urban anthropology is going to progress beyond analysis and description, a decision-making model must be instrumental to understanding and planning for migration. When urban planners and social administrators have some way of predicting migration, they will also be in a position to plan for migration and for the avenues of mobility. In an increasingly densely populated world this subject could be just another theme for graduate student papers, or it could become a meeting place of scientists, administrators, and planners.

REFERENCES

BEIJER, G.
   1969   "Modern patterns of international migratory movements," in *Migration*. Edited by J. A. Jackson, 11–59. Cambridge: Cambridge University Press.
BERG, ELLIOTT J.
   1965   "The economics of the migrant labor system," in *Urbanization and migration in West Africa*. Edited by Hilda Kuper, 160–181.
BERGLUND, AXEL-IVAR
   1970   "Transition from traditional to a Westernized outlook on life," in *Migrant labour and church involvement*. Distributed by Mapumulo, Natal: Missiological Institute.
BOTT, ELIZABETH
   1957   *Family and social network*. London: Tavistock.
BUSIA, KOFI A.
   1950   *Report on a social survey of Sekondi-Takoradi*. London.
CALDWELL, JOHN C.
   1969   *African rural-urban migration*. New York: Columbia University Press.
CALDWELL, J. C., C. OKONJO
   1968   *The population of tropical Africa*. New York: Columbia University Press.
COHEN, ABNER
   1969   *Custom and politics in urban Africa*. Berkeley: University of California Press.
DU TOIT, BRIAN M.
   1968   "Cultural continuity and African urbanization," in *Urban anthropology, research perspectives and strategies*. Edited by E. Eddy. Athens: University of Georgia Press.
EJIOGU, C. N.
   1968   "African rural-urban migrants in the main migrant areas of the Lagos Federal territory," in *The population of tropical Africa*. Edited by

John C. Caldwell and Chukuka Okonjo. New York: Columbia University Press.

FLINN, WILLIAM L.
1971   "Rural and intra-urban migration in Columbia, two case studies in Bogotà," in *Latin American urban research*, volume one. Edited by F. F. Rabinowitz and F. M. Trueblood. Beverly Hills: Sage.

FORTES, MEYER
1965   "Culture contact as a dynamic process," in *Methods of study of culture contact in Africa*. Edited by L. P. Mair. Memorandum XV, International African Institute, London.
1969   *Kinship and the social order*. Chicago: Aldine.

FREILICH, MORRIS
1970   "Toward a formalization of field work," in *Marginal natives: anthropologists at work*. Edited by Morris Freilich, 485–594. New York: Harper and Row.

GARBETT, G. K.
1960   *Growth and change in a Shona ward*. Department of African Studies, University College of Rhodesia and Nyasaland, Occasional Paper 1. Salisbury.
1967   Prestige, status and power in a modern valley Korekore chiefdom, Rhodesia. *Africa* 37: 307–326.

GROSSKOPF, J. F. W.
1932   *The poor white problem in South Africa*. Stellenbosch: Pro Ecclesia Press.

GUGLER, JOSEF
1969   "On the theory of rural-urban migration: the case of sub-Saharan Africa," in *Migration*. Edited by J. A. Jackson, 134-155. Cambridge: Cambridge University Press.

GULLIVER, P.
1957   Nyakyusa labour migration. *Rhodes Livingstone Institute* 21: 32–63.
1960   Incentives in labor migration. *Human Organization* 19:159–163.

HELLMANN, ELLEN P.
1935   Native life in a Johannesburg slum yard. *Africa* 8:34–62.
1937   "The native in the towns," in *The Bantu-speaking tribes of South Africa*. Edited by I. Schapera, 405–34. Cape Town: Maskew Miller.
1948   *Rooiyard*. Rhodes Livingstone Paper 13. Cape Town: Oxford University Press.

HERSKOVITS, M. J.
1957   *Anthropology and cultural change in Africa*. Communication of the University of South Africa. Pretoria.

HOLZNER, L., GRAHAM H. T. HART
1970   Cultural-genetic aspects of Bantu urbanization in South Africa. *The Professional Geographer* 22(2):67–73.

HOUGHTON, D. HOBART
1958   "Migrant labour," in *Africa in transition*. Edited by P. Smith 39–46. London: Max Reinhardt.

HOUGHTON, D. H., E. M. WALTON
1952   *The economy of a native reserve*. Keiskammahoek Rural Survey, volume eleven. Pietermaritzburg: Shuter and Shooter.

HOWARD, ALAN
  1963   Land activity systems, and decision-making models in Rotuma. *Ethnology* 2:407–440.
KRIGE, E. J.
  1936   Changing conditions in marital relations and parental duties among urbanized natives. *Africa* 9:1–23.
KRIGE, J. D.
  1947   The social function of witchcraft. *Theoria* 1:8–21.
KUPER, LEO, HILSTAN WATTS, RONALD DAVIES, *editors*
  1958   *Durban: a study in racial ecology.* London: Jonathan Cape.
LESLIE, GERALD R., ARTHUR H. RICHARDSON
  1961   Life cycle, career pattern and the decision to move. *American Sociological Review* 26:894–902.
LEVIN, R.
  1947   "Marriage in Langa native location." Communication from the School of African Studies, University of Cape Town.
MABOGUNJE, AKIN L.
  1962   *Yoruba towns.* Ibadan: The University Press.
  1970   Systems approach to a theory of rural-urban migration. *Geographical Analysis* 2:1–18.
MAGUBANE, BERNARD
  1971   A critical look at indices used in the study of social change in Colonial Africa. *Current Anthropology* 12:419–445.
MARWICK, M. G.
  1965a   *Sorcery in its social setting.* Manchester: Manchester University Press.
  1965b   "Some problems in the sociology of sorcery and witchcraft," in *African systems of thought.* Edited by M. Fortes and G. Dieterlen, 171–91. London: Oxford University Press.
MAYER, P.
  1961   *Townsmen or tribesmen: conservatism and the process of urbanization in a South African city.* Cape Town: Oxford University Press.
  1962   Migrancy and the study of Africans in towns. *American Anthropologist* 64:576–592.
  1964   "Labour migrancy and the social network," in *Problems of Transition.* Edited by J. F. Holleman, et al., 21–51. Pietermaritzburg: Natal University Press.
MITCHELL, J. CLYDE
  1956   *The Yao village.* Manchester: University Press.
  1969   "Structural plurality, urbanization and labour circulation in Southern Rhodesia," in *Migration.* Edited by J. A. Jackson, 156–801. Cambridge: Cambridge University Press.
  1970   "Tribalism and the plural society," in *Black Africa.* Edited by John Middleton 257–69. New York: Macmillan.
NIDDRIE, DAVID
  1954   The road to work. *Rhodes-Livingstone Institute Journal* 15:31–42.
PAUW, B. A.
  1963   *The second generation: a study of the family among urbanized Bantu in East London.* Cape Town: Oxford University Press.

PROTHERO, R. M.
1957   Migratory labour from north-western Nigeria. *Africa* 27:251–261.
1962   Migrant labour in west Africa. *Journal of Local Administration Overseas* 1:149–155.
1965   Socio-economic aspects of rural/urban migration in Africa south of the Sahara. *Scientia.*

RAVENSTEIN, E. G.
1885   The laws of migration. *Journal of the Royal Statistical Society* 48.

READ, MARGARET
1942   Migrant labour in Africa and its effects on tribal life. *International Labour Review* 45.

RHEINALLT JONES, J. D.
1934   "Social and economic conditions of the urban native," in *Western civilization and the natives of South Africa.* Edited by T. Schapera, 159–192. London: George Routledge and Sons.

ROSSI, PETER H.
1955   *Why families move.* Glencoe: The Free Press.

ROTBERG, ROBERT I.
1965   *A political history of tropical Africa.* New York: Harcourt, Brace and World.

SANDERSON, F. E.
1961   The development of labour migration from Nyasaland, 1891–1914. *Journal of African History* 2:259–271.

SCHAPERA, I.
1934   Labour migration from a Bechuanaland Native Reserve, part two. *Journal of the African Society* 33:60–69.
1947   *Migrant labour and tribal life.* London: Oxford University Press.

SCOTT, PETER
1954   Migrant labour in Southern Rhodesia. *The Geographical Review* 44:29–48.

THOMPSON, LEONARD
1969   "Cooperation and conflict: the high veld," in *The Oxford history of South Africa,* volume one. Edited by Monica Wilson and Leonard Thompson, 391–446. London: Oxford University Press.

UNION OF SOUTH AFRICA PARLIAMENTARY PAPERS
1932   *Report of the Native Economic Commission, 1930–1932* (=U.G.22).

VAN VELSEN, J.
1961   "Labour migration as a positive factor in the continuity of Tonga tribal society," in *Social change in modern Africa.* Edited by Aidan Southall, 230–241. Studies presented and discussed at the First International African Seminar, Makerere College. London: Oxford University Press.

WATSON, W.
1967   "Migrant labor in Africa: a consideration of its various forms and their relation to traditional and bureaucratic socio-economic system." Paper read at the Tenth Annual Meeting of the *African Studies Association.* New York.

WILSON, F.
1970   "Economics of migrant labour in South Africa," in *Migrant labour and church involvement.* Mapumulo, Natal: Missiological Institute.

WILSON, G. H.

1941   *An essay on the economics of detribalization in Northern Rhodesia.* Rhodes Livingstone Paper 6.

WILSON, MONICA

1951   With beliefs and social structure. *American Journal of Sociology* 56:307–13.

Some Perspectives on Balkan Migration Patterns (with Particular Reference to Yugoslavia)

JOEL M. HALPERN

To understand fully the meaning of contemporary population movements a view of the past is essential. In the period after World War II in the Balkans, mass population movements within countries have been influenced particularly by urban industrial developments. These reflect a delayed process when compared with Western Europe. Within the past decade and a half there has also been a movement of workers from the Balkan countries with open borders — Greece and Yugoslavia — to the labor-deficit countries of Western Europe. These population movements relate not only to altered individual social and economic value systems, but also to questions of ethnic identity. We are too close to these events to delineate them in a comprehensive manner, as both processes are on-going. However, we can gain needed perspective by viewing them in the context of earlier mass movements, whether unique or regular movements.

Some of the variables that must be taken into account in discussing migration patterns are: individual life span, sex, and familial and kin affiliations; economic and occupational factors; governments actions; and such historical factors as war and revolution. Migration simply means passing from one place to another, or moving from one place of residence to another. In its broadest interpretation, it could refer to a trip of almost any kind, particularly one repeated with a certain kind of regularity. A more restricted and useful meaning of the term, and one that will be employed here, is either a change of residence without immediate intention to return to the former home (thus eliminating casual travel for personal-kin reasons or occasional occupation-related trips) or a regularized pattern of movement for a specific purpose (i.e. daily, weekly, or seasonal movements related to employment). This paper examines the origins of migratory movements in a Balkan context and, in so doing, raises questions about the kinds of values associated with residential and occupational stability or mobility from a long-term perspective. It is not the intention here to suggest that a simplistic categorization is possible with respect to the attachment of long-term values either to stability or to mobility. Rather it is to suggest that motivations for mobility and movement are not simply conditioned by perceived economic opportunity; indeed, they are perceived through a cultural screen in which conditioned historical perspectives play a key role.

A specific historical perspective may be useful in understanding the development of migration patterns. The region of Sumadija in central Serbia provides an example related to factors of ethnic identity and national history. Here a complicated series of advancing and retreating movements has occurred in the historically recent past.

As a result of Turkish conquests Sumadija was depopulated after the fifteenth century, when ancestors of the present population sought refuge in the Dinaric uplands to the south. Depopulation was virtually total. A traveler in the region in the second decade of the sixteenth century wrote that Sumadija was completely deserted, whereas a traveler through the same area a century earlier had written about seeing many towns and villages (Stoianovich 1967:28–29; Halpern 1967a: 9–11; Drobnjakovic 1932). In the late seventeenth and the eighteenth centuries, when the area had a dense cover of oak forest, it began to be repopulated (Popovic 1950). Those who then came to Sumadija from the Dinaric mountain regions were pioneers clearing the land and building log houses (Kojic 1949).

This migration experience is vital in defining the social structure of contemporary villages in Sumadija. The men of any village community are able to trace individual descent to the ancestor who originally settled there, established the patrilineal descent group, and gave rise to the family name (Halpern 1967a: 23, 150–161). Contemporary village neighborhoods are also based on this original pattern of settlement (Halpern 1956:323, Table 58). Historic migrations of this type are of such great importance in defining traditional settlement patterns and state territorial boundaries that a school of analysis concerned with tracing migrations developed in Serbian ethnology. Such migrations also occurred in great measure somewhat prior to the emergence of the Serbian state in the nineteenth century.[1] Studies based on them formed some of the back-

---

[1]   The Serbian scholar Jovan Cvijic stated that patterns of migrations were intimately linked with the development of national consciousness after the destruction of the medieval Serbian state at the Battle of Kosovo. This view is presented in summary form

ground to memoranda presented at the peace conference at Versailles after World War I, when the Yugoslav state was established.[2] In sum, this group migration for political-economic reasons is of historic importance.

Once settled in new homes, the inhabitants modified the tribal-lineage organization they had brought with them from the Dinaric mountains. They established large extended family units (*zadrugas*) in which all adult males had a right to inherit.[3]

Such units were ideally adapted to the mixed economy of livestock raising, subsistence farming, and local crafts that developed. However, many of the men soon became involved in two other types of activities which took them from their homes. The first was for economic reasons and had a degree of regularity; the second was irregular and was related to war and revolution.

The *zadruga,* in addition to being a unit adapted to agriculture and extensive livestock herding, was also a trading unit. In the late eighteenth and early nineteenth centuries an extensive trade developed in acorn-fattened pigs, brought by peasants to Austrian traders. Oxen and cattle were driven to Turkish-controlled areas in Bosnia. (Warriner 1965:287–288, 299, 301; Auty 1963). Because there were a number of adult males in the relatively large *zadruga* households, the periodic absence of a member or even several members did not drastically upset the household agricultural economy. This flexibility in structural organization was subsequently used by the Austro-Hungarian government in recruiting *zadruga* households to the frontier areas with the Turks. Here men were able to go on regular service in these military colonies and their households were able to continue to be productive.[4]

The bands of *hajduks* [brigands] that roamed the Balkans in Turkish times could in a sense be considered seasonal migrants, because their activities did tend to have a seasonal focus. The relationship of these *hajduks* to the existing settled *zadrugas* is not clear. Some sources claim that the true brigands rejected kin ties, but this does not appear to be the

---

in Cvijic (1918a) and in more detailed form in Cvijic (1918b). Earlier, Cvijic had initiated an anthropological-geographical series of monographs (Cvijic 1902), which traced the origins and migratory movements of populations of particular regions.

[2] The principles of nationality played a vital role in defining the borders of the new Yugoslav state. It was intended that the basis of the frontiers would be "ethnographic." See Lederer (1963:93, 126–128), who specifically refers to the participation of Cvijic and other Yugoslav ethnologists.

[3] Hammel (1968:13–38) gives a summary of *zadruga* structure.

[4] Rothenberg (1966) describes how this extended family unit fitted into the military organization of the Hapsburg frontier with the Ottomans.

case with Cossack bands in the Ukraine. The distinctions between brigandage, political struggle against the Turkish oppressor, and commercial activities do not always appear clear-cut. (Nor is the interlinking of these activities peculiar to the Balkans, as the New World struggle between the Spanish and the English bears out.) In the Balkan context the importance of mobility for at least certain groups of men in all three types of activity, however intermixed, is clear.[5]

Thus in the Balkans brigandage, crafts, and trade have long been involved with patterns of temporary or permanent migration in the course of villagers' attempts to better themselves economically. Often those most active in these occupations have been villagers who lived in mountainous areas where agriculture was marginal and who already were accustomed to a partially mobile existence because of the requirements of seeking pastures for their flocks. Stoianovich (1960:276) comments on these relationships:

The Greek and Vlach highland inhabitants of Thessaly, Epirus, and Macedonia present another example of the "free" but "wretched" who make fortunes. The pastoral folk of these highlands obtained a livelihood from five principal occupations: the men were herdsmen, brigands, seasonal migratory workers and mercenary soldiers, and muleteers, while the women were skilled weavers. The [people] of the Pindus often did not dwell in a fixed place throughout the year. Seeking green pastures, they climbed the mountains in summer and descended into the lowlands and approached the sea in winter. Since small numbers of individuals can supervise large herds, men tended to become superfluous. Men unable to earn a living through the exercise of economic functions consequently turned to banditry... The expansion of towns in the sixteenth century subsequently opened other occupations to the pastoral rural folk. Younger sons and men who lacked herds or the urge to highway robbery departed from their homes for a season or a year to work as pecalbari or semi-skilled and unskilled laborers in distant towns, even in the Ottoman capital.

He goes on to state:

The availability of raw-material surpluses — wool, cheese, and skins — and craft products, the migratory habits of the men and their intimate knowledge of the difficult routes, their special privileges, which allowed them to bear arms, persuaded a portion of the pastoral folk to become carriers and traders of goods.

[5] Hobsbawn defines the *hajduk* as an insurrectionary, one who became part of a recognized social group and "a more ambitious, permanent and institutionalized challenge to official authority than the scattering of Robin Hoods... which emerged from any normal peasant society" (1969:66). But he maintains that they were primarily a voluntary group detached from kin ties and not a normal social unit. By contrast, Edwards defines a *hajduk* as a brigand, but an individual who is considered a national hero and glorified in the epic ballads (1969:225). The latter definition does not seem to exclude family ties.

Around 1800 it was observed that the Balkan merchants in Hungary were often "from the most wretched villages of Macedonia and other parts of Turkey." By contrast, those peasants in the most prosperous villages were either bound to the soil or worked for landlords (Stoianovich 1960:277).

For the premodern period the historian Braudel (1972) depicts the seasonal rhythm involved in migrations in the Mediterranean area. He cites St. George's Day in April and St. Demetrius's Day at the end of October as the times of the migratory activity. These were the two occasions on which an apprentice entered the service of a master. In April migratory craftsmen left for distant areas, laborers hired themselves out, and the brigands came together. In October the Ottoman armies ceased their campaigns, laborers and craftsmen returned home, shepherds and their flocks left the mountain pastures for the plains, and the highwaymen disbanded (Stoianovich 1967:66–67).

In the 1930's the Yugoslav-American writer Louis Adamic found the *pecalba* tradition functioning in Macedonia in approximately the same sense that Stoianovich described it for the premodern period:

The village of Galichnik — nearly three thousand feet above sea-level in the barren and not easily accessible mountains... is a village of grass widows. For approximately eleven months out of the year, no men – aside from a priest or two and a few octo- and ono-genarians — live in the hundred-odd homes... Their husbands and oldest sons (if more than fifteen years of age) are scattered over Central and Western Europe, Greece, Rumania, and Yugoslavia, the north coast of Africa, parts of Asia Minor, Russia, and the United States, where, during the building seasons, they work at highly specialized trades of masonry, stonecutting, wood-carving, cabinet-making...

Once a year, between the 1st and 15th of July, most of the men return from the big world. Those working in Europe, in Asia Minor, or in North Africa get home yearly; those in America and the distant parts of Russia return but every two or three years... the communal wedding day, when all the couples married that year are wedded simultaneously... occurs on July 12th. When we were there, sixteen couples entered matrimony. All the bridegrooms were from Galichnik. All but two were regular pechalbari. The other two were sheepmen whose flocks' grazing-ground was several hours distant from the village... (Adamic 1934:115–124).[6]

Closely paralleling this journalistic account are more recent descriptions of *pecalba* elicited from villagers in southern Macedonia in the early 1960's. Their accounts stress the importance of kin and village ties.

---

[6] This abbreviated account of approximately forty years ago has taken on a distinct historic flavor. According to a current comment (1973) by a Macedonian scholar, the village is now largely abandoned and most of the former inhabitants have migrated to towns.

Ethnic determinants — Orthodox villagers work in Belgrade and Muslim villagers serve as intermediaries with Turkish officials — are also emphasized.

As a result of earlier Turkish conquests, the society that developed in late eighteenth and early nineteenth century Serbia lacked a native ruling class. The Turks and other foreigners lived in the towns, and the Serbs dominated the countryside (Vucinich 1962:597–616). The more prosperous *zadrugas* which engaged in extensive trade also came to political prominence, and it was from this group that the leadership of the early nineteenth century Serbian revolts against the Turks was derived. During this period there was no organized military recruitment as such; rather the local village and district headmen enlisted men, probably with a degree of coercion, to fight against the Turks (see Edwards 1969).

Contrasting with the individual, kin-linked, economically motivated *pecalba* migratory movements are those involuntary movements linked to state requirements or governmental conflicts, war, and revolution. With the growth of the Serbian state during the nineteenth century, an organized militia developed, and the obligatory military service introduced in 1883 required a term of service for all men twenty years of age.[7] This continues to the present time, and therefore all able-bodied village men serve a period of time in the army, during which they are often posted to distant parts of the country and mix with men of other ethnic origins. All the periodic struggles, two world wars, and their associated conflicts, have resulted in mobilization and periods of conflict in which men were absent from home for years at a time. Although the Serbs and Yugoslavia were ultimately victorious in both world wars, large numbers of men were taken prisoners and as a result traveled extensively. Many men recalled these involuntary migrations as life's most exciting experience. Often villagers were influenced by the period of imprisonment in the more technologically advanced countries of Austria and Germany and returned to their villages with new ideas that contributed to subsequent innovations.

A man in his seventies recalls:

I first served in the army in 1914. I was taken as a young man into the army

---

[7]   (See Sread 1909:80–92). This article also makes the point that the army had its origins in *hajduk* bands, which were of key importance in initiating the First Revolt against the Turks in 1804. Certainly it is possible to see a degree of continuity between the role of the *hajduks* and the subsequent bureaucratization and regularization of military service, in that both involved absences of adult males from the village. Army duty was, of course, universal, compulsory, and of a specified time limit, while *hajduk* activity was the antithesis.

when the Germans invaded our country. The president of the village took a group of us by ox-cart to a town near Valjevo, where we trained for three months... After we succeeded in throwing the Germans [Hapsburg armies] out of Serbia in 1914, we went to the Bulgarian frontier. There, when the Austrians and Germans invaded again in 1915 we were defeated. King Peter returned to Salonica and I was taken prisoner by the Germans. But in 1916 I was interned in Czechoslovakia where I worked in a factory. Later I was sent to work for a farmer in Hungary. There I worked as a peasant. In most ways it was like here. But I was impressed by their use of scythes. Here before the war we used sickles to cut wheat. Our people thought that cutting wheat with a scythe would scatter it. They used to grab a few stalks of wheat and cut them. It took many people 10 to 15 days to cut the wheat. I told my father, "Let's go reap the wheat." He said that it would scatter. I said it wouldn't. So this is the way we changed (Halpern and Halpern 1972:65).

Combined with these experiences of discovery as prisoners is the generally strong positive feeling about military service and pride in one's history and ethnicity. This tradition is reinforced by folk epics, dating back to Turkish times, that speak of heroic, although sometimes futile, overt resistance to the Turkish conquest.

While war-related travel could be beneficial, the obvious suffering should not be overlooked. The Serbian historian Dragoljub Jovanovic describes the enforced migrations within Serbia of World War I:

The most clear-cut impression of the Serbian campaign is the motley, pitiful spectacle of the bezanija, that endless, disorderly flight of fugitives muffled to the eyes, old women, children, on foot or in wooden carts patiently drawn by emaciated and exhausted oxen, driving in front of them some cattle and carrying on their backs or under their arms some chattels, the number and importance of which grew less with every stage of this removal which was always beginning again and never coming to an end (quoted in Stoianovich 1967).

Similar experiences occurred in World War II. One of the consequences of wartime bombing of cities was an inverse, although clearly temporary, migration of city people to the countryside. Also, because of problems in security and food distribution, many city people felt that they could better survive in the countryside (Rayner 1957).[8] The struggle in Yugoslavia during World War II, both a civil war and a fight against the German invaders, involved enormous population movements of the fighting forces as well as of the affected civilian populations. There are certain parallels to World War I and in certain respects the activities of the guerrillas are reminiscent of the struggle against the Turks in the nine-

---

[8] Rayner was an Englishwoman married to a Serb in prewar Beograd who wrote of her experiences in a village outside the capital.

teenth century, in that both were waged to a significant extent from forest and mountain strongholds.[9]

Another direct consequence of World War II in Yugoslavia and the coming to power of a communist government was that many of the defeated forces sought political refuge abroad. These, then, are what might be called forced historic migrations, some of them having major long-term effects. This was particularly true, for example, for two ethnic groups in Yugoslavia. The ethnic Germans, who had been settled in Yugoslavia in an organized manner by the Hapsburgs several centuries previously, sided with the invading Germans and retreated with them.[10] Many of the Yugoslav Jews who survived the occupiers' attempts at extermination moved to Israel soon after the war.

Kosinski (1969) has classified war-related migrations in East-Central Europe into two categories; (1) war transfers from 1939 to 1944 and (2) evacuations and flight at the end of the war, including postwar transfers of populations. Focusing only on Yugoslavia, in the first category he lists 86,000 Serbs and Croats deported from areas made part of Germany and Italy; 190,000 persons transferred within Serbia and Croatia; 40,000 persons deported from Macedonia and incorporated into Bulgaria; and 50,000 Hungarians repatriated from Yugoslavia. A good portion of this movement was related to the wartime dismemberment of the Yugoslav state; the incorporation of bordering areas into Italy, Hungary, and Bulgaria respectively; and the emergence of the independent state, Croatia. Presumably not included in these movements of civilians was the mass transfer of captured Yugoslav army troops to Germany. In the second category were 270,000 ethnic Germans from Yugoslavia who eventually reached West Germany, 40,000 Serbs and Croats repatriated from Hungary, and 200,000 Italians transferred from Yugoslavia to Italy; in 1946–1955 some 28,000 Yugoslav Muslims went to Turkey. Furthermore, approximately 200,000 new settlers came to the Vojvodina from within Yugoslavia, mainly from the mountainous areas. A number of Yugoslav soldiers and civilians who had been prisoners in Germany did not return. In addition, many of the defeated forces of Serbian Royalist Cetniks and Croatian supporters of the fascist wartime Croatian state ended up in West Germany; along with Danubian Germans, many of

[9]   The retreat of the Serbian army through Montenegro into Albania and eventually to Corfu is described in Adams (1942). The eventual victory of the partisans is depicted in diary extracts in Dedijerts (1951). Both contain accounts of civilian population movements, although that is not their main focus.

[10]   Paikert (1967) describes the founding of German colonies in Yugoslavia, mainly in the eighteenth century, the elimination of the ethnic Germans at the end of the World War II and their migration to Germany.

these people migrated to North America and Australia in the postwar period.

As a planned process, the emigration of Yugoslav villagers from marginal agricultural lands in the mountainous areas south of the Danube to the rich, flat Vojvodina plains has been studied significantly by Yugoslav scholars. There were considerable problems in adaptation, and a number of the new settlers moved from farming into industry.[11]

Looking at migration patterns in the Balkans in broad historical terms, we can see a part of the overall process as the dynamic of interaction between mountain and plain. Writing of the Mediterranean world in the latter part of the sixteenth century, Braudel noted a cycle, spanning centuries, of oscillation from nomadism to transhumance or from mountain residence to plains dwelling. This involves, for a given span of time, a period when the mountainous regions begin to lose population as the plains area absorbs all the migrants it can (Braudel 1972; 101–102). This dynamic of interaction entails banditry as well as trade, as noted above. But as Stoianovich (1960) indicates in a discussion of kin-linked Greek commerce, the descent of the mountain dwellers means not only simply settlement in the plains, but also wider interaction in the Mediterranean world. Braudel (1972:48–69) makes a similar point: in the sixteenth century, Albanian soldiers found careers throughout the Mediterranean (in such disparate areas as Cyprus, Venice, Mantua, Rome, Naples, Sicily, and Madrid) and subsequently even in the Low Countries, England, and France. Later, as administrators within the Ottoman Empire, they reached the highest levels with notable frequency (McNeill 1964:134–135).

There is no clear-cut distinction between migrations forced by governmental and political activities, on the one hand, and migration of an individual for economic reasons in a kin-linked context, on the other. Migrations in a kin-linked context imply not only regional affiliations, but common ethnicity as well. The latter is easily tied to political motives. Joyce Cary's description (1960) of his participation in a British Red Cross unit affiliated with the Montenegrin army, which was engaged in a struggle with the Turks as part of the First Balkan War in 1912, illustrates this point. Cary describes Montenegrins who went to America in the 1870's and later participated in mining camps in the West or who worked in restaurants in San Francisco and subsequently returned to

11   There is considerable literature on postwar migration to the Vojvodina. See especially Kostic (1963). There are also individual studies by Matica Srpska in Novi Sad during the period 1957–1964. These include monographs on the settlement of Croatians, Montenegrins, and Macedonians in the Vojvodina, as well as some analysis of resettlement, connected with initial land reforms in the area, which took place after the First World War.

their homeland to fight the Turks, while at the same time retaining positive images of their life in America (Cary 1960:49, 101, 108). For these Montenegrins, as for the *pecalbari* from Galichnik, the descent to the "plains" was represented not only by Balkan valleys and the Mediterranean world of the sixteenth century, but in the late nineteenth and early twentieth centuries by North America as well. The mountain-plains dichotomy is not totally extinct even in our time: after the Czech invasion in 1968, it was widely reported that the Yugoslav army was considering withdrawal from the Danubian plains to the mountains in the event of a possible Russian invasion.

The greatest population movements in Yugoslav history have occurred since the postwar period. Yet the historically defined patterns of movement from mountain to plains — kin-linked, regionally affiliated, ethnically associated, economically motivated with political overtones, and influenced by governmental activity — remain important. The enormously complex postwar movements, which can be summarized here only briefly, can be viewed under a number of general categories. First, there is the overall pattern of rural depopulation and urban growth viewed within both a Yugoslav and a general European context. Second, there is migration viewed strictly in spatial terms, as daily movement from a village or small community to a job in a town or larger city. Third, there is seasonal or long-term migration to towns or urban centers within Yugoslavia. And fourth, there is short- and long-term migration of Yugoslavs abroad.

With regard to the general pattern of rural depopulation and urban growth, basic statistical data help to provide overall perspective. Between 1921 and 1961, the percentage of the agricultural population of Yugoslavia declined from 79 to 49, while the total population increased from 12,500,000 to approximately 16,000,000 in the same period. Within an agriculturally based population of 9,170,000, approximately 1,306,000 commuted to jobs off the farm in 1960. Significantly, between 1949 and 1960, some 2,162,000 Yugoslavs migrated from rural to urban areas. This means that almost 19 percent of the total population either had moved from villages or was working outside villages by the beginning of the 1960's.[12]

By 1970 the agricultural population had declined to 42 percent of the population, half of what it had been in 1890. If the situation is viewed, not specifically in terms of a rural to urban migration, but rather in in terms of a shift out of agriculture as a primary occupation, with its

---

[12] Some basic background data is given in Halpern (1967b:356–381).

implied large-scale daily commuting, by 1961, 2,848,000 persons had abandoned agriculture as a primary source of income in the postwar period. From 1961 to 1970 an additional 1,550,000 did so, making a grand total of almost 4,500,000. At the same time, Yugoslavia has not become highly urbanized, as almost 59 percent of the population still lives in settlements of fewer than 2,000 inhabitants. This, however, does not take into account the pattern of daily commuting to work in larger towns. This labor force of peasant-workers amounted to approximately 1,400,00 in 1970. In addition, it is estimated that there are approximately 1,500,000 Yugoslav emigrants abroad (although this figure does appear high), in addition to the 1,000,000 or so workers who are now considered to be temporarily residents abroad (Livada 1972: 127–142).

Putting aside the horrors of World War II with its approximately 3,000,000 casualties, actual war-induced population movements seem relatively small when contrasted with the magnitude of peaceful postwar movements.

In terms of overall patterns of migration, the contemporary daily pattern of the peasant-worker is one of the most important in Yugoslavia. It is very much a compromise situation for all concerned. For the worker himself, who must rise early in the morning, struggle with commuting by bicycle, bus, train, or foot through all kinds of weather, and then return to farm his land in the afternoon, it is a compromise between the security of wages and the security of independent subsistence. Wages are often felt to be comparatively low in unskilled or semiskilled jobs, but this is offset to a significant extent by social benefits in the form of paid vacations, pensions, provision for disability, and expecially in the largely free medical care available to the worker and his family. For the private peasant such benefits are either not available or open to only a limited extent.

To work at two demanding jobs is most tiring and frequently tends to detract from the quality of work performed in both situations. At home it means that the worker's wife has to assume a larger share of the agricultural work than was formerly the case in larger extended rural families, when the wife did mostly household chores, child care, and relatively light agricultural work. Today women sometimes tend the major livestock and even do such heavy work as plowing and harrowing, which they formerly performed only in wartime or emergency situations. On the other hand, there are now fewer children to care for because of a reduced birth rate and the children are getting an education. There is improved agricultural machinery, a better diet to sustain work, and superior medical care available in case of traumatic accidents. Home produce is also an important supplement to wages, a cushion against inflation and other insecurities.

From the point of view of management and general state policy, it may be considered more desirable to incorporate the worker fully into the productive process, including participation in the system of self-management so important to the Yugoslav socialist system. But the commuting peasant-worker makes fewer demands on the system although he has, in effect, a double job. Urban communities already straining to accommodate the influx of postwar migrants do not have to provide housing, schooling, and other urban amenities for the peasant-worker and his family, who continue to reside in the village. The provision of bus service and usable roads, for example, cannot be considered unreasonable social overhead because these have clear benefits to those who are primarily farmers as well. Medical facilities have to be built to serve the general population in any case. There may also be some side benefits in that larger numbers of dependents, particularly elderly relatives, are more easily supported and even gainfully employed in a rural setting. In addition, minor children are less likely to be social and law enforcement problems in rural areas, where they usually have chores to do and appear to be subject to more traditional familial authority. This is not to say that rural Yugoslavia does not have many problems, ranging from questions of agricultural productivity to underemployment to the status of elderly couples whose children have moved to town.[13] However, when viewed on a broad, comparative basis, the Yugoslav situation of migrant workers can be seen as positive: none of the more highly industrialized states of the West (least of all the United States, with its frustrated commuters, central city ethnic conflicts, and agricultural migrant populations living in debased conditions), or the East, for that matter, have successfully solved the twentieth century problems of urbanization and industrialization.

Some conflicts in the role of the peasant-worker as seen from a village perspective are evident in the following accounts. The first is from a middle-aged villager in the vicinity of Zagreb in the early 1960's:

For the past eight years I have worked in a factory in Zagreb. Every day I travel to work by train and return home in the afternoon. I leave for work at 6:30 in the morning and return at 3:00 and then often help my parents in the fields. I would like to move to the city and work there and also find a job for my wife, but I have old parents and a son who goes to school here...

[13]   There is a significant literature on peasant-workers in Yugoslavia. For a bibliography of Serbo-Croatian sources see Livada 1972: 248–260. For English-language sources see Halpern and Halpern (1972: 149–152) and Simic (1973: 167–174).

I want my son to obtain a university education, for since I could not get academic training he at least should have it. If I had other children I would not let a single one work the land. There is no future in farming (Halpern 1967c: 116–117).

In 1969 a Slovenian villager commented on his situation:

We work in the factory so that we can continue to hold onto the land, and we hold onto the land because no one knows what is sure. It may be hell but we still hold on. If we did not have the factory, life would be bad. Now at least the young people live well, but the old ones suffer because they have so much work. It used to be that the old could stop working and the young could take over, but now the old must work the land while the young go to the factory.

Said another:

Yes, you are right, but it is exhausting for the young also, for they both cultivate and work in the factory. It is all right while the old are here to help, but when they are alone and we are — how can they do it? (Winner 1971:108).

There are a number of significant differences between the households of the peasant-workers and those of the full-time agriculturalists. According to the agricultural census of 1969, the number of farms with peasant-workers increased by approximately 10 percent over 1960. According to a 1968 survey, those farms with part-time workers were larger in terms of number of household members than were farms with full-time agriculturalists (5.5 to 4.6). However, the former had less land, on the average 3.8 hectares, than did full-time farmers, with 4.8 hectares. In addition, those farms with peasant-workers had less desirable holdings from the point of view of land quality; they tended to sell land more frequently than did the full-time farmers; and their labor force was composed to a larger extent of women, the aged, and children. They also had less agricultural equipment and were oriented more toward home consumption and less toward marketing produce than were the full-time agriculturalists. As for standard of living, the peasant-worker households tended to invest more in building new homes, repairing old ones, and purchasing furniture, and to spend more for recreation. Puljiz (1972: 127–142), a Yugoslav observer, sees the development of the village-based peasant-worker as a consequence of the economic needs of the poor peasantry and their struggle for income parity. He also feels that many of the present peasant-worker holdings will not be maintained into the next generation because the children will continue to choose nonagricultural occupations, probably outside the village.

The major migratory step, of course, has been the permanent move to a town or city from a village. There has been intercity migration as well, but it has not been as significant in demographic, economic, social, or cultural terms as the migration from rural to urban areas. This is not something that began in Yugoslavia only after World War I. A major development of the nineteenth century was the replacement by the South Slavs of the Turkish, Greek, and other foreign ethnic groups in the cities. This was particularly marked in Serbia and was related to the gradual acquisition of independence from the Turks, for at the beginning of the nineteenth century cities in the Balkans were populated almost exclusively by foreigners. This view is summarized by the Serbian chronicler Vuk Karadzic, writing at the beginning of the nineteenth century:

Among the Serbian people there are no people other than peasants. (Those few Serbs who do live in towns as tradesmen — virtually only shopkeepers — and craftsmen, are called townspeople. Since they dress as Turks and live according to Turkish customs, and since during revolts and wars they either shut themselves up with the Turks in cities or run away to Germany [presumably across the Danube to Austrian territory], not only can they not be counted among the Serbs, but the Serbs despise them. Serbs, as peasants, live only from their land and livestock (quoted in Halpern and Halpern 1972:12).

Vuk concludes that even though there are a few who are traders, their home life is like that of other peasants.

But there was an ambivalence about the city. In their language peasants saw their own way of life as *crni svet* [dark world], while the big, wide world was *beli svet* [white world]. The city, of course, was Beograd [White City]. The city was in a sense a center of oppression under the Turks, because the origins of the First Revolt go back to a redress of grievances rather than an absolute desire for independence. An eighteenth century Turkish administrator in Beograd, Hadji Mustafa-pasha, who was regarded as a just ruler, was called "Mother of the Serbs" (Edwards 1969: xiii). After successful insurrections against subsequent Turkish rulers, who were much harsher in the period 1818–1836, some 10,000 Serbian peasants left their villages to settle in towns (Stoianovich 1970: 109). But during the nineteenth century, both Beograd and Zagreb grew relatively slowly, neither having reached 100,000 by the first decade of the twentieth century.[14] In the past sixty years Beograd has grown from 90,000 to 1,200,00 in 1971, and Zagreb from 80,000 to 602,000. Despite this impressive growth, Yugoslavia remains proportionately one of the least urbanized countries in Europe, with 35 percent of its population in urban centers. (Rumania has 39 percent and Bulgaria 48 percent, while England

---

[14]   Beograd had a population of some 25,000 in 1867, which increased to 35,000 in 1884 and 90,000 in 1910. Zagreb ahd 20,000 in 1869, 30,000 in 1880, and 80,000 in 1910. See Halpern (1965: 172).

and Sweden have 79 percent and 77 percent respectively.) Partly this is a matter of definition. The urban population of Yugoslavia has grown by over 80 percent in the period 1953–1971, while the overall population has grown by only about 20 percent (Ginic 1971:25–41). Thus the formalized percentage of urbanization conceals the dynamics of the growth of the nonagricultural sector of the economy, which is already dominant.[15]

The rural to urban migration process within Yugoslavia follows a number of distinct paths. One important way has been through education. In the recent past, relatively few children who managed to go beyond the eighth-grade village school remained in the village.[16] A second way has been through job mobility of more mature individuals who might move to a nearby town or a large city, depending on how the opportunities were structured.

The prevailing opinion among a number of foreign anthropologists who have studied rural to urban migration in Yugoslavia is that the kin network has formed a kind of bridge that can operate successfully in both directions. It is often through kin or fellow villagers that initial educational and job opportunities are perceived and that advancement, up to a point, is obtained. Frequently a young villager attending a high school or specialized trade school stays with relatives in town. As partial compensation the relatives may be supplied with food from the family farm. Fellow villagers who have settled in a town are often helpful, especially if native associations are reinforced by common descent or affinal ties. The village home remains a place where city grandchildren can visit grandparents during summer vacations. The village can provide a place of refuge and in certain instances a place of retirement. Retirement in the village is particularly feasible where the village is located in an area attractive to tourism and therefore to other kinds of supporting development. In most cases it appears that initial departure from the village is a one-way avenue with occasional return visits to relatives and for vacations. Sometimes these vacations include helping with the harvest.

[15] See, for example, discussion of the definition of "rural" and "urban" in the Yugoslav context by Halpern (1969:323–329).

[16] Some case study data from a rural community provide insight. In the Serbian village of Orasac, surveys were taken from 1962 to 1965 by the district school authorities among the eighth-grade graduating class of the village school to determine occupational preferences. Boys overwhelmingly wanted to be skilled workers of various types, while a few wanted professional careers. In 1966 it was possible to get follow-up information on half of those surveyed. Among the thirty-one boys in the sample, twelve had learned or were learning a trade, ten were continuing their schooling, and nine were farming, at least for the time being. Among the thirty-eight girls, almost all went on further in school, while three had jobs and three remained at home (Halpern 1967a: 314–315).

If the move is to a nearby market town, the relationships may continue to be close. Often village parents help to provide a son (or sometimes a daughter) with building materials for a new house he is constructing for his own family in the town's suburbs.[17]

Baric characterizes Yugoslavia as a "kinship" society and says that rights and obligations among kin are viewed as having greater force there than in English society. Because the family farm is viewed as a holiday residence, a source of supplemental food, a place to send children for vacations or other reasons, and a locus of security, it cannot be viewed primarily as a firm or business (Baric 1967a:266–267). Baric also notes that kin links are vital in helping to find housing in the city and that such links are essential in a society that relies more on personal communication than on formal written communication (Baric 1967b: 12–13).

Such attitudes are, of course, not unique to Yugoslavia or to Eastern Europe, and favoritism to kin seems to exist in all societies, even in those sometimes termed post-industrial. However, certain shared features of East European societies have resulted in a post-revolutionary mass movement of rural folk to urban centers. The values that these people carry with them, including a kinship orientation, take on broad cultural dimensions and result in what some observers have called the ruralization of the town or the peasantization of the city (Halpern 1967d:34–35).

The Polish sociologist Galeski has suggested certain analytical categories. He views the prewar peasantry as a substantially undifferentiated stratum of small family farmers that has, in the postwar period, broken into four differentiated groups: (1) small-scale landholders who have remained in the village; (2) peasant-workers who, as we have described, live on their holdings and commute to town; (3) worker-peasants who live in town but bring to the urban setting value complexes derived from the rural setting; and (4) bureaucrats. Industrialization, urbanization, and the centralization of all European socialist societies, even if done on a regional republic basis as in Yugoslavia, have resulted in a tremendous expansion of the civil service. In most of Eastern Europe, because the old ruling strata have been excluded (and often in part have emigrated) and because the working and middle classes were small, the new administrative class has had to come from the peasantry. This has been particularly true in Yugoslavia. Many of the postwar administrators came to their positions through their service with the Partisan forces, experience which, however heroic, did not necessarily qualify them for complex

[17]   For a description of the situation in central Serbia and Slovenia see Halpern (1963:167–171).

administrative tasks. It is only now, a quarter of a century after the war, that this class is gradually passing into retirement; the succeeding generation, some of peasant origin and some the children of Partisans and others who moved to town immediately after the war, is now becoming important. The point is that the administrative cadre is of peasant origin, particularly at the lower levels. This bureaucracy shares many values with the peasantry from which it originated. Industrialization on a regional basis, which was conceived as amalgamating the peasantry into the postwar industrial process, is approved. Corruption, too, unites peasant and bureaucrat in an alliance of kin and personal ties and strengthens resistance to the depersonalization of administration and justice. Such considerations are particularly important in a state where the commercial sector is socialized and in effect part of the state apparatus (Galeski 1972, summarized in Simons 1973). In Yugoslavia there have been vigorous efforts to keep the two apart through the role of enterprise Workers' Councils,[18] the distinction between social property and state property, and the differentiation of both of these from private ownership, which is restricted.[19]

Changes in cultural values and large-scale categories provide a useful overview, but these are made comprehensible only in terms of specific cases.[20] Bette Denich (1970:133–148) has used structured interviews

[18] Lukic (n.d.: 25–44) maintains that workers self-management influences the adoption of "the progressive way of life" and causes "a rapid disappearance of class differences," while the peasant-worker gradually introduces progressive changes into village life.

[19] These distinctions are discussed in Chloros (1970).

[20] In a 1960 investigation conducted by the Institute of Social Sciences in Belgrade, more than 5,000 workers of various skill levels in all parts of the country were surveyed. Approximately 3,000 of these workers were the sons of peasants, compared with 940 who were the sons of workers or craftsmen. Ten percent of the 3,000 sons of peasants were highly skilled workers and 24 percent were skilled workers, whereas 28 percent of the sons of workers became highly skilled workers and 31 percent became skilled workers. These figures indicate that peasant-worker or worker-peasant migrants have experienced some disadvantage because of mobility. Those who had attained the greatest skill appeared to be the permanent migrants who had given up association with the the land (Institut Drustvenih Nauka 1963:257–288). By the early 1960's a significant proportion of white-collar workers was also of peasant origin. Of office workers with elementary schooling, 55 percent were from villages, as were 32 percent of those with middle and higher schooling and 37 percent of executive personnel (Begovic 1964:3). The empirical studies published in such Serbo-Croatian journals as *Sociologija* (Belgrade) and *Sociologija Sela* (Zagreb) are pertinent. There are also a large number of statistical bulletins and census reports issued by the Yugoslav Federal Bureau of Statistics and the republic bureaus. Other than statistical studies on migration, the interests of Yugoslav sociology have focused on problems of class stratification and the workers' councils as a way of coping with social differentiation in an industrializing society. There has been relatively little interest in case studies of migration seen from

carried out in 1965–1966 on a sample of 200 people who migrated after World War II from villages to Titovo Uzice in western Serbia, a town that has undergone intensive industrialization and a fourfold population increase since the end of the war. Immediately after the war, labor was recruited by governmental directive for work on large-scale construction projects. People came to work in town from the surrounding mountain villages, following an old pattern of interaction with the lowland area. After 1949 migration to town was not officially mandated but left to individual option. At that point, kin-linked networks played an important role, a role exemplified by the use of such terms as *veze i posnanstvo* [connections and acquaintanceship]. Both the relationships between people of equal status and the asymmetrical ties between those of unequal power were stressed. A more powerful member of a kin or friendship dyad within a network could bestow *protekcija* (patronage); this was done by political officials and industrial managers.

As mentioned above, patronage was often dispensed by ex-Partisans, producing a situation that exemplifies Galeski's concept of the peasantization of the bureaucracy. Such activities did result in much subsequent criticism of the party structure by those at the top, who were concerned with ideology and the overall functioning of the state apparatus, as well as by those who might not receive favors at a particular time. The need to rely on network contacts was emphasized in terms of access to scarce goods, to some extent to jobs, and particularly to housing and later to educational opportunities for one's children.

Denich includes not only kin in her analysis of migrant networks but also workmates, neighbors, schoolmates, and migrants from the same village. She depicts consanguineal kin and affines as minor in terms of urban friendship. However, kin ties are regularly reinforced — half her sample stated that they visited their native villages at least once a month. Denich also believes that the initial material success of migrants reinforces the desire of others to leave and that a primary motivation is not economic necessity but rather the general attractions of urban life, which overwhelm the allegiance to family farm and succession, even when the migrating son is the last child at home. A conclusion drawn from her study is that the significant degree of orderliness in the fast-paced growth of Uzice and comparable Yugoslav towns relates, at least partly, to the use by migrants of social networks that also carry information to the

---

the viewpoint of cultural-social anthropology, emphasizing social networks and cultural values. See, for example Tomovic (1968:96–125). A more recent overview is given by Bogdan Denitch (1971:1–26).

villages, encouraging new groups to leave. In this and other respects the migrant acts as a culture broker.

In another study, approached from a broad cultural, historical, and social perspective, Hammel (1969a) traces the origins and development of kin ties, mainly in Montenegro and Serbia, from medieval times to the present. His survey combines ecological, psychological, and historical explanations that argue for the continuity of kinship relations into the period of industrialization. The viability of the family core is emphasized. Rather than being weakened by the growth of mining and industry in rural areas, kin ties are strengthened, as when employed sons contribute cash to meet family needs. Family and kin units are not destroyed by the upheavals and rapid mobility of industrialization but serve as "the orienting thread and conduit of mobility." According to Hammel, more important than any theoretical or systematic notions of how an industrial society should work is the question of how it must work when people move into a strange cultural environment. There is a need to trust someone to show the way. "Who better," asks Hammel, "than an uncle?" He also notes that these ties can be maintained because the movement has been carried out within a relatively small geographic area.

Changes in urban culture are rapidly transmitted to the village "in knowledge if not in fact," so that modernization and industrialization do not realize their potential to divide the nation. Hammel cites a central dilemma in the overt conflict between modernization and a sense of national identity: "How can one damn the idiocy of rural life when that life is the cradle of national consciousness?" (Hammel 1969a).

Many city-bound migrants cannot wait to shake the village mud from their boots, and for those who remain in the village, agriculture is viewed as a very low-status occupation, essentially one of last resort (Halpern 1967b) (although this may be subject to change in the 1970's because job opportunities have decreased). The recent migrant of village origin may wish strongly to disassociate himself from village life in an overt sense and may strive for an education as a means of entering a non-manual occupation far removed from toil in the fields, but he does not, in so doing, cut his ties to the past. Factors in the peasantization of the city bring about basic changes from the elite nature of the pre-industrial city, where, in the limited growth period of the nineteenth century, each successive group of village migrants looked down upon the new arrivals. Moreover, the postwar movements to the town from the village have overwhelmed the incipient working-class ideology that was at the core of the Communist party's historic perspective. The new cities, like Novi Beograd, with their burgeoning new suburbs of high-rise apartments, have overwhelmed everyone's perceptions. Just as historic landmarks take on increased importance, so kin ties take on great importance, particularly in initial generations in the city. In investigating kin ties in Belgrade, Hammel found that among the workers surveyed, kin were more important than friends, with linkages specified largely in agnatic terms. The important family assets remain within the control of men. "The maps in peoples' heads really are the last thing to go."[21]

In another study of Belgrade, Hammel (1969b) calls attention to the importance of the military as a channel of mobility. This phenomenon, obviously difficult to study yet of great importance, recalls Braudel's comments about the Albanians, with whom the Montenegrins share adjoining mountainous territory — the latter have been the proto-typical military officers of the Yugoslav army up to and including the postwar period. The position of the Partisans as a new elite in postwar Yugoslav society has already been mentioned.

However, background, education, and personal connections continue to be important even in a postwar era of great opportunities, one in which Horatio Alger-type stories abound. Hammel concludes:

What is most impressive about the evidence is the way in which the raw forces of economic change have shaped the general outlines of mobility, and the way in which impersonal and universal accidents of date of birth, class or origin, ordinal rank in a sibling set,... predict the average moblity of segments of the population (1969b:91).

From the perspective of his study, Hammel believes that the population is under the influence of impersonal restraints, "in the grip of historical forces beyond the control and even the understanding of the population" (1969b:91). (One might add that these sometimes elude the analyst as well.)

A most comprehensive description of long-distance migration and permanent resettlement is Simic's (1973) study of Belgrade. Both Simic and Halpern have spoken of the peasantization of Belgrade, one from the point of view of the arriving migrant, the other from the perspective of the sending village. Halpern has also discussed the villager's influence on the small town. Simic cites case histories of those who have left the poverty of villages and found relative fulfillment in the city, or at least greater opportunity there. Halpern cites autobiographies that relate past rural poverty, narrations of those who have seen the world beyond the village and returned, and even some who have achieved modest prosperity

---

[21]   For discussion and bibliography of Hammel's work see Halpern 1970:21–25).

within a rural context, as well as those who have migrated to the nearby market town and those who leave the village daily to gain a living outside. The conclusions to Simic's Beograd study parallel in many respects those of the Halperns' most recent study of the Serbian village of Orasac.

Simic comments that it was the remarkable expansion of the economy in the postwar period that made the journey of the peasant migrant possible. He sees the peasantization of Beograd as having affected all levels of society and points out that even the old intelligentsia and aristocracy had ties with the peasantry. Given the specific history of Serbian society in the nineteenth century, this is readily understandable. The migrant encounters in Beograd a cultural situation that bears considerable resemblance, ethnically and linguistically, to what he left in the village.

Simic views the urbanization process in terms of a series of events, with a succession of spatial relocations set in motion by the initial decision of an individual, usually a male, to leave the village. Motivations include personal reasons as well as those external to the individual. Important variables are not only the pattern of inheritance, limited land, and restricted educational and employment opportunities, but also the desire for the greater stimulation, variety, and degree of individual expression offered in the city. Simic stresses this. The important kin ties are also reflected in perceptions of others, and thus a person may be called "Montenegrin" even if he came to Beograd as an infant and has little or no firsthand knowledge of his ancestral home. The transformation of the migrant is seen by Simic as economic rather than sociocultural, with rural-urban exchange continuing to function across kin lines but conditioned by a number of variables: the nearness of the village, the precise nature of the kin relationships, the degree of prosperity of the particular rural community, the affective quality of the existing interpersonal relationships, and the degree of alienation from village norms.

Often, Simic postulates, the migrant may see himself as an urban component of the rural household, with the ties that he maintains with his village or origin acting as a kind of insurance policy against possible failure in the city. The ties linking the urban and rural components of society act as important communication links and help to promote integration of rural and urban norms as well as further movement out of the village. The positive nature of these integrative mechanisms in the Yugoslav context is furthered by the fact that migration usually takes place within a republic or within a cultural area. There is very little movement between culturally different republics; e.g. between Slovenia and Macedonia, to cite an extreme case, or even between Croatia and Serbia.[22]

This is not to say that there are no discontinuities or ethnic conflicts inherent in the urbanization process. A very common observation in Beograd is that Albanian migrants from the Kosovo Autonomous Region of Serbia, the center of the Albanian ethnic group, perform some of the least desirable jobs in the capital (e.g. collecting garbage and carting wood and lignite for heating). The highly successful Serbian commercial film *The Feather Collector* gives a view of life as experienced by another low-status ethnic group, the Gypsies. Several scenes follow a young Gypsy girl from a plains village north of the capital on her trip to Beograd in search of work. She is told bluntly by a Gypsy in the city that she has a choice of either working as a trash collector and rag trader or being a prostitute. Her search for help in a series of Gypsy neighborhoods is seen against the background of the modern city, with posters announcing bathing beauty contests and glamorous television programs, a culture she does not share. Some Gypsies have achieved success through the stereotyped role of entertainer and in other ways, but there is no question that traditional kinds of discrimination exist, despite the demolition of the old Gypsy quarter of Beograd.

Migration abroad or to great distances has existed since the time of Greek trading colonies in Dalmatia. In medieval times migrations occurred within the Mediterranean area and involved both coastal seamen and mountaineers. The late nineteenth and early twentieth centuries saw

[22]   The matter is complex because of overlapping border areas in such multiethnic areas as the Vojvodina, an autonomous province within the Republic of Serbia. According to the 1961 census, of some 960,000 migrants recorded who moved between republics, very few made long-distance moves. Macedonians and Montenegrins tend to go to Serbia. From Bosnia ethnic Serbs move mainly to Serbia and ethnic Croats mainly to Croatia. Slovenians who cross republic borders go mainly to Croatia. Croatians move mainly to Croatia from Bosnia and Serbia. These data are set forth in great detail in a publication of the Institut Drustvenih Nauka (1971:214–215, Table 30).
There also seems to be a trend toward greater ethnic homogeneity in certain areas. Between 1961 and 1971 the proportion of Albanians in the Autonomous Province of Kosovo has risen from 67 to 74 percent while the relative number of Serbs has declined from 23 to 18 percent. This obviously has involved migrations and is related to what was called, in the late 1960's, the national re-awakening of the Albanian minority in Yugoslavia. The Albanian presence is related to an earlier series of migrations subsequent to Ottoman occupation, when Serbs moved north out of this area and across the Danube. These developments are clearly linked to the growing economic inequality and accompanying political functions between such regions as Kosovo and the other more developed areas in Slovenia, Croatia, and Serbia. All areas have developed in the postwar period, but the gap has increased. (See also Singleton 1973: 281–304.)

pecalbari as well as migrations both temporary and permanent to North America, as exemplified by some of the Montenegrins about whom Cary wrote.[23]

Much of the migration of the approximately 1,000,000 Yugoslavs who are currently abroad has been to Western Europe.[24] Interestingly, some

[23] Migrations to the United States can only be touched on in this survey, which focuses on continuity within Yugoslavia. There does not seem to be any detailed literature on returnees from North America as a specific group. Two useful sources for Yugoslavs in the United States are Govorchin (1961) and more recently Colakovic (1970). Migration to North America has been on a comparatively small scale, with respect to both the numbers of other immigrant groups who came to the United States and the migratory movements within Yugoslavia. Between 1908 and 1923, statistics indicate that 105,000 Bulgarian, Serbian and Montenegrin immigrants arrived; approximately 89 percent of these eventually returned. A higher proportion of Croats and Slovenes stayed, 226,000 making the trip and 51 percent of these eventually returning. By contrast the Dalmatian, Bosnian, and Hercegovinian (probably mainly Dalmatian) migrants, who numbered 31,000, had a return rate of only 29 percent.

Clearly, the *pecalba* tradition was very strong in southern regions, which were the least developed economically. The cultural differences were also greatest, and this migration appears to have been overwhelmingly male at first (Colakovic 1970:85, Tables 4–11). In 1940, of 11,000,000 immigrants recorded in the United States, only 147,000 were Serbs, Croats, and Slovenes; of that number, 76,000 were Slovenes from the most highly developed area in Yugoslavia and also the smallest of the major ethnic groups (Govorchin 1961:335). There was also a significant post-war migration. Between 1946 and 1968 some 66,000 persons were admitted from Yugoslavia as refugees and displaced persons. Of this number, 16,000 were ethnic Germans (Colakovic 1970:112). The postwar group had somewhat different settlement patterns, most going to New York, Illinois, Ohio, New Jersey, and California, particularly to the metropolitan areas of New York City, Chicago, and Cleveland, the destinations of two-thirds of the immigrants. Relatively few settled in Pennsylvania, West Virginia, Minnesota, Montana, or Colorado and went into the mining and steel industries, as formerly (1970:113). The movement to the United States, in both the pre- and post-war periods, has evidently been smaller than the recent temporary or permanent movement to Western Europe. The early movements to the United States, both temporary and permanent, were overwhelmingly by males in the period 1899–1910 (85 percent of the Croats and Slovenes and 96 percent of the Bulgarians, Serbians, and Montenegrins) (Govorchin 1961: 55). By 1920 only 68 percent of the Yugoslav-born population was male, and this declined to 55 percent by 1960 (Colakovic 1970:150, Table 5–14,)

By contrast, Yugoslav workers officially listed as working abroad in 1971 were 69 percent male, indicating a significant female participation. (See Begtic 1972:20).

[24] A recent Yugoslav publication gives the figure of 800,000 Yugoslavs temporarily employed abroad, of whom some 470,000 are in West Germany, 120,000 in Austria, 60–70,000 in France, more than 30,000 in Sweden, about 30,000 in Switzerland, and some 10,000 in Belgium (Vujovic 1972:12). These figures contrast with the 672,000 listed in *Yugoslav Survey* (February, 1972) articles and cited as being derived from the 1971 census (Begtic 1972:17–31; Nikolic 1972:1–16).

Politika (Beograd) (June 4, 1970) gives a figure of 750,000 ,with 500,000 listed as being in Western Europe and more than 250,000 overseas. A brief report in the *Economist* (London) (September 5, 1970:39) cites a round figure of 1,000,000. The matter is conplex because some workers go on short-term labor assignments for several months, and there is constant movement back and forth, the countries of Western Europe being near and communications excellent.

of this movement has along been very traditional patterns. Lockwood
(1970), in a study of a Muslim village community and marketing patterns in a town in Bosnia, discusses migrant agricultural workers, who
approximate patterns noted in a historic framework by such scholars
as Cvijic (1918b:408–413) and Tomasevich (1955:456)[25] For western
Bosnia, Lockwood states that migration to Austria began about 1960.
The first workers went from the more accessible areas of Livno, Duvna,
and Kupres and subsequently from the area of Skoplje Polje, which
Lockwood studied. This migration began in the mid-sixties as other workers from western Bosnia began to push on to better jobs in West Germany and Sweden. Those who go to Austria travel in groups and usually
stay from three to six months. The entrance permit is a negotiable com-
modity, and in order to raise the money a potential migrant worker may
sell some of his livestock. Despite the many difficulties, the lure is great
because of the wage differential. Some save their money to invest in land
and livestock when they return home, while others bring home material
gifts. The inventory of consumer goods in relatively marginal agricultural
villages has increased as a consequence.

This type of migrant labor is contrasted with temporary labor from
the same region that goes to more prosperous and highly industrialized
areas within Yugoslavia. Such seasonal domestic migrations, e.g. to work
in the cornfields of the fertile Vojvodina Plain, began in 1945 as an organized government effort but have since continued on the basis of voluntary
association.

The longer-term migrations outside Yugoslavia usually involve men
only, although increasingly families go too. Such movements, naturally,
increase the adjustment problem for the migrant worker and his family
and for the receiving society. The impact of the presence of foreign workers, even in the tens of thousands (small numbers by American, English,
or French standards), looms very large in the ethnically homogeneous and
relatively small-scale societies of Scandinavia and Holland. While those
countries project what is sometimes thought to be a "liberal" image with
regard to political and social policies, the presence of numbers of southern Europeans, whose accustomed way of life is very different, can
easily provoke outcries with decidely racist overtones, especially given
the ultimately provincial nature of those societies as concerns their
internal affairs.[26] These problems are, of course, also present in the lar-

---

[25] Cvijic refers to the *pecalba* tradition, and Tomasevich refers more generally to
periodic migrations for seasonal labor in industry, construction, or agriculture in
various parts of the country.
[26] According to official statistics, employment abroad is considered temporary if

ger-scale societies of Germany and France and even in multiethnic Switzerland.

From many points of view, the shorter-term migration, in which firm family ties and a strong intention to return to Yugoslavia are maintained, is perhaps in the most bearable situation. Even if the migrant and his family experience discrimination and live in substandard housing, their ability to save for the building of a new house or to acquire capital for a small-scale enterprise based on new trade skills is key. So are the remittances to relatives who remain at home. These remittances now constitute a significant part of Yugoslavia's foreign exchange earnings.[27]

The nature of individual and family adjustment is of vital importance, and outside appearances can be misleading. During a stay in a small community in southern Germany, I became fairly well acquainted with a Yugoslav migrant family. The household was relatively large, reflecting extended family patterns common at home. The family originated from the relatively prosperous area of Slavonia (Croatia) and had retained its village home, to which the family members planned to return.[28] The worker and his wife were in their mid-forties; with them were their eldest son and his wife, both in their early twenties, and two younger sons, ages eighteen and twelve. They were later joined by the man's mother-in-law. All worked except the daughter-in-law, the younger sons, and the mother-in-law. From an outside (host country) view, they presented

---

its average length is about 3 years, with a lower limit of 1 year and an upper limit of 5 years. It is not clear, however, how individuals are counted if they return home on a vacation after having quit one job in a foreign country and then go abroad again to another job. The census figures give the average length of employment abroad as 2.4 years. About 100,000 individuals are recorded as having been abroad longer than 5 years, and 20,000 longer than 10 years, with a low rate of return. From 1965 to 1971, only 85,000 are listed as having returned.

A comprehensive study in Sweden (Meurle and Andric 1971) clearly indicates that this movement is a very recent phenomenon. Yugoslav migrants in Sweden increased from slightly over 100 in 1950 to 1,300 in 1960, but by 1967 they had reached 22,500 and by 1969 they had increased to 28,300. Approximately half are in the twenty-six to thirty-five age group, but significantly, 44 percent are women, many of these probably dependents, as 72 percent of the migrants are married. Some 73 percent were in mining and factory work, predominantly the latter, as over half lived in or near large cities. Migration is seen as positive by both the employee and the employer, because it entails a foreign language, housing, social interaction with Swedes in general, and relationships to employer and fellow employees.

[27] Remittances totaled some $870,000,000 in 1972, up from $96,000,000 in 1966 and $500,000,000 in 1970 (Hoffman 1973).

[28] Croatia, which has 22 percent of the total Yugoslav population, contributed 33 percent of those working abroad, while Serbia, with 41 percent of the population, contributed 30 percent of the foreign workers. (Begtic 1972:17–31) This seems to be an old pattern reflected in century immigration to America.

socially undesirable aspects and multiple problems. They lived in one of the poorest houses in town. This was partly because of discrimination, but from their point of view, it minimized rent and at the same time allowed all of them to be together. The father was a skilled mason, worked successively at several jobs, and was not infrequently in conflict with his employers. The eldest son had a diverse job history in Germany, and he, too, had trouble holding a job. The mother had steady work although she was ill. The local inhabitants held strongly negative feelings toward these people. The family itself, although beset with problems and full of conflict over changing roles, still remained faithful to its goal of returning home. Because of frequent bus service to Yugoslavia, occasional trips home for the purchase of land and the construction of a house did not present problems.

The younger members of the family were very impressed by the German standard of living, and a few tentative friendships with young German workers were formed by the two older sons. All working members of the family were learning new skills. But clearly this family did not share the local passion for sobriety, neatness, and orderliness.[29]

Although minor in terms of total emigration, the Yugoslav "brain drain" has been significant.[30] Yugoslav architects in Paris, engineers in Switzerland, and doctors in the United States are not rare.[31] Their adaptation is, of course, drastically different from that of semi-skilled workers. Given the high desirability of their skills, their prosperity is assured in most cases. Their standard of living is high, but here, too, conflicts of adjustment arise. The experience of an ophthalmologist in Switzerland illustrates some of the contradictions. Both the eye doctor and his wife, an obstetrician, had easily found employment in a medium-sized Swiss town, and their two children were enrolled in local schools. Both husband and wife had post-graduate training in North America in addition to their professional educations and early work experiences in Yugoslavia.

[29]   The condition of this family paralleled the description of migrant workers in Sweden on a number of counts. The Swedish apartments were also overcrowded, with more than two people to a room and were "mostly little better than slums;" the workers in the group surveyed were mainly of peasant origin and they came to save money and then return to Yugoslavia to buy a car, build a house, or purchase agricultural machinery (Meurle and Andric 1971).

[30]   Only 1 percent (a total of 6,900) are listed as having had university training; almost all of them come from Croatia (3,000) and Serbia (2,700) (Begtic 1972: 24). These figures would seem to be rather conservative and possibly reflect only those who have gone to work through official channels, probably a minority of those actually working abroad.

[31]   There are more than 100 medical doctors of Yugoslav origin in the New York City area alone, most having come since World War II and now permanent residents or United States citizens.

They had decided to settle in Switzerland because of the favorable financial opportunities. They resided in a modern and comfortably furnished apartment and had a servant recruited from Yugoslavia, but they were both dissatisfied with their working conditions. They felt that they were being exploited because Swiss physicians received greater reimbursement for work requiring the same degree of skill. The husband, unable to establish a private practice, was employed by a local specialist with less training and experience; eventually, because of the conflict in this situation, he felt forced to take a position in a fairly distant town. As his wife was satisfactorily established locally, he had to resort to long-distance commuting. Nevertheless, these disadvantages were somewhat offset by the family's ability to vacation every summer in a small villa they had built on the Dalmatian coast. They were ambivalent about the possibility of ultimately returning to Yugoslavia and concerned with their ability to maintain their standard of living there.

In both of the above cases, the families lived to a large degree in isolation from the surrounding societies. The professional couple had a few Swiss acquaintances but no Swiss friends, and they interacted mainly with other Yugoslav professionals in the area.

Established immigrant communities of Yugoslavs abroad range from Croatian villages in Italy, which have existed for several centuries, to communities established in the nineteenth century in the mining towns and steel mills of Pennsylvania and Ohio, to groups in California engaged in fishing and farming (see, for example, Babic 1964 and Lovrich 1966–1967). These communities are, of course, ethnically specific, with particular Macedonian, Croatian, Serb, Slovene, Albanian, and former Volkdeutsch settlements. The Orthodox and Catholic churches with their ethnically defined parishes have historically played a major role in giving these communities form, although their influence is lessening with suburbanization. These communities were basically formed by waves of economic immigrants (many of whom came before World War I), and these continue to arrive up to the present.

Another situation is presented by the arrival of dispossessed bureaucrats, military officers, and intellectuals who were not able to co-exist with the postwar Yugoslav government. Some of them have come to public attention because such groups as the Croatian fascist Ustashi have continued to maintain their organizations in Germany and to some extent in North America, South America, and Australia. They recently staged several spectacular exploits — the assassination of the Yugoslav ambassador to Sweden, the blowing up of a Yugoslav airliner, and even a small-scale invasion of Bosnia, in which all the protagonists, along with a number of local people, were killed. Unlike both the permanent and the temporary economic migrants, who were concerned either with establishing a new life and community or with saving and remittances at home, political exiles have been preoccupied with the reconstruction of past history and what might have been. In a sense this is similar to the epics that recreate the Serbs' defeat by the Turks in the fourteenth century in the laments of Kosovo, but it takes place in a foreign land and by means of printed matter with limited circulation. These émigré political groups are divided politically as well as ethnically, so that among Serbs and Croats there are separate groups embracing a range of political viewpoints.

The large-scale movement of Yugoslav workers to Western Europe reflects the unique experience of a socialist state that opened its borders not only to foreign tourists but also, in the early 1960's, to its own citizens. There has been great concern about the outflow of youthful labor, and it appears that restrictive measures are being considered.[32] This movement abroad has, of course, been smaller in scale than the rural to urban movement within Yugoslavia; from all points of view, the latter has been the most important migratory movement in Yugoslav history and the one with the most far-reaching consequences.

The Balkans in general and Yugoslavia in particular have long had a mobile population, although it is difficult to measure such matters on an absolute scale. Barring the catastrophe of another war and what appears to be the likely slowing down of the movement abroad, through restrictive measures from the Yugoslav government or increasingly attractive opportunities within Yugoslavia, the question arises as to whether the Yugoslav population will now enjoy a greater stability. Will the most significant moves in the future be for summer vacations or for short-term recreational travel, study, and work abroad? That is, once a villager has moved to a republic capital, perhaps via a provincial staging area, are other moves likely? As indicated, large-scale movement across republic lines does not appear very likely, although from this point of view Serbia and Montenegro constitute one area, and Croats residing in Bosnia often move to Zagreb. Job opportunities may influence succeeding generations to shift, for example, from Beograd to Nis

---

[32]   President Tito has remarked on the absence of 300,000 men of military age, "enough to man three whole armies." Some 60,000 Yugoslav children abroad with their parents attend Western schools and are being assimilated into the societies in which they live; this is viewed with concern. Although some 400,000 Yugoslavs are said to be looking for work within the country, and remittances are said to be approaching the billion-dollar-a-year mark, there is concern that more than half of the 1,000,000 workers have gone abroad through private channels and not through government offices. Tighter restrictions are said to be contemplated (Anderson 1973:5).

or from Novi Sad to a smaller town, although there is great resistance to this because of the perceived concentration of amenities in the larger places. Large-scale mobility on the American pattern does not appear likely because of ethnic differences. Suburbanization in a planned context does, however, indicate certain kinds of moves. Thus, Novi Beograd, across the river from the main city, has more easily available housing, as do a number of growing satellite communities but these are primarily housing areas with some limited services.

With the increasing spread of amenities, it is not inconceivable that in another generation small towns may again become attractive as job opportunities become more restricted in the cities. This has already begun to happen, and there has been some movement of technically trained personnel, e.g. for staffing factories in small centers. Beyond these considerations, there is the question of the long-term attractiveness of large population centers. Yugoslav cities are still relatively small by New York, Tokyo, or London standards, but as cultural centers they are preeminent, on the pattern of Moscow or Paris.

As in the past, it seems likely that there will be a continuing dialectic between the supra-individual and personal factors. The context will change, but long-term stability need not be a future condition any more than it has been in the past. If one considers the dynamism of a society as a positive asset, then a certain degree of migratory movement can be seen as a convenient way of aiding in the resolution of future social problems, inevitable as long as change and conflict, preferably within limits, remain a part of human culture.

In conclusion there are at least two key matters to consider.

First, there is the complexity of relationships between migration and mobility. The latter term can refer to a complex of changes involving spatial, economic, cultural, social, and class or class-like dimensions, and can overlap with various kinds of migration experiences. Of great importance, as has been stressed here, is the time dimension in viewing such matters.

Second, and much more speculative, is the question of migration and mobility with respect to the changing dynamic of rural-urban relationships and the evolving nature of cities in Yugoslavia and elsewhere. This is linked in part to the future of the peasantry, the ultimate reservoir of past migration and also the ultimate reference point for measurement.

Several kinds of historically based generalizations emerge from the data presented. There can be limited spatial migration without innovation; such migration is necessary to the maintenance of the social structure. This type of migration is best illustrated by the movement of women at marriage, most frequently from one village to another relatively nearby. This process has continued up to the present.[33] More important from the point of view of change have been the social-ecological shifts conditioned by historical factors. As noted above, the Ottoman invasions of the Balkans forced a considerable portion of the population up into the mountains and gave a new lease on life to tribal and *zadruga* organizations. This was related to the destruction of the medieval Serbian state and its associated class structures and gave rise to a relatively homogeneous peasantry with strong pastoral specialization and a closely linked national church.

A third pattern is that of circular migration; this results in economic change but with a more restricted sociocultural change component, i.e. the village of origin remains the ultimate reference point and a place to which to return. This has characterized the *pecalba* tradition for the past several centuries and has continued to modern times. It marked the late nineteenth and early twentieth century migrations to America, with their high rates of return to native villages. Some of these migrants stayed away long enough to qualify for American social security benefits and often returned to their native villages several times before final retirement there. The "Americans" described by Cary are of this group. The experiences of the *hajduks*, the more recent and more limited experiences of those in military service, and the unplanned experiences of prisoners-of-war also followed this circular pattern. Villagers who worked for a time as apprentices or in service-related occupations (e.g. waiters), as common laborers on construction, or as seasonal migrant farm laborers fit into this classification. The contemporary peasant-worker falls in part in this category, although he is a daily or weekly commuter, and the secondary sociocultural impact is greater by virtue of the continuing daily contact.

Permanent migration, with its accompanying social, cultural, economic, and class changes, is distinct. Here socioeconomic mobility is combined with migration. In the pre-industrial period these opportunities were restricted essentially to the state service and involved military, administrative, and religious careers, in both Hapsburg and Ottoman areas. Individuals could rise spectacularly, but large groups could not. Trade and crafts provided some opportunities, but these were also limited.

In addition, there are large group movements resulting from political change and, within the last generation, related to political and ideological factors. After the successful revolts in Serbia in the nineteenth century,

---

[33]   Livada (1972) cites "marital mobility" as the most important motivation for moving. The Orasac village study in Serbia (Halpern 1956:373, Table 61) indicates that these migration patterns have had considerable constancy.

there was movement to towns to replace the departing foreigners and to fill the opening positions in the state administration and commercial ventures, the latter often linked to political activity, particularly at the level of the new elite. (The founders of two rival dynasties in Serbia, one of which ruled Yugoslavia until World War II, were both of peasant origin and were both engaged in trade.) Related to this type of movement were the population transfers during and immediately after the war, many of them involuntary, some voluntary, but all connected with the politics of war and revolution.

But most important of all has been the postwar decline in the peasantry as the majority reference group and its related ideological eclipse as a conceptual embodiment of valued national characteristics. The village has also become less important as a place of return in the context of the massive rural to urban migrations. These have been mostly within Yugoslavia, but beginning in the 1960's, they have also been abroad. Yugoslavia, like other Mediterranean nations — Turkey, Greece, Italy, Spain — sends her surplus or underemployed rural and urban labor to Western and Northern Europe. But socialist Yugoslavia has given certain of these movements a singular twist. Restrictions on the ownership of land and machinery in the private agriculture sector have been a factor there. The role of the worker was initially glorified and has continued to be stressed. In addition, there has been concern with the class role of the migrant as a worker in the socialized ownership sector. Accompanying this trend has been great emphasis on education as a channel of mobility.

Although the rural-urban gap has narrowed, most migrants do not seem to return to the village. Greater equality seems to have been a consequence of this massive shift out of the villages. The massive migrations of the twenty-five-year postwar period have obviously been a unique historical process that cannot be repeated, although movement can continue at a reduced rate because there are still potential rural migrants. The process does contain within it forces for a new dialectic based on the nature of the future opportunity structure, in which access to advanced training and education obviously will be a factor. Peasant origins will probably be less important as a frame of reference. Although many Yugoslav scholars have questioned the extent of the opportunities for socioeconomic mobility in mass migration, it seems clear that future mobility opportunities will be somewhat more restricted, in part because the major migratory moves have already been made.

The fate of children will be determined to some extent by the path taken by their parents. Movement from peasant to professional, managerial to bureaucratic elite will not be open to as many, nor will movement from peasant to skilled or semiskilled worker be possible for as many. The children of workers will probably be able to become professionals or managers in an urban area (mobility without migration), but the restrictions are already evident. Citing limitations, however, does not in any way minimize the profound changes that have taken place in the past quarter-century, changes that have clearly involved more migration and mobility than in any previous period in Yugoslav history.

A final question is the relationship, or perhaps more accurately stated, the series of relationships between migration and mobility and what has been called the nationalities question. There is a sizable literature on the subject, although most of it does not bear on the interrelationships defined above. The prominent Yugoslav scholar Branko Horvat (1969) suggests that the overall rapid urbanization of the population in the postwar period has created a climate of insecurity which in turn has led to the intensification of nationalist feelings. He maintains that individuals have felt isolated.[34]

This would seem to be at variance with the findings of anthropologists who have stressed the role of kinship and friendship networks in the migration and urbanization processes. Suvar (1972[1971]) depicts the political managers, the "so-called humanistic intellectuals," and increasingly the students as preoccupied with this problem of nationality, in contrast to the workers and peasants, who are engaged in "the minimum

[34] Horvat (1969) defines a "hierarchy of social groups," although he states that existing research is inadequate. He lists six groups: (1) government political figures, economic and other leaders who have the highest incomes and prestige and who make the most important social decisions; (2) intellectual workers, those of a technological economic sub-group, upper-echelon bureaucrats, and the humanist intelligentsia; (3) routine office workers or white-collar workers; (4) highly skilled, semi-skilled, and unskilled workers, including peasant-workers; (5) artisans; and (6) peasants. As indicative of mobility problems, he cites data showing that workers' children have only one-ninth the chance and peasants' children one-twentieth the chance of attaining the leadership category that children born to families within that group possess (Horvat 1969: 147–149). However, by implication he does see continued significant mobility between the social groups he defines. He sees an intensive exodus of 2 percent per annum under way from agriculture and expects during the lifetime of the present generation (presumably the one now economically active) a further drop of 15 percent (1969:158). However, he cites data on the social composition of the League of Communists that indicate a decrease in mobility. Thus, peasants, who composed half of the party in 1946 and 43 percent in 1952, were only 7 percent in 1966. By contrast, those in state employment went from 10 to 19 percent to 39 percent while worker representation increased only from 28 to 32 to 34 percent (1969:199). Put in another context, among children of secondary school age, virtually all those from the families of the first three categories listed by Horvat go on in their schooling, only one-third of the children of workers continue, and one-seventh of the children of peasants do so (1969:237).

struggle for existence." A number of writers have remarked that increasing nationalist and also religious identification is related not only to the social traumas associated with the general process of modernization, but also to a certain disillusionment with the initial promises of Yugoslav socialism, in Suvar's words "an ideology which destroyed everything old and stable and projected quick happiness."

It is not possible to relate the crucial question of the role of nationalism, on which the future of the Yugoslav state rests, in any simple way to a carry-over of rural or small-community values into an urban milieu. Suvar maintains that the peasantry has disintegrated and at the same time a "modern" urban population has failed to emerge:

About four million peasants moved to the city, but as many still have nowhere to move but can no longer live in the traditional conditions of village life, which are poor and limited.[35]

From the perspective of an outsider, this would seem to overstate the case, for change and migration have not been restricted to the postwar period. In addition to kinship networks, ties to villages have remained and there is much movement back and forth. Undoubtedly, as Suvar points out, the struggle for professions, careers, and income under conditions in which there is a great deal less than full employment will be a real one. As Horvat (1972) puts it, "The number of those who are abroad or who are unemployed today already approaches the number employed in all of Yugoslav industry." (Horvat gives this number as 1.2 million, which is not far from the 1.5 million in manufacturing: a total of 3.9 million were employed in the social sector in 1971.)

The question of allocation of limited resources is a crucial one, clearly related to ties of identity which, although redefined, have strong historical bases. However, because migration patterns have by and large followed republic lines (and have not, as in the American case, involved massive relocation of ethnic and racial groups in new areas), migration did not create the historical consciousness, nor did it pose direct confrontations on a major scale because of geographic proximity in an urban context. Nationalist consciousness seems to be an urban phenomenon primarily articulated by professional intellectuals within Yugoslavia as well by *émigré* groups residing abroad, including those with and those without a clearly defined political ideology for or against socialist Yugoslavia.

[35] A useful recent treatment is in a special 1972 issue of the *International Journal of Politics, The Nationalities Question in Yugoslavia*. See especially the articles by Horvat (1972: 19–46) and Suvar (1972:47–77) translated from the journal *Gledista* (1971). For general background and bibliography see Shoup (1968).

The Yugoslav problem needs to be seen in a broader European and perhaps world context. Within Europe there is great population movement: Southern Europeans migrate to work in Northern Europe, and Northern Europeans vacation in Southern Europe. Despite these movements and the growth of regional economic units in Eastern and Western Europe, local nationalisms thrive both on a national level and within the country. In the United Kingdom and Belgium, the Industrial Revolution developed early, and there is an old established working class within an urban framework predating this century.

Yet Yugoslavia's six republics and associated regions do represent historically and politically defined interest groups, with official ideological sanction within a multi-national state, whose economic possibilities are finite. Modernization as a generalized process is partly responsible for our quandary because it implies completion, just as migration implies a fixed goal. It is unlikely that in the near future Yugoslavs of various nationalities will move between republics the way Americans cross state or regional lines. However, there is no reason to assume that the predominantly rural to urban migration of the past quarter-century is the end of a historical process and implies a future stability with respect to population movement.

In the nineteenth century national consciousness among South Slav intellectuals in a largely rural society developed with respect to the domination of foreign powers; now it is developing with respect to one another in a society in which a peasant population, in a formal occupational sense, is now a minority. In the nineteenth century national identity focused on the idealized characteristics of a peasant society; today it stresses articulated, urban-focused economic needs and, to a degree, a shared historical past. The conceptualization of cultural continuity can have conservative ideological overtones, but the projection of future change, in which cultural inheritances will function in new ways, leaves open the question of whether population mobility will cease with this generation in Yugoslavia.

REFERENCES

ADAMIC, LOUIS
   1934   *The native's return*. New York: Harper and Brothers.
ADAMS, JOHN C.
   1942   *Flight in winter*. Princeton: Princeton University Press.
ANDERSON, RAYMOND H.
   1973   "Belgrade to curb worker outflow." *New York Times*. June 3, 1973:5.

AUTY, PHYLLIS
  1963 Article in *Yugoslavia at the Paris Peace Conference: a study in frontier-making.* By Ivo J. Lederer. New Haven: Yale University Press.

BABIC, WALTER
  1964 "Assimilation of Yugoslavs in Franklin County, Ohio." Unpublished doctoral dissertation, Ohio State University.

BARIC, LORRAINE
  1967a "Traditional groups and new economic opportunities in rural Yugoslavia," in *Themes in economic anthropology.* Edited by Raymond Firth. London: Tavistock.
  1967b "Levels of change in Yugoslav kinship," in *Social organization.* Edited by Maurice Freedman. London: Cass.

BEGOVIC, VLAJKO
  1964 "Current themes on the eve of the VII [Party] Congress." *Kumunist.* April 12, 1964:3.

BEGTIC, MUSTAFA
  1972 Yugoslav nationals temporarily working abroad. *Yugoslav Survey* (February): 17–31.

BRAUDEL, FERNAND
  1972 *The Mediterranean and the Mediterranean world in the age of Philip II,* volume one. Translated from French by Sian Reynolds. New York: Harper and Row.

CARY, JOYCE
  1960 *Memoir of the Bobotes.* Austin: University of Texas Press.

CHLOROS, A. G.
  1970 *Yugoslav civil law.* Oxford: Clarendon Press.

COLAKOVIC, BRANKO M.
  1970 "Yugoslav migrations to America." Unpublished doctoral dissertation, University of Minnesota.

CVIJIC, JOVAN
  1902 *Naselja i poreklo stanovnista* [Settlements and origin of populations]. Serbian Academy of Sciences.
  1918a The geographical distribution of the Balkan peoples. *The Geographical Review* 5(5).
  1918b *La Peninsule Balkanique.* Paris: Colin.

DEDIJERTS, VLADIMIR
  1951 *With Tito through the war, 1941–44.* London: Alexander Hamilton.

DENICH, BETTE S.
  1970 "Migration and network manipulation in Yugoslavia," in *Migration and anthropology: proceedings of the 1970 Annual Spring Meeting of the American Ethnological Society.* Edited by Robert F. Spencer, 133–148. University of Washington Press: Seattle.

DENITCH, BOGDAN
  1971 Sociology in Eastern Europe: the human factor. *The Journal of the Graduate Sociology Student Union of Columbia* (summer): 1–26.

Economist
  1970 September 5:39. London.

EDWARDS, LOVETT, *translator*
  1969 *The memoirs of Prota Matija Nenadovic.* Oxford: Clarendon Press.

GALESKI, BOGUSLAW
 1972   *Basic concepts of rural sociology.* Manchester: Manchester University Press.

GINIC, IVANKA
 1971   Dinamika Gradeskog Stanovnistva Jugoslavije Preme Prvim Rezultatima Popisa od 1971 Godine [Dynamics of the Yugoslav urban population according to the first results of the 1971 population census]. *Stanovnistvo* (January-June):25–41.

GLEDISTA
 1971   Articles in *Gledista* (5–6).

GOVORCHIN, GERALD G.
 1961   *Americans from Yugoslavia.* Gainesville: University of Florida Press.

HALPERN, JOEL
 1956   *Social and cultural change in a Serbian village.* New Haven: Human Relations Area Files.
 1963   Yugoslav peasant society in transition — stability in change. *Anthropological Quarterly* 36 (July):167–171.
 1965   Peasant culture and urbanization in Yugoslavia. *Human Organization* 24(2):172.
 1967a *A Serbian village.* New York: Harper and Row.
 1967b "Farming as a way of life: Yugoslav peasant attitudes," in *Soviet and East European agriculture.* Edited by Jerzy F. Karcz, 356–381. Berkeley: University of California Press.
 1967c "The process of modernization as reflected in Yugoslav peasant biographies," in *Kroeber Anthropological Society papers*, special publications 1.
 1967d *The changing village community.* Englewood Cliffs: Prentice-Hall.
 1969   "Yugoslavia: modernization in an ethnically diverse state," in *Contemporary Yugoslavia: twenty years of socialist experiment.* Edited by Wayne S. Vucinich, 323–329. Berkeley: University of California Press.
 1970   "A brief survey of English language research in Yugoslav cultural and social anthropology and ethnology," in *A symposium on East European ethnography.* Edited by Zdenek Salzmann, 21–25. Research Reports 6. Amherst: Department of Anthropology, University of Massachusetts.

HALPERN, JOEL, BARBARA HALPERN
 1972   *A Serbian village in historical perspective.* New York: Holt, Rinehart and Winston.

HAMMEL, EUGENE A.
 1968   *Alternative social structures and ritual relations in the Balkans.* Englewood Cliffs: Prentice-Hall.
 1969a "The Balkan peasant — a view from Serbia," in *Peasants in the contemporary world.* Edited by Phillip K. Bock. Albuquerque: University of New Mexico Press.
 1969b *The pink yo-yo, occupational mobility in Belgrade, ca. 1915–1965.* Institute of International Studies, Research Series 13. Berkeley: University of California.

HOBSBAWN, E. J.
1969   *Bandits*. London: Weidenfeld and Nicolson.

HOFFMAN, GEORGE W.
1973   "Migration, urbanization and problems of social transformation: the case of Yugoslavia," in *Problems of communism*.

HORVAT, BRANKO
1969   *An essay on Yugoslav society*. White Plains, New York: International Arts and Sciences Press.
1972   "Nationalism and nationality," in *The nationalities question in Yugoslavia*, 19–46. *International Journal of Politics*, special issue 2(1).

INSTITUT DRUSTVENIH NAUKA
1963   "Odeljeje za sociologiju," in *Socijalna struktura i pokretljivost radnicke klase Jugoslavije*, volume one, 257–288. Beograd: Institut Drustvenih Nauka.
1971   *Migracije Stanovnista Jugoslavije*. Beograd: Institut Drustvenih Nauka.

International Journal of Politics
1972   *The nationalities question in Yugoslavia*. *International Journal of Politics*, special issue 2(1).

KOJIC, BRANISLAW
1949   *Stara Gradska: Seoska Arhitektura u Srbiji* [Old town and village architecture in Serbia]. Beograd: Prosveta.

KOSINSKI, LESZEK A.
1969   Migration of population in East-Central Europe, 1939–1955. *Canadian Slavonic Papers* 11 (3):359–373.

KOSTIC, DARINKA M.
1963   *Promene u Drustvenom Zirotu Kolonista* [Change in the social life of the colonists]. Beograd: Institut Drustvenih Nauka.

LEDERER, IVO J.
1963   *Yugoslavia at the Paris Peace Conference: a study in frontiermaking*. New Haven: Yale University Press.

LIVADA, SVETOZAR
1972   "The basic structures and mobility of Yugoslavia's rural and agricultural population," in *The Yugoslav village*. Zagreb: Department of Rural Sociology, Institute of Agriculture Economics.

LOCKWOOD, WILLIAM G.
1970   "Selo and Carsija: the peasant market place as a mechanism of social integration in western Bosnia." Unpublished doctoral dissertation, University of California, Berkeley.

LOVRICH, FRANK M.
1966–1967   Croatians in Louisiana. *Journal of Croatian Studies* 7–8. New York.

LUKIC, RADOMIR
n.d.   "Influence of the Worroks' self-management on the class system in the Yugoslav society," in *Sociologija, selected articles, 1959–1969*, 25–44.

MCNEILL, WILLIAM H.
1964   *Europe's steppe frontier, 1500–1800*. Chicago: University of Chicago Press.

MEURLE, KRISTINA, MILE ANDRIC
  1971   *Background to the Yugoslav migration to Sweden, case study of a group of Yugoslav workers at a factory in Sweden.* Lund, Sweden: Department of Sociology, Lund University.

NIKOLIC, MILOJE
  1972   Some basic features of Yugoslav external migration. *Yugoslav Survey* (February): 1–16.

PAIKERT, G. C.
  1967   *The Danube Swabians.* The Hague: Martinus Nijhoff.

Politika
  1970   June 4. Beograd.

POPOVIC, DUSAN
  1950   *Srbya i Beograd.* Beograd: Srpska Knjizerna Zadruga.

PULJIZ, VLADO
  1972   "Part-time farms in the socio-economic structure of Yugoslav rural areas," in *The Yugoslav village,* 127–142. Zagreb: Department of Rural Sociology, Institute of Agriculture Economics.

RAYNER, LOUISE
  1957   *Women in a village.* London: Heinemann.

ROTHENBERG, GUNTHER E.
  1966   *The military border in Croatia, 1740–1881.* Chicago: University of Chicago Press.

SHOUP, PAUL
  1968   *Communism and the Yugoslav national question.* New York: Columbia University Press.

SIMIC, ANDREI
  1973   *The peasant urbanities: a study of rural-urban mobility in Serbia.* New York: Seminar Press.

SIMONS, THOMAS W., JR.
  1973   "The peasantry in the East European political process: a typology." Paper presented at the seminar, "What is a Peasant?," at a symposium on East European Peasant Sociietes sponsored by Boston University, Brown University, and Harvard University, January 1973.

SINGLETON, FRED B.
  1973   "The economic background to tensions between the nationalities in Yugoslavia," in *Festschrift fur Hans Raupach, Problemen des Industrialismus in Ost und West.* Munich: Gunter Olzog Verlag. (Reprinted from Werner Gumpel and Dietmar Keese.)

SREAD, ALFRED, *editor*
  1909   "The army," in *Servia by the Serbians,* 80–92. London: Heinemann.

STOIANOVICH, TRAIAN
  1960   The conquering Balkan Orthodox merchant. *Journal of Economic History* 20 (June): 276.
  1967   *A study in Balkan civilization.* New York: Alfred A. Knopf.
  1970   "Model and mirror of the premodern Balkan city," in *La ville Balkanique XVe–XIXe SS.* Sofia: Academie Bulgare des Sciences.

SUVAR, STIPE
  1972 [1971]   "Marginal notes on the nationalism question," in *The na-*

tionalities question in Yugoslavia, 47–77. *International Journal of Politics*, special issue 2(1). Translated from *Gledista* (5–6) 1971.

TOMASEVICH, JOVO
1955 *Peasants, politics and economic change in Yugoslavia*. Stanford: Stanford University Press.

TOMOVIC, VLADISLAV A.
1968 *Post World War II sociology in Yugoslavia*. Windsor, Ontario: University of Windsor.

VUCINICH, WAYNE S.
1962 The nature of Balkan society under Ottoman rule. *Slavic Review* (December): 597–616.

VUJOVIC, RADE
1972 Workers abroad. *Review* 9–10:12. Beograd.

WINNER, IRENE
1971 *A Slovenian village*. Providence, Rhode Island: Brown University Press.

Migration, Population Change, and Ethnicity in Argentina

ALFREDO E. LATTES

Even though studies on human migration are nothing new,[1] it has only been in recent decades that learning about their causes and consequences has begun to be considered important in the case of internal as well as international migrations. This acknowledgement of the importance of migration in relation to a long series of social, cultural, and economic aspects of the transformation process of societies has produced an increase in the scientific study of this phenomenon; and there is a growing number of studies, essentially empirical, on the net and gross migration, migration differentials, migration streams, etc.

The larger number of researches has made it possible to make important progress in the improvement of the techniques and methods for the measurement and description of the phenomenon. The recent manual on methods of measuring internal migration (United Nations 1970) illustrates this progress.

Around 1950, approximately 80 percent of the world population was enumerated. These censuses collected a great deal of data for the study of migration. In the censuses of 1960 and 1970 new questions were added in relation to this topic. The large amount of collected data, though not completely adequate, undoubtedly constitutes the main bulk of data for the study of migration in most countries of the world.

In addition, a growing number of countries are collecting demographic data through sample surveys which also include the collection of information for the study of migration. Thus new variables are incorporated

---

[1] In 1885, the British demographer Ravenstein (Ravenstein 1885) presented his celebrated paper on the Laws of Migration before the Royal Statistical Society.

which make it possible to widen the approach of the studies. The sample surveys in migration analysis appear to be a most fruitful instrument, both in themselves and as an aid with information from other sources.

Many of the studies carried out on the basis of censuses have not been aimed solely at the study of migration in the past decades. Much research has dealt with the analysis of this phenomenon in the present as well as in the past.

From a different angle, however, in spite of the just mentioned boom, there is not yet much that can be regarded as common knowledge in the field of migration. Several authors (Mangalam and Schwarzweller 1968, 1970; Goldscheider 1971) have called our attention to such an important point in recent articles. Among the main reasons hindering effective progress in the knowledge of migration, Elizaga (1970:2) summarizes the following:

A. A coherent and satisfactory system of operational definitions is still missing.

B. Data not wholly adequate are used, especially for the study of migration in the social, cultural and economic context.

C. There is neither a comprehensive theory nor even a systematic frame of reference to guide the research carried out.

All these reasons are valid. A quick look at the literature shows an abundance of descriptive research that, in general, lacks an orientation necessary to obtain more fruitful production and accumulation of knowledge.

The present concern about the lack of theoretical guidelines expressed by many researchers is justifiable, but we must also keep in mind that we are going through a necessary and unavoidable stage in scientific knowledge. A start has been made by describing reality, albeit in an imperfect way. This situation is not remedied with theoretical statements made hastily without a good empirical basis. On the contrary, a rush in this direction would be of little use and would contribute to make the present situation more chaotic.

However, a true process of inventory, assessment, and ordering of the empirical knowledge existing in each country may be and must be attempted at once. We could then detect empirical regularities — or irregularities — for different periods, different socioeconomic contexts, etc. The task must be carried out in such a way that everything that has actually been done can be placed in the proper frame or substratum of reference of the field — demography, sociology, anthropology, economics, etc.

A comprehensive theory of migration is a future possibility, and all research should aim at it. But there are concrete tasks to carry out now:

tasks proper to the stage of knowledge of this phenomenon, tasks which with a relatively low investment will allow us to profit greatly from the large effort already made.

A CASE OF INTEREST IN MIGRATION ANALYSIS

In the long process of social, cultural, and economic change which has taken place in Argentina, mainly from the middle of the nineteenth century up to the present, two phenomena have been particularly relevant: the mass immigration of foreign born and the internal migration of natives.

Table 1. Main countries of European immigration

Country of immigration	Total (thousands)
United States (1821–1932) (1946–1954)	33,958
Argentina (1853–1932) (1946–1954)	7,166
Canada (1821–1932) (1946–1954)	6,318
Brazil (1821–1932) (1946–1954)	4,842
Australia (1861–1932) (1946–1954)	3,810

Source: before 1932: Thomas 1961: 12; 1946–1954: Borrie 1959: 17

Argentina ranks second among the nations that have received European immigration since the beginning of the nineteenth century (see Table 1). On the other hand, Argentina is at present one of the most urbanized nations in the world, with slightly over 70 percent of its population living in urban areas and one-third of the people clustered in Greater Buenos Aires, one of the largest metropolises in the world. Because of these characteristics, Argentina is an interesting case in the area of study of internal and international migration.

SCOPE AND DATA

Some aspects of migration in Argentina are considered here. The analysis is rather limited. We focus on migration only as one of the factors of change in the population; and within this change, we pay attention to some parts which, in turn, are of interest for the process of ethnic configuration of the population in Argentina.

The approach is essentially demographic, or more precisely, macro-demographic. Thus the units of analysis are populations, and the phenomena under study affect these units.

In the process that demographers usually call population change, three characteristic aspects are generally distinguished for reasons that facilitate the analysis. These aspects are the changes taking place in (1) the size, (2) the spatial distribution, and (3) the composition[2] of the populations.

We try to understand in what way migration is a factor of change, that is, how it generates growth, spatial redistribution, and changes in the composition of a population. These changes are, in turn, part of the process of formation of the ethnic identity of the population. To summarize, we analyze some of the links between migration and ethnicity. The area and the period of time studied are Argentina and its provinces between 1869 and 1960.

In any country that has received important groups of immigrants from other countries, censuses almost invariably contain questions related to ethnic origin. In their simplest form these questions ask only about the place of birth; the total population can thus be classified into natives and foreign born. In this way the foreign born constitute a group that can be isolated for analysis. This classification is, of course, very limited, and it hardly allows us to have an image of the cultural pluralism of the receiving population. However, for a study of population with a macro-demographic approach which covers a long period of time, censuses constitute the main source of information, though one must point out that censuses are only sporadic snapshots of a long and complex process of change. In the case of Argentina this remark is absolutely true, for the censuses here occurred less often than in other countries. Specifically, we shall analyze information from the first five national population censuses taken in the years 1869, 1895, 1914, 1947, and 1960, respectively.

In relation to the foreign born, these five censuses allow us to analyze, in addition to their number for the total of the country and for provinces, some individual characteristics such as age, sex, country of birth, etc. With this information and through the use of appropriate techniques, it is

---

[2] Population composition includes, besides age and sex characteristics, marital status, literacy or educational attainment, economic characteristics, nation of birth, etc.

possible to estimate — with a certain approximation — the intercensual net migration (gains or losses) for the total of the country as well as for the provinces. Analyzing the available tables, this can also be done for sex and age, and for sex and country of birth.

If we start from this knowledge, keeping aware also of the change that took place in the total population, it is possible to study the role of the net migration of the foreign born in the growth, interprovince distribution, and changes in the composition by sex, age, and nationality.

The natives also have migrated. These migrations, which have been rather important in Argentina, also are a factor of change in the population. The five censuses provide for the natives the information already described for the foreign born, and we can therefore estimate the net migration (gains or losses) for each province and for each intercensual period. Both migrations — native and foreign born — act as factors of change in the population. It is interesting to analyze, in addition to the individual contribution of each of them, the interaction and the differences existing between them.

The basic definition of migrant is the same for the natives as well as for the foreign born. A migrant (lifetime migrant) is a person whose area of residence at the census date differs from his area of birth: a different country for the immigrants, a different province for the natives.

This definition — a consequence of the available data — has important limitations. It is impossible to deal here with all the diverse and complex problems that it offers, but we will mention some of them, and we refer to the discussions on this topic contained in the manual on methods of measuring internal migration (United Nations 1970). This definition does not allow us to know at what point in the intercensual period the migration took place, nor does it tell us how many times the migrants have moved; it also hides the cases of return migration. The fact that it is possible to make an analysis only at the province level excludes important intraprovince movements. The estimates of the intercensual net migration contain, in addition to typical census errors, those errors in the method used for their calculation, especially those related to the census survival ratios which are utilized. As a corollary to this, we want to point out the approximative level that these estimates have.

BRIEF HISTORICAL SETTING BEFORE 1869

The knowledge we have on the evolution of the population of the country during the first part of the colonial period is hardly anything but conjectures which scarcely allow us to have an idea of what could have been the tendency followed.

At the beginning of the sixteenth century (the arrival of the conquerors) the total number of Indians — the total population — was probably not over 400,000. From then up to the middle of the seventeenth century, the population decreased in number. It is estimated that at that time the total was about 300,000, of which 80 percent must have been Indians, and the rest mestizos, Creoles,[3] Spaniards, Negroes, and mulattoes.

It was only in 1778 that the so-called census of Vertiz enumerated the largest part of the population of the territory occupied by the Spaniards. The results of that census plus the estimates of the population not covered by the census yield a total of about 420,000. Of these, 200,000 must have been Indians who lived in areas not in touch with the Spaniards. Of the remaining 220,000, 25 percent must have been peaceful Indians, another 25 percent Negroes and mulattoes, and the rest mestizos, Creoles, and Spaniards. At the beginning of the nineteenth century, the total estimated population was approximately 550,000.[4]

Among the important changes that took place during the first half of the nineteenth century were a larger rate of growth of the population and changes in its racial composition, which included the disappearance of the Negro and a decrease in the proportion of the indigenous population. In the middle of the century the population rose to 1,200,000, of which 15 to 20 percent was the indigenous population; 10 percent, the foreign born; and the rest — the largest proportion — Creoles and mestizos plus a few Negroes and mulattoes.

In the 1850's, the immigration, which up to that time had not numbered over a few thousands per year, began to increase rapidly. In 1869, the first national population census shows more than 210,000 foreign born.

MIGRATION AS A DETERMINANT OF THE STATE OF POPULATION IN 1869

The 1869 census in Argentina opens the "statistical era" in the study of its population. We can obtain a fairly clear picture of the population at that time and can infer some characteristics of the change of population which took place a few years prior to that date. The total of the population enumerated was 1,736,923. To this figure we must add an estimate of

[3] Creoles: Spanish-speaking persons born in the New World.
[4] All population estimations for dates previous to 1869 are from the author's unpublished research.

93,138 Indians who lived out of touch with the rest of the population, for a total of 1,830,061. In recent evaluations (Lattes 1968) we find that the result of this census has, as is to be expected of every census, omissions which would raise the total figure up to about 1,900,000. Although this figure is given as an illustration of the total size of the population at that time, when we analyze characteristics of the population we must use the figure that constitutes the actually enumerated total.

We summarize next some of the characteristics of the state of the population in Argentina in 1869, especially those characteristics that are relevant here. According to the figures of the actually enumerated population, in 1869, 12.1 percent of the population was foreign-born. Some characteristic aspects of the foreign-born population made its influence have greater weight than that represented by its proportion of the total population.

The spatial distribution of the foreign-born population in the country was much more concentrated than that of the native population. Thus in three provinces the relative importance of the foreign born was greater than for the whole of the country. These three provinces (Buenos Aires, Santa Fe, and Entre Ríos) contained 87 percent of the total of the foreign born.

Another characteristic of the spatial distribution of the foreign born in the territory was their greater concentration in urban areas than in rural ones. Within the urban population we must stress the special case of Buenos Aires City, where the foreign-born population was almost 50 percent of the total, and the foreign-born males largely outnumbered the natives.

The age and sex pyramids of the country's population enumerated in 1869 (Figure 1) clearly show the high proportion of males among the foreign born (sex ratio = 250) and also the higher concentration of foreign born in the young adult groups.

The relative weight of the foreign-born population is more evident if we consider the economically active male population. The foreign-born males constituted more than 26 percent of the whole of active males, as a direct consequence of the different structures of ages among natives and foreign born.

Another characteristic that stands out is the higher level of education of the foreign-born population in comparison to the native. The proportion of literate males among the foreign born was remarkably higher than among the natives. For both sexes, the literates made up 55.5 percent of the foreign born and only 22.5 percent of the native population. Among foreign-born males, the proportion of literates was as high as 60 percent.

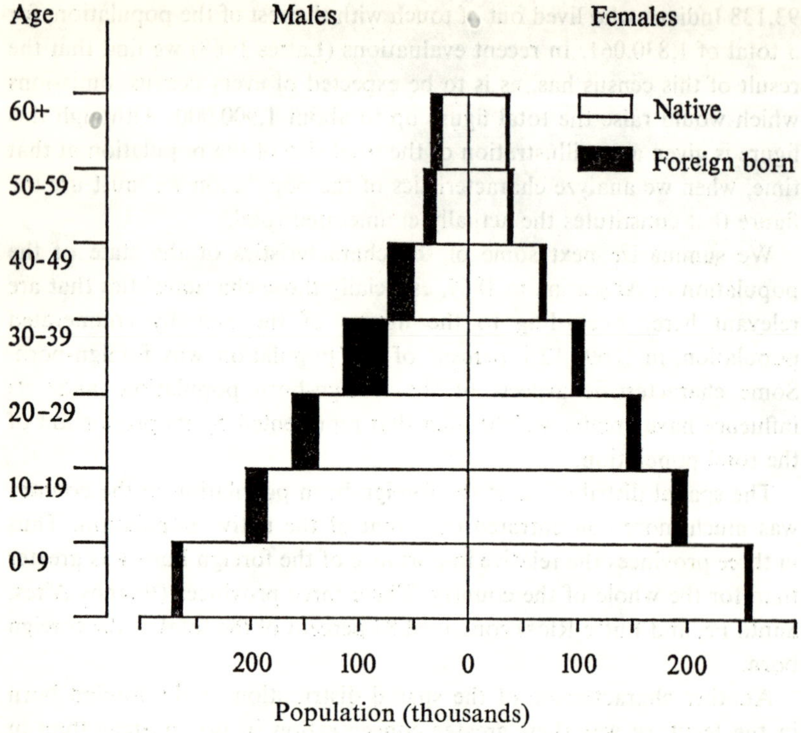

Figure 1.   Age-sex and nativity structure of the population, Argentina, 1869.
Source: Somoza and Lattes 1967

These are some of the several differential characteristics of the foreign-born population that stressed the significance of their presence in the country beyond their numerical proportion of the total.

Although it is impossible to reach an exact measure of the composition of the population in the following categories, we can present a gross estimate of them. The categories are:

A.   foreign born
B.   native of foreign parents
C.   native of mixed parentage
    a.   foreign-born father, native mother
    b.   foreign-born mother, native father
D.   native of native parents (descendents of foreign born)
E.   native of native parents (descendents of mestizo)
F.   native Indians.

As a consequence of the particular composition of the foreign-born population by sex and age, an important proportion of the natives must have belonged to categories B and C. It is estimated that the foreign born — who represented 12.1 percent of the enumerated population — plus their children added up to 30 percent of the total population (categories A, B, and C).

Argentine censuses do not allow us to distinguish the indigenous population within the total population in the censuses. In the 1869 census there are approximately 5,000 people classified as Indians, besides the estimate of the non-enumerated Indians. From the reading of the introductory chapters to this census, as well as from the writings related to the population in the period prior to 1869, we find that, in general, the presence of the indigenous population has been either ignored or forgotten. Our opinion is that, in addition to the 100,000 Indians (from the census and the estimate of the non-enumerated Indians), the population actually contained a larger number of them. We base our opinion on the examination of the original census schedule of the 1869 census, particularly those censuses of the provinces in the northwest of the country. In them, the frequent omission of characteristics such as age, marital status, literacy, etc., in small communities or in whole population groups suggests that they are rural communities of indigenous population. On account of this we think that the indigenous population — though not all Indians preserved their natural way of life — could not be less than 10 percent of the total population.

Summarizing this outline of the composition of the population, we would have at the date of the first national census 30 percent of the total made up by what might be called "the foreign stock," 10 percent by indigenous population, and the remaining 60 percent by the descendents of Creoles and mestizos, who would thus constitute the dominant group. Among the foreign born, though they were from almost all the European countries and even from others in Asia and Africa, the three Mediterranean countries — Italy, Spain, and France — and the neighboring ones — Chile, Bolivia, Paraguay, Brazil, and Uruguay — represented the largest proportion with about 85 percent of the total (see Table 2).

The 1869 census is the first source of information about internal migration of natives that covers the whole of the country. Only for a few provinces or cities is it possible to find information about internal migration of natives prior to that date.[5] We mention briefly some clues and characteristics of migratory internal movements of native population which took place mostly in the two decades prior to the 1869 census.

---

[5] As an example, for Buenos Aires City see Recchini de Lattes 1971.

Table 2.   Nationality of major foreign-born groups residing in Argentina in 1869

Nationality	Percent of total foreign-born population
Italian	33.6
Neighbors[a]	19.8
Spaniards	16.1
French	15.3
English	5.1
Swiss	2.8
German	2.4
All others	4.9

[a] Chileans, Bolivians, Paraguayans, Brazilians, and Uruguayans.

Source: Argentina 1872

The proportion of native migrants in the total native population was 8.3 percent at the time of the 1869 census. If we consider Buenos Aires City as a separate spatial unit, this proportion rises to 14.4 percent.

Among the native migrants there were more men than women. The sex ratio was 138. Migrants also were concentrated in the young adult ages in comparison to non-migrants (see Table 3). Although each migrant

Table 3.   Distribution of lifetime migrants and non-migrants by sex and age groups, Argentina, 1869

Age groups	Migrants		Non-migrants	
	Males	Females	Males	Females
0–9	10.6	14.0	37.3	33.7
10–19	17.6	17.3	25.3	24.2
20–29	24.4	22.6	14.1	16.6
30–39	20.0	18.4	9.4	10.7
40–49	13.8	13.7	6.6	7.1
50–59	8.0	7.2	3.8	4.1
60 +	5.6	6.8	3.5	3.6
Total	100.0	100.0	100.0	100.0

Source and references: These distributions have been calculated from special tables from a sample of the original schedules of the population enumerated in 1869. For more details about this sample see Somoza and Lattes 1967.

might have migrated at any time during the period from his birth to the date of the census, it suffices to presume that children migrate with their parents to find that not less than 50 percent of the migrants that appear in the 1869 census migrated in the 1860's.

Other characteristics of native migrants are the following: the level of literacy among migrants was lower than among non-migrants in all age groups (see Table 4); the level of economic activity in males was higher

Table 4. Percentage of literate lifetime migrants and non-migrants by sex and age groups, Argentina, 1869

Age groups Total ages	Migrants		Non-migrants	
	Males	Females	Males	Females
(15 +)	22.6	16.2	26.8	20.5
15–19	24.6	25.5	27.3	29.8
20–29	23.5	19.1	26.5	21.5
30–39	21.5	13.1	28.3	17.9
40–49	20.6	14.4	27.0	14.2
50–59	26.8	11.7	27.3	15.0
60 +	18.6	10.9	21.3	11.7

Source and references: These distributions have been calculated from special tables from a sample of the original schedules of the population enumerated in 1869. For more details about this sample see Somoza and Lattes 1967.

among migrants, but in females it was higher among non-migrants. This might indicate that in many cases migrant females accompanied their husbands and did not take part in the economic activity.

The spatial distribution of the (native) migrant population was some-what different from the distribution of the non-migrant natives. The former were much more concentrated in some provinces. For instance, Buenos Aires (Buenos Aires City included), Santa Fe, and Entre Ríos held 58 percent of the total number of migrants and 33 percent of the non-migrants. We must keep in mind that these provinces were also those in which the largest proportion of the foreign born were concentrated (87 percent).

Because the provincial populations varied greatly in size, it is interesting to observe the relative importance of migration in relation to the size of the population. As can be seen in Table 5, in-migration had been higher in Santa Fe and Entre Ríos than in the other provinces. Buenos Aires, which had the largest number of lifetime in-migrants, in relative terms, had a value similar to that of other provinces such as Salta, San Juan, Men-doza, Tucumán, etc. Also in Table 5, we can see, in relative terms, the loss of population per province. Santiago del Estero appears as the province which had lost the highest proportion of its population, and the one which — with the exception of Corrientes — had attracted the lowest proportion. The situation clearly opposite to that of Santiago del Estero

Table 5.   Lifetime in-migrants by province[a] of destination and out-migrants by province of origin, Argentina, 1869

Province of destination and origin	Lifetime in-migrants (percent)	Lifetime out-migrants (percent)
Buenos Aires[b]	9.0	2.6
Catamarca	6.1	9.4
Córdoba	3.6	12.5
Corrientes	1.0	7.3
Entre Ríos	14.2	2.4
Jujuy	9.7	5.1
La Rioja	5.7	11.6
Mendoza	8.7	9.0
Salta	8.7	5.8
San Juan	9.8	8.6
San Luís	7.8	14.8
Santa Fe	35.0	11.7
Santiago del Estero	1.4	15.1
Tucumán	8.9	8.4
Total country	8.3	8.3

[a] No population was enumerated in Territorios Nacionales in 1869.
[b] It including Buenos Aires City.

Source: Recchini de Lattes and Lattes 1969: 90

was that of Entre Ríos, which was second in terms of attraction of migrants, and first in terms of loss of population.

Finally, in relation to the migration of natives and foreign born, let us keep in mind that the various differential characteristics were observed at the level of migrant populations as a whole. Neither migrant nor non-migrant populations constitute homogeneous groups in themselves. Both contain subgroups which are, in turn, highly differentiated among themselves. It has been shown (Lattes 1970) that among native migrants, if characteristics are analyzed by interprovincial streams, these are significantly different from each other. As we shall see later, there are also differences among foreign-born groups of different origins.

Up to this point we have been concerned with a brief description of the state of the population in Argentina in 1869. At that time, the state of the population and some aspects of the ethnic identity were already, to a great extent, a direct consequence of the migrations — internal as well as international — which had taken place up to that time.

A LONG-RANGE VIEW OF MIGRATION AS A FACTOR OF POPULATION CHANGE BETWEEN 1869 AND 1960

The net migration of foreign born was far from being a constant or stable phenomenon during the years between 1869 and 1960. As a consequence, its effect on the growth of the population differed for the various periods. Our observations about the long and unequal intercensual periods, though not completely adequate to indicate what we are pointing out, serve as a good illustration of these differences. Table 6 shows what the role of

Table 6. Net migration, natural increase, and total increase for intercensual periods. Numbers and rates for Argentina, 1869–1960

| Periods | Numbers in thousands | | | | Annual rates per 1,000 average population | | |
	Net migration	Natural increase	Total increase	Average population	Net migration	Natural increase	Total increase
1869–1895	1,270	948	2,218	2,846	17	13	30
1895–1914	2,097	1,834	3,930	5,920	19	16	35
1914–1947	1,790	6,219	8,009	11,890	5	16	20
1947–1960	969	3,086	4,056	17,922	4	13	17

Source and references: Population: Data taken directly from census report.
Migration: Net migration has been estimated using the Average Survival Ratio Method for all ages together. Symbolically:

$$\text{Net M} = (I^{t+n} - SI^t) \frac{(1 + S)}{2 S}$$

M is the estimate of net migration on the assumption that deaths and migrations were evenly distributed over the period. I^{t+n} and I^t are the total foreign-born population at times t and t+n. S is an overall Census Survival Ratio computed for native (closed) population (ratio of persons aged n years and over in the country at the second census to persons of all ages in the first census). This ratio was adjusted to account for the differences in the level of mortality and age distribution that exist between native and foreign-born populations.
Natural Increase: Obtained as an indirect estimation:
Total Increase – Net Migration = Natural Increase
Rates: All rates are based on the average population of the period. In order to facilitate comparisons over time, annual rates have been computed by dividing the rate for each period by the number of years in the period.

international migration has been, and the way in which it stopped being the main factor of growth of the total population after the first two intercensual periods.

It is important to emphasize that we refer only to the DIRECT contribution of migration to the population growth, that is, to its capacity to subtract and add people. Therefore we shall not take into account any of the INDIRECT contributions it makes, such as its own natural growth, the structural demographic changes it originates in the receiving population and which modify in turn the levels of natality and mortality, etc.

The composition by sex of the foreign-born migration, in addition to varying among the different intercensual periods, has always been different from that of the natives, which has generated a changing composition by sex of the total population of the country. Table 9 shows the variations which the composition by sex of the net migration of foreign born undergoes through the different intercensual periods. Moreover, we can observe that the important decrease of the net migration of foreign born — which took place in the last two intercensual periods — was accompanied by an important change in the composition by sex. During the first two periods, the high rates of net migration show a high male predominance. In the third period, along with the abrupt drop of the rate of net migration, the proportion of males also declines to some extent, and then it continues dropping in the fourth period to the point where females predominate.

The method used to obtain the net migration of foreign born by sex and intercensual period does not allow us to distinguish between net immigration and net emigration. Therefore the change in the composition by sex observed for the net migration in each period might have other differential characteristics in terms of these two components of the migratory process.

Finally, Table 7, which shows the composition by sex of the native,

Table 7. Sex ratio of native, foreign born, and total population at census years, Argentina, 1869–1960

Year	Total enumerated population	Sex ratio		
		Total	Native	Foreign born
1869	1,736,923	104.9	93.6	249.6
1895	3,954,911	113.3	98.3	175.2
1914	7,885,237	117.6	100.9	171.0
1947	15,893,827	105.1	100.1	138.5
1960	20,013,793	103.1	99.8	129.2

Source: Recchini de Lattes and Lattes 1969

foreign born, and total populations at the different censual dates, illustrates the process of change in the composition by sex at the level of the total country between 1869 and 1960.

We have seen, on the one hand, the DIRECT contribution of the net migration of foreign born to the growth of the total population. On the other hand, we have seen how its differential composition by sex modified the composition by sex of the population of the country. As a consequence of both effects, another aspect of the composition of the population is modified. We refer to its composition regarding natives and foreign born by sex. Table 8 shows how in 1914 the proportion of foreign born in the total population reaches its highest value, and how this value, in turn, differs for the sexes.

Table 8. Percentage of foreign born in the total population and by sex at census year, Argentina, 1869–1960

| Year | Percentages of foreign born | | |
	Total population	Male population	Female population
1869	12.1	16.9	7.1
1895	25.4	30.4	19.8
1914	29.9	34.9	24.2
1947	15.3	17.4	13.2
1960	13.0	14.2	11.8

Source: Recchini de Lattes and Lattes 1969

We have already seen that in 1869 the enumerated foreign born came from different places. The composition by origin of the net migration of the country will determine whether that composition will remain the same or change. Table 9 presents the composition of net migration for each intercensual period by sex and by five major groups of place of origin. The first two correspond to the nationalities which, since the middle of the nineteenth century, have predominated among the foreign born in the country. Those grouped under Rest of Europe have had, in general, one or two dominant nationalities in the different intercensual periods, but they have not remained constant. Italians make up slightly over 50 percent of the total net migration during the first period, and, along with Spaniards, they are the dominant nationalities of migration. Both together make up 71 percent of the total. Among those coming from the rest of Europe in that period, Russians (most of them Jewish immigrants), Austrians, and Hungarians prevailed.

In the 1895–1914 period, the proportion of Italians decreases and the Spaniards (41.2 percent) are the largest group. Both together represent a still higher proportion of the net migration of the period (77 percent) as compared to the earlier period. Among the other Europeans, Russians

Table 9.   Foreign-born net migration. Distribution and sex ratio by major groups of origin, intercensual periods, Argentina, 1869–1960

Origin	1869–1895		1895–1914		1914–1947		1947–1960	
	Percent distribu-tion	Sex ratio	Percent distribu-tion	Sex ratio	Percent distribu-tion	Sex ratio	Percent distribu-tion	Sex ratio
Italy	50.7	173.7	35.7	173.0	25.0	124.0	36.8	90.8
Spain	20.2	179.1	41.2	161.2	26.2	79.4	20.4	62.5
Rest of Europe	17.6	149.6	11.5	176.8	26.2	140.4	8.3	60.8
Neigh-boring countries	10.5	132.3	7.5	127.8	17.2	111.9	28.9	116.2
Rest of the world	1.0	207.2	4.1	405.0	5.4	140.6	5.6	102.3
Total net migration	100.0	165.6	100.0	169.4	100.0	112.6	100.0	88.2

Sources and references: The methods followed for estimating major groups of origin and sex of foreign-born net migration by intercensual periods were the same as that for total net migration, described in the sources and methods of Table 6. Mortality level was assumed the same for all groups and by sex.

and Polish prevail in this period. The Syrians and Armenians also constitute an important group within the category Rest of the World.

In the 1914–1947 period, the composition by origin of the net migration of foreign born shows important changes. The three main groups — Italians, Spaniards, and Rest of Europe — make similar contributions. Among the last-named, the Polish and German prevailed. It is also worth noting the important increase in the proportion of immigrants from neighboring countries.

In the last intercensual period analyzed, Italians are again the dominant group. Together with Spaniards, they make up approximately 57 percent of the net migration. The important decrease of the group Rest of Europe and the new increase in the proportion of immigrants from neighboring countries are the other two important characteristics of the net migration of this period.

As a result of the changes produced in the net migration of foreign born by origin, the various nationalities represent very different proportions of the total population at the dates of the five censuses. Table 10 shows the nationality of the five major foreign-born groups enumerated at each census date and its proportion in the total population.

As a final remark in this brief and partial analysis of the effect of the net migration of foreign born on the total population of the country, we turn

Table 10. Nationality of major foreign-born groups enumerated at the date of each census, Argentina, 1869–1960

1869		1895		1914		1947		1960	
Nationality	Percent of total	Nationality	Percent of total	Nationality	Percent of total	Nationality	Percent of total	Nationality	Percent of total
Italians	4.1	Italians	12.5	Italians	11.9	Italians	4.9	Italians	4.4
Spaniards	2.0	Spaniards	5.0	Spaniards	10.7	Spaniards	4.7	Spaniards	3.6
French	1.9	French	2.4	Russians	1.2	Polish	0.7	Paraguayans	0.8
Uruguayans	0.9	Uruguayans	1.2	French	1.0	Russians	0.6	Chileans	0.6
Chileans	0.6	Brazilians	0.6	Turks	0.8	Uruguayans	0.5	Polish	0.5

Source: Data taken directly from census report.

to a point we have already mentioned. We referred to only one aspect of migration as a factor of growth in the population: its DIRECT contribution. But we also must point out that migration has some effects on the natural growth; that is, a new situation is generated which results from the interaction of the migration and the natural growth that take place in the period analyzed. Besides, this effect of migration, though with different characteristics, continues affecting the change of population of later periods. We shall not attempt here an estimate of what the dimension and the direction of this INDIRECT effect of migration on the population growth has been. For the Argentine case some measurements have already been made of this phenomenon at the level of the total population and for the population of Buenos Aires City (Recchini de Lattes 1965, 1971). In both cases the results obtained indicate that the DIRECT contribution must be increased in a significant way as a consequence of this INDIRECT effect of migration. Therefore, it may be stated that the contribution of the net migration of foreign born to the total population of the country was larger than what the rates in Table 6 indicate.

The process that we call spatial redistribution of the population or, more precisely, interprovince redistribution of the population, takes place because of the differences existing among the rates of growth of the different provinces. These differences, in turn, are generated by the action of the basic components of growth: migration and natural increase. At the level of analysis of provincial population, net migration includes migration of foreign born as well as migration of natives, and it also includes internal as well as international migration of both populations. We shall consider this joint migration, which we call net total migration, a combination of internal and international migration; and we separate as

Table 11.   Total increase, natural increase, total net migration, foreign-born net migration, and native net migration by intercesual periods. Annual rates per 1,000 average population, Argentina, 1869–1960

	Intercensual Periods																			
	1869–1895					1895–1914					1914–1947					1947–1960				
Provinces	TOT INC	NAT INC	TOT MIG	F–B MIG	NAT MIG	TOT INC	NAT INC	TOT MIG	F–B MIG	NAT MIG	TOT INC	NAT INC	TOT MIG	F–B MIG	NAT MIG	TOT INC	NAT INC	TOT MIG	F–B MIG	NAT MIG
	(1)	(2)	(3)	(4)	(5)	(1)	(2)	(3)	(4)	(5)	(1)	(2)	(3)	(4)	(5)	(1)	(2)	(3)	(4)	(5)
Buenos Aires[a]	41	12	29	29	0	41	15	27	26	0	20	10	10	7	3	21	7	14	6	7
Catamarca	5	15	−11	1	−11	6	16	−10	1	−12	11	19	−7	0	−7	10	24	−14	0	−14
Córdoba	20	14	5	7	−2	37	16	21	15	6	21	20	1	2	−1	12	14	−21	1	−3
Corrientes	23	23	0	5	−5	19	25	−6	2	−8	12	22	−10	0	−10	1	14	−13	0	−13
Chaco[b]	78	35	43	31	13	66	13	53	18	35	49	26	23	7	16	17	26	−9	0	−9
Chubut[b]	78	19	59	45	13	76	13	63	47	16	39	22	17	12	5	23	16	7	8	−2
Entre Ríos	29	18	11	14	−3	20	19	0	5	−5	18	26	−7	0	−8	2	20	−18	0	−18
Formosa[b]	78	0	77	56	21	63	8	55	39	16	43	21	22	19	2	33	25	8	10	−2
Jujuy	8	−1	9	4	5	23	2	21	14	6	22	13	9	8	1	27	21	6	10	−3
La Pampa[b]	78	−3	81	19	62	62	15	47	35	12	15	28	−13	1	−14	−5	17	−22	−2	−20
La Rioja	14	18	−5	1	−5	7	18	−10	1	−11	10	18	−8	0	−8	11	24	−13	0	−14
Mendoza	22	11	11	8	3	43	12	31	26	5	22	18	4	2	2	25	20	5	4	1
Misiones[b]	78	3	75	55	19	25	10	15	14	1	39	22	17	16	1	28	25	3	10	−7
Neuquén[b]	78	4	74	69	5	35	19	16	22	−6	30	22	8	4	4	17	20	−3	5	−8
Río Negro[b]	78	31	47	20	28	67	20	47	35	13	32	21	11	8	3	27	17	10	12	−2
Salta	11	12	−1	2	−1	10	9	1	4	−4	21	16	5	4	1	26	21	5	5	0
San Juan	13	17	−4	3	−8	18	15	3	8	−5	23	22	1	2	−1	22	21	1	2	−1
San Luís	16	22	−6	2	−7	18	19	−1	6	−7	11	22	−11	0	−11	4	19	−15	0	−16
Santa Cruz y Tierra del Fuego[b]	78	−2	80	51	29	82	−3	85	73	12	30	8	22	21	0	38	−1	39	23	16
Santa Fé	49	6	44	36	7	41	20	21	21	0	19	18	1	2	−1	7	12	−4	0	−5
Santiago	8	9	−2	1	−3	25	25	0	2	−2	18	28	−10	0	−10	0	18	−18	0	−19
Tucumán	26	12	13	4	10	22	14	8	6	2	17	20	−3	1	−4	20	22	−2	0	−3
Total country	30	13	17	17	0	35	16	19	19	0	20	16	5	5	0	17	13	4	4	0

For Notes, see bottom of p. 135.

its components, the net migration of natives, which is essentially internal migration, and the net migration of foreign born, which is a combination of internal and international migration.

Once the net total migration and its components, the net migrations of natives and foreign born, were estimated, the total growth was calculated by province and for the four intercensual periods. Estimates of net total migration were subtracted from the total growth to yield INDIRECT estimates of natural increase. With these five series — total growth, natural increase, net total migration, net migration of natives, and net migration of foreign born — we carried out the analysis by province and for the four intercensual periods. We emphasize that its purpose was to find out what role was played by these five demographic variables in the growth and redistribution of the population by province for the four intercensual periods.

Table 11 summarizes the results obtained in terms of rates. A quick look at the total growth rates of the different provinces for each intercensual period shows that these have always been highly differential. This implies, then, that in the four intercensual periods there have been important redistributions of population among the provinces. First we compare natural increase and net total migration as the two factors of growth. We can see that the two variables have had different effects among the provinces as well as among the different periods. The following is a summary of the role of these variables in the growth of provincial populations.

The phenomenon described for the country is partially reflected in what has happened with the growth of provincial populations. In the first two intercensual periods, net total migration is the main factor of growth of the population in eleven of twenty-two provinces. In the third period this

---

a Including Buenos Aires City.
b Territorios Nacionales. No population was enumerated in 1869.

Source and references: Population: Data taken directly from census report.
Migration: Native net migration:

$$\text{Net M} = [(I^{t+n} - O^{t+n}) - S\,(I^t - O^t)]\,\frac{(1 + S)}{2S}$$

where I^t and I^{t+n} are the numbers of lifetime in-migrants in a particular province at two censuses at times t and t + n respectively, and O^t and O^{t+n} are the corresponding lifetime out-migrants; S is the intercensual survival ratio that gives the proportions of I_t and O_t that survive the intercensual period.
Foreign born net migration: same as for Table 6.
Natural increase: same as for Table 6.
Rates: All rates are based on dividing the average population of the period by the number of years in the period.
Note: In some cases the difference of 1 between the total and the sum of its components is due to rounding off procedures.

is true for only one province, and in the fourth for only two. The provinces thus show a new role of net migration: that of acting as a factor of depopulation. The phenomenon becomes increasingly clear as we move through the last three intercensual periods, in which in four, eight, and twelve provinces respectively the net total migration had a negative sign (i.e. is a factor of depopulation). In general, the situation in the first two intercensual periods was similar. In both periods, the net total migration and the natural increase affected the same number of provinces in respect to their roles as dominant components of growth.

The last two intercensual periods also shared similar characteristics. In both, natural increase was for almost all the provinces the main factor of growth, and the net total migration emphasized its role as a factor of depopulation.

As regards the role of the net total migration in the first two intercensual periods, the situation was essentially different in the various provinces. In some provinces, the so-called Territorios Nacionales were lands that were just beginning to be settled, whereas in other provinces they were the site of populations of fair size. This difference not only affected the comparison between the calculated rates for one province and another, but it also gave a different significance to a certain migration which took place then: because the ex-Territorios Nacionales were uninhabited lands, migration necessarily had to be the dominant variable.

Up to this point the analysis shows the role of natural increase and net total migration in the growth of the provincial populations during the various intercensual periods. The other aspect of interest for analysis is the role played by these two variables in relation to the different rates of total growth of the provincial populations. A quick way of showing the degree of association of the net total migration rates and the natural increase rates with the rates of total growth is by means of coefficients of rank correlation. Table 12, which includes the correlation coefficients

Table 12.   Correlation coefficient between the rate of total growth and the rates of net migration and natural increase by intercensus periods, Argentina, 1869–1960

Variables correlated[a]	1869–1895	1895–1914	1914–1947	1947–1960
Total growth and net migration	.54	.94	.94	.90
Total growth and natural increase	.12	.06	.50	.46

[a] Spearman's formula for rank correlation.

Source: Table 10.

obtained for the various intercensual periods, clearly shows the closer relationship between the net total migration and the total growth. Thus net total migration constitutes the main variable in relation to the different growth rates of provincial populations, and because these differences generate the interprovince redistribution of the population, net total migration appears as the main factor of this characteristic aspect of the change of population.

Now that we know the role played by net total migration in relation to the growth of provincial populations and the redistribution of the population among them, it is of interest to know what role was played by the net migration of foreign born and the net migration of natives.

With the information contained in columns 4 and 5 of Table 11, we can summarize this aspect of the analysis. From an overall view of the net migration rates of foreign born for all the provinces and for the four intercensual periods, it is clear that this factor in varying degrees always — with the exception of two cases — produced gains in population. Thus in most of the provinces where net total migration was the main factor of population growth, the role of the foreign born was most important. In general, in all the intercensual periods the net migration of natives was the main factor of loss of population in the provinces. In all the provinces where the net total migration had a negative sign, the net migration of natives prevailed. This role of net migration of natives kept growing over time. In the first and second intercensual periods, eleven provinces lost population as an effect of this variable; in the third period, thirteen, and in the fourth, nineteen. On the other hand, the net migration of foreign born diminishes as a factor of population growth after the first two periods, as a consequence of the important decrease of this phenomenon in the country. In the last intercensual period there were, for the first time, provinces that suffered losses of population as an effect of the net migration of foreign born.

Finally, we have pointed out that the net migration of natives as a factor of provincial depopulation increases in the third and, especially, in the fourth intercensual period. A situation where this did not happen — Buenos Aires — should be specifically discussed because of its peculiar characteristics. In the 1947–1960 intercensual period, net total migration was the main component of growth in Buenos Aires, which in this study includes Buenos Aires City. Within the migration components, the net migration of natives predominated slightly. Except in the case of Santa Cruz and Tierra del Fuego — of little significance because of the reduced size of its population — Buenos Aires is the only province where the net migration of natives was highly significant as a factor of growth of the population. The level of its rate is not so high (0.7 per thousand) owing to the large size of the population of Buenos Aires. But the volume of the net migration was high, as it reached 97.1 percent of the country's net total migration in that intercensal period. Almost all of this gain in population corresponded specifically to the area called Greater Buenos Aires. This characteristic aspect of the migration of natives which took place partially explains why in this reduced area of 1,550 square miles there is a concentration of 33.7 percent of the total population of the country or 45.7 percent of the country's urban population.

CONCLUDING REMARKS

We have presented an overview of some characteristics of the internal and international migrations and some of their demographic consequences.

The analysis was carried out exclusively with data from the national population censuses. Undoubtedly, this is the information source offering the best possibilities for obtaining a perspective of the role of migrations in the process of social and economic transformation that has taken place in Argentina since the middle of the past century. The censuses of Argentine population, even with their many limitations, may be further exploited. In order to do this, not only do we need to apply all the available techniques, but we also have to improve them and conceive of new ones.

After the brief historical setting of the population of the country before 1869, we saw how the state of the population in 1869 showed clearly the effects of the internal as well as the international migrations which had taken place before that date, particularly in the two decades immediately preceding the census year. The quick look we had at some results of that census allowed us to see, among other aspects, the absolute and relative sizes of the foreign-born population in the country, its direct and indirect contributions to the size of the total population, its greater concentration in some provinces and in urban areas, and, in general, its differential spatial distribution relative to the native population. We also pointed out some characteristics of the composition of the foreign-born population as compared to the native population, such as a larger proportion of males, the predominance of young adults, the higher level of male economic activity, and the higher level of literacy. We also analyzed the composition of the foreign born according to main countries of origin.

In relation to the internal migrations of natives, a phenomenon of a significant dimension already in 1869, we also saw some of its main characteristics. Native migrants as a population were different from the population of non-migrant natives. They had a larger proportion of males and of young adults and a smaller proportion of literates. Male migrants had higher levels of economic activity than non-migrants, but for females the situation was the opposite. Native migrants presented a spatial distribution different from that of non-migrants: the former were more concentrated in some provinces in the same way as the larger concentrations of foreign born. There were provinces that specially attracted migrants and others which pushed them out.

In a long view of the years between 1869 and 1960, we can see some characteristics of the migration that took place, as well as some of their main effects on the process of change of population. The net migration of foreign born was far from being a phenomenon with stable characteristics over time. These were important differences in the net migration of foreign born in the two halves of that long period. Besides its volume, it also had a changing composition by sex and place of origin among the various intercensual periods, and thus it produced important changes in these aspects of the total population. We saw how, in general, migration became the main factor of the process of spatial redistribution of the population, and how the foreign born played a role different from that of the native migrants. Moreover, there were changes in the various intercensual periods for both cases. All this was analyzed in a historical perspective which allows us to have a more comprehensive view of the process.

We may still put many questions to these data. We could continue the analysis on more detailed levels, and also in other directions or aspects of the phenomenon not included here. One can ask methodological questions, or, simply, questions about other temporal and spatial factual evidences which would contribute to the knowledge of the role that migration had in the process of change of the population. Our approach did not include such fundamental aspects as that of the causes of migration, nor did we consider other kinds of consequences other than the just mentioned demographic ones. Neither did we make any reference to other aspects of the economic and social changes which were taking place simultaneously with migrations, and to which they were surely related in a process of mutual interdependence. We concerned ourselves only with measuring and giving a partial description of the phenomenon, and with analyzing some of its consequences. However, in relation to the characteristics of the population, we chose some that are of particular interest for the study of the process of ethnic configuration of the population. We think that in this sense we have illustrated some channels which, through the process of change of the population, link the phenomenon of migrations to that of the ethnic identity of the population.

It is hoped that the work presented here will provide new bases for continuing exploration of the migration in Argentina. There is clearly a need for more intensive research on the actual experiences of nations, present and past.

REFERENCES

ARGENTINA
  1872   *Primer censo de la República Argentina — 1869.* Buenos Aires: Imprenta del Porvenir.

BORRIE, W. D.
  1959   *The cultural integration of immigrants.* Paris: UNESCO.

ELIZAGA, JUAN C.
  1970   "Migraciones interiores: el proceso de urbanización. Mobilidad social," (documento del organizador de la sección 3), in *Conferencia regional latinoamericana de población.* México: El Colegio de México.

GOLDSCHEIDER, CALVIN D.
  1971   "An outline of the migration system," in *International population conference: London 1969,* volume 4. Edited by International Union for the Scientific Study of Population. Great Britain: Henry Ling.

LATTES, ALFREDO E.
  1968   *Evaluación y ajuste de algunos resultados de los tres primeros censos nacionales de población,* documento de trabajo 51. Buenos Aires: Instituto Torcuato Di Tella, Centro de Investigaciones Sociales.
  1970   "Algunos indicios de migración interna diferencial en Argentina antes de 1869," in *Conferencia regional latinoamericana de población.* México: El Colegio de México.

MANGALAM, J. J., H. K. SCHWARZWELLER
  1968   General theory in the study of migration: current needs and difficulties. *The International Migration Review* 3 (1):3–18.
  1970   Some theoretical guidelines toward a sociology of migration. *The International Migration Review* 4 (11):5–21.

RAVENSTEIN, E. G.
  1885   The laws of migration. *Journal of the Royal Statistical Society* 48, part 2; reprint S–482 in the Bobbs-Merrill Series in the Social Sciences.

RECCHINI DE LATTES, ZULMA L.
  1965   "Demographic consequences of international migratory movements in the Argentine Republic, 1870–1960," in *World population conference,* 1965, volume 4. New York: United Nations, Department of Economic and Social Affairs.
  1971   *La población de la ciudad de Buenos Aires: componentes demográficos del crecimiento entre 1855–1960.* Buenos Aires: Editorial del Instituto.

RECCHINI DE LATTES, Z. L., A. E. LATTES

1969 *Migraciones en Argentina: estudio de las migraciones internas e internacionales, basado en datos censales, 1869–1960.* Buenos Aires: Editorial del Instituto.

SOMOZA, J. L., A. E. LATTES

1967 *Muestras de los dos primeros censos nacionales de población, 1869 y 1895,* documento de trabajo 46. Buenos Aires: Instituto Torcuato Di Tella, Centro de Investigaciones Sociales.

THOMAS, BRINLEY

1961 *International migration and economic development.* Paris: UNESCO.

UNITED NATIONS

1970 *Manual 6: methods of measuring internal migration.* Population Studies 47. New York: United Nations, Department of Economic and Social Affairs.

Malay Migration to Kuala Lumpur City: Individual Adaptation to the City

T. G. Mc GEE

If there is something specific and peculiar to the Marxist approach to the study of man, it is in its stubborn effort to combine into a unified whole the multifarious and divergent images of man as seen from different points of observation. To use the modern technical terminology we can say that Marxist social science aims at a 'hologram' of man instead of series of photographs.

ZYGMUNT BAUMAN[1]

INTRODUCTION

Few urbanologists would deny the complexity of the city. Many would assert a simplicity in their assessment of the reactions of an individual who shifts his place of residence from the country to the city. In the analysis of the rural-urban movement of populations in developed societies, most notably the United States, the focus of sociological research has been largely on the maladjustment of the migrant in the urban milieu.[2]

[1] In: Modern times, modern Marxism, page 399.

[2] The most comprehensive review of prewar studies in Europe and the United States is found in Thomas (1938). Since World War II migration studies have proliferated in both the developed and underdeveloped world. Useful summaries of the literature can be found in Bogue (1959) and the Milbank Memorial Fund (1958). Reviews of the literature pertaining to rural-urban migration can be found in Epstein (1967); Mitchell (1966); Turner (1962); McGee (1964); Hauser (1957, 1961); Eames (1954); and Pryor (1971). The seminal theoretical papers on the subject still remain Simmel (1900: 635-646) and Wirth (1938:46-63).

Of course, much of this work has been carried out in "capitalist" or "capitalist-penetrated" societies, but there is also some evidence of problems of adjustment to the urban environment occurring within socialist societies (Turski 1967:17). To some extent problems of adaptation are to be expected in situations where people move from peasant and tribal worlds into the different socioeconomic structures of the city, for there will be new situations relating to work patterns and to relations with work partners and neighbors.

However, in the postwar period, research focusing on the problems of migrants in the cities of the Third World, while indicating severe economic problems, has not always supported the assertion that the migrants suffer grave problems of social adaptation. For instance, Lewis' study in Mexico was one of the first to highlight this point when he said:

The preliminary findings of the present study of urbanization in Mexico City indicate quite different trends, and suggest the possibility of urbanization without breakdown. They also show that some of the hitherto unquestioned sociological generalizations about urbanization may be culture-bound and in need of reexamination in the light of comparative studies of urbanization in other areas (1952:31).

Work by Bruner among the Toba Batak of Medan led him to a similar conclusion: "It is clear that the social concomitants of the transition from rural to urban life are not the same in Southeast Asia as in Western society" (1961:508).

Janet Abu-Lughod has made a similar point with respect to absorption of migrants into Cairo City (Abu-Lughod 1961:22-32). The work of Mayer among the Bantu in East London provides additional evidence that there are many migrants who never become committed to urban society no matter how long they live in the city (Mayer 1962). During the sixties the work of Mangin and others has further strengthened the conclusions of these earlier researchers (Mangin 1970), so much so that the cohesive aspects of the migrants' adaptative process to the city — associations, etc. — are being held up by planners as concrete elements which can aid the urbanization process (Turner 1967). An important research thrust among political scientists has found migrants more conservative and satisfied with their conditions than the Western-based theories predicted (Nelson 1970).

Thus all these studies, despite the diversity of the cultural milieux in which they have been carried out, reach much the same conclusion — migrants to the cities of the Third World are not experiencing severe problems of social adaption. Many reasons are produced to explain this phenomenon, but few researchers contest the original hypothesis that cities are places where social maladjustments occur. They simply state that the hypothesis is not valid in their field area. It is the writer's view that this original hypothesis, framed as it was within the context of the rural-urban continuum, was quite false, for the constructed model of rural and urban behavior which was elaborated was inaccurate. I have already discussed this point at some length elsewhere (McGee 1971). It is sufficient to point out here that the assumption of a unilinear shift from rural to urban behavior associated with the shift from country to town was severely criticized.

I will try to show here that the level of individual adaptation indicates that the majority of migrants retain attitudes which may be regarded as both urban and rural at the same time. Perhaps these attitudes will change after long periods of residence and work in the city, but it is dangerous to argue that they will necessarily change because of the influence of the city. We do tend to underestimate the considerable capacity of the individual to hold seemingly antithetical attitudes at the same time and the range of choice that individuals have in deciding these questions. The following study of Malay migrants in Kuala Lumpur City is an attempt to test these assumptions.

MALAY MOVEMENT TO KUALA LUMPUR[3]

Malaysia is a multiracial society in which Malays, Chinese, Indians, and other ethnic groups form what has been labeled a "plural society." Today it consists of three distinct geographic territories — the Malayan peninsula, Sabah, and Sarawak — but historically the development of Malaya and Singapore has been inseparable.[4]

This "plural society" grew up as a consequence of the extension of British control over the Malayan peninsula and Singapore during the nineteenth and twentieth centuries. The indigenous Malay population remained primarily in the countryside while the Chinese and Indians who arrived during the extension of British control tended to occupy the commercial sectors of the cities and the plantation labor forces. This created a situation in which the Malays were largely encapsulated within the peasant sector outside the cities. Only in some of the towns — in the predominantly Malay areas of the east coast and Kedah — did the Malay populations assume any dominance.

[3]   This section is a considerably abridged version of McGee (1968, 1971).
[4]   Despite the fact that today these are two separate states it is unrealistic to analyze them separately.

In the majority of the large towns of the west coast the Malays were historically a minority, a small community dominated by the Chinese. The capital of the present Malaysian Federation is Kuala Lumpur, founded in the 1840's, first as a raw and rambunctious Chinese mining camp. Later, in the 1890's, it became a major administrative center for the British as well as an important commercial center for the west coast as the rubber plantation industry expanded. Accompanying the expansion of these functions was a considerable increase of city population from 18,000 in 1891 to 175,000 in 1947. Throughout this period the city remained essentially an administrative and commercial center — a colonial city ruled by Europeans, dominated numerically by the immigrant Chinese and Indians, while the indigenous Malays remained marginal participants except for the Malay aristocrats who cooperated with the European rulers (Gullick 1956).

The period of the Japanese invasion in the early 1940's disrupted the structure of political power but did little to change the ethnic composition of the city or its functions. The reassertion of British control, the failure of the attempt to set up the Malayan Union, and the creation of the Federation of Malaya in 1948 with Kuala Lumpur as its capital led to a further concentration of administrative and commercial activities in that city. There was also a period of rapid devolution towards independence and of political instability associated with the communist revolt.

The 1955 elections saw the victory of the Malay-dominated Alliance Party in the newly-created House of Representatives in Kuala Lumpur, continuing the trend to centralize political control in that city. The rapid onset of independence precipitated the movement of civil servants, police, and army personnel to Kuala Lumpur. Many of the Malays from other states came to the capital so that for the first time in over a century the proportion of Malays in the total city population increased from 12.4 to 15.0 per cent. The period since 1957 has seen an even more rapid growth of the city's population to almost half a million, increasing the proportion of Malays to 25 percent (Provencher 1971; Chander 1972).

The accelerated migration of Malays in this period appears to have comprised two broad streams. One stream of older married migrants moved with their families on transfer to take up government posts; a second stream of younger single males moved to Kuala Lumpur from the countryside in an effort to find jobs or for advanced education. On the whole, Malays have tended to occupy government jobs rather than commercial jobs which have been dominated by the Chinese.

In this movement of the Malays to the cities, there was, of course, a potential danger for if the Malays did not find jobs in the Chinese-dominated city, they would put pressure on the Malay political parties to achieve this end. Thus the Alliance government encouraged programs of rural development and improved educational facilities to keep the Malays in the countryside. In this they were not markedly successful, and the communal riots of May 1969 between Malays and Chinese, while sparked by immediate political tensions, were fueled by this underlying failure.

INDIVIDUAL ANALYSIS: A HOLISTIC PICTURE

It is against this background of accelerating Malay movement to Kuala Lumpur and other cities along with the associated increase in Malay political power that the researcher has to assess the features of the Malay migrants in Kuala Lumpur. In 1962 and 1963 the author carried out a survey of 560 Malay households in Kuala Lumpur designed to obtain basic socioeconomic information and to assess their degree of adaptation to the urban setting. This was organized on a quota sample basis which represented a 5 percent sample of the estimated Malay population at that time. The following analysis is based on the data collected in that survey and during follow-up interviews and is an attempt to see the individual Malay in this city in his "totality."

I have not chosen to present the data in terms of a series of statistics categorizing a group — by date of arrival, for example — for this inevitably leads the researcher to argue that the group will act in the same manner, make demands in the same way or relate to the "urban situation" similarly. For as Bauman says, this group type of analysis is but a series of photographs departing from "man as such, pursuing the process of living through and by his social and cultural environment" (1967:399). Thus I have developed here an attempt to see each individual in the context of his urban situation. Twenty-eight indices have been chosen to measure each individual's urban adaptation to the "urban situation" of Kuala Lumpur.

It is at this individual level that the influence of SITUATIONAL CHANGE, to use Mitchell's term, seems most appropriate (1966:37-68). The forces of limited STRUCTURAL CHANGE have already allotted the individual to a broad socioeconomic position within the total society, but within that position the individual has certain possibilities of adaptation. The Malay in the city is encouraged to ACCOMMODATE at a group level and ADAPT at an individual level. In this situation, the role of government is obtrusive and the pre-eminence of the non-Malay groups prohibiting. It is within this framework that individual adaptation occurs.

In choosing these indices, I have made certain assumptions that are generally in line with what we may label Western assertions concerning the urbanization process. Thus, for instance, I assume that the longer a person has resided in Kuala Lumpur, the more capable he is of adapting to the urban situation. I assume that if an individual is well educated, he will be more adaptable to the urban situation than the individual who had no education. I assume, too, that traditional stereotypes with respect to the city, for instance, the assertion that people are less friendly in the city than in rural areas, is a more traditional and less urban assertion than the claim that Malays in the city are more friendly. It must be emphasized that I do not claim that these assertions are necessarily a reflection of reality, simply that they are a reflection of a manner in which reality has been interpreted.

The twenty-eight indices which have been chosen are divided into seven main sectors:

1. Background situation
2. Respondent's socioeconomic background
3. Urban commitment
4. Respondent's present socioeconomic characteristics
5. Urban-rural ties
6. Communications and contact in the city
7. Urban attitudes

Within each of these sectors, a varied number of indices have been ranked according to a scale from 1 to 4. In every case, it is assumed that level 4 is the most urbanized, 1 is the least urbanized, while 2 and 3 represent points on a continuum between these two extremes. These are referred to as levels of urban adaptation throughout the remainder of the study and are equated with the four circles of the hologram. The outermost circle is thus level 4; the innermost circle, level 0.

Each individual household head was then assessed according to these twenty-eight indices grouped in seven broad sectors, and these were diagramatically shown on the holograms (see Figures 1–3 and Appendix). The numbers in the center of the hologram indicate the average score obtained by each individual on the four-point scale for the twenty-eight indices. Thus those individuals whose average score fell between 1 and 1.99 were least urbanized; those with scores between 2.00 and 2.99 more urbanized and those with scores of 3.00 and above the most urbanized.

The advantage of the hologram[5] is simply stated: It enables a quick,

[5] These holograms are used to show a wide variety of socioeconomic data by place in Centre National Française de la Recherche Scientifique (1959).

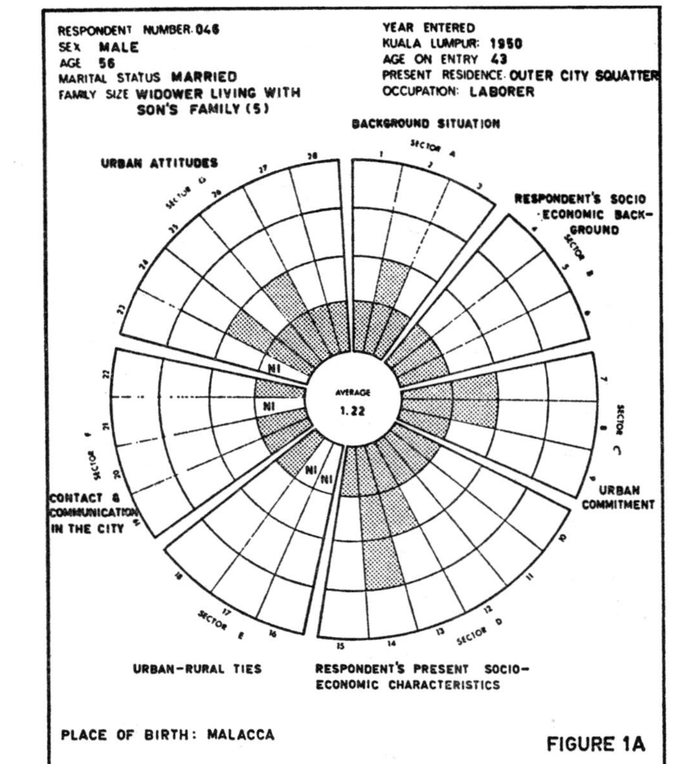

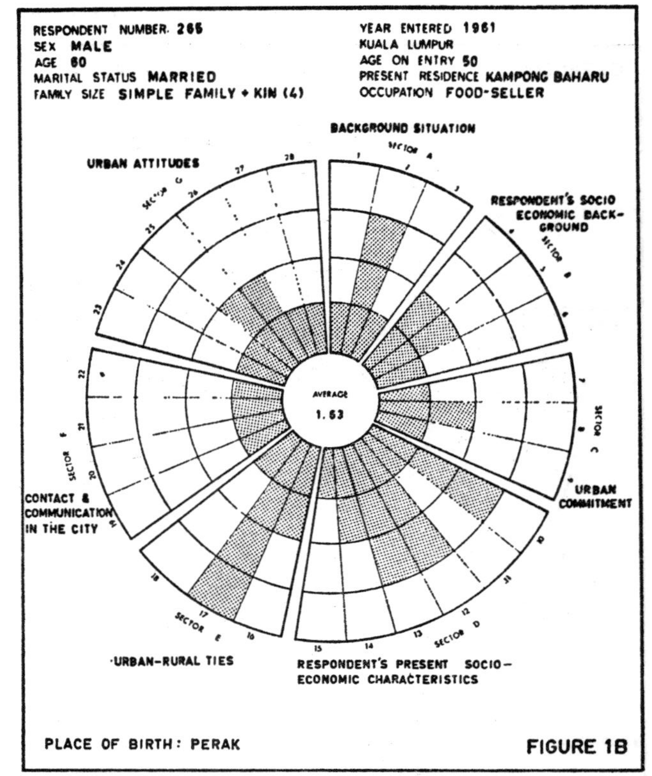

Figure 1 (A and B). Holograms of two individuals whose adaptation to the city is less than satisfactory

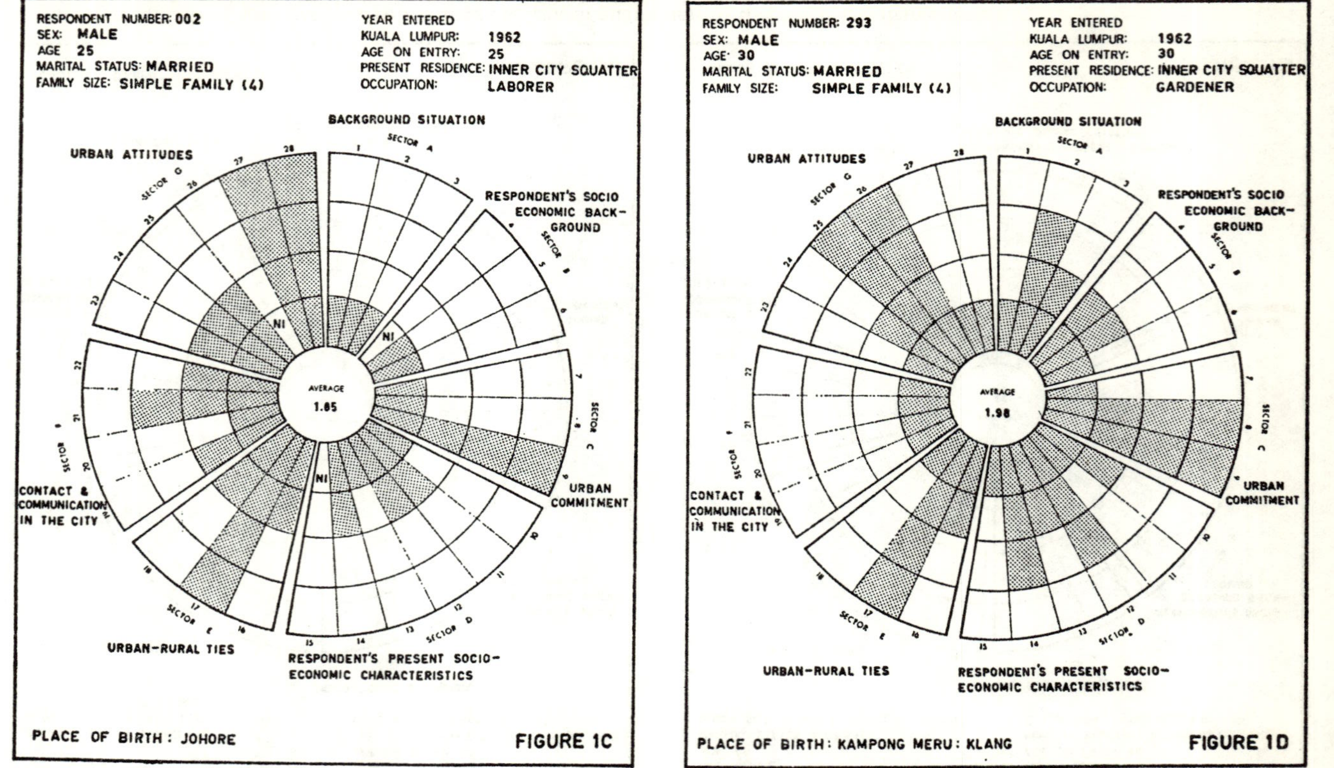

Figure 1 (C and D).   Holograms of two individuals whose adaptation to the city is less than satisfactory

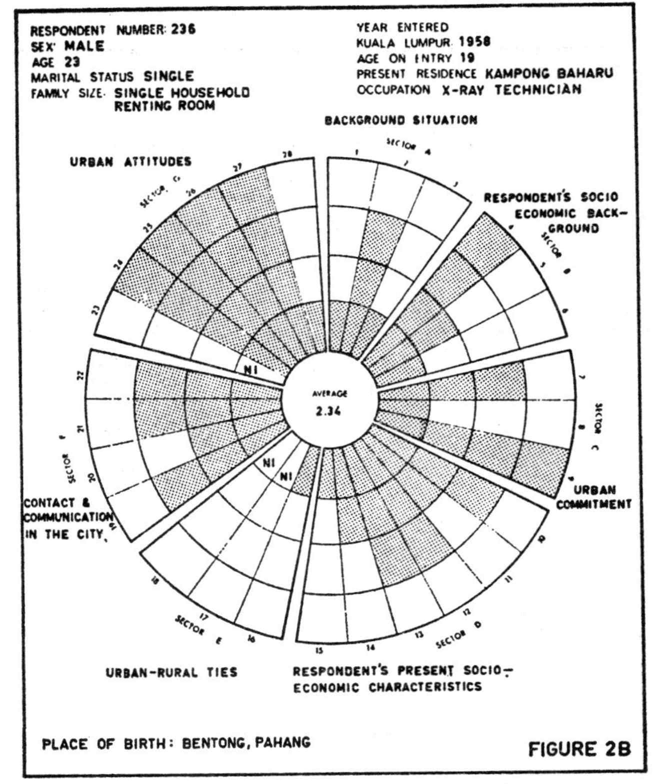

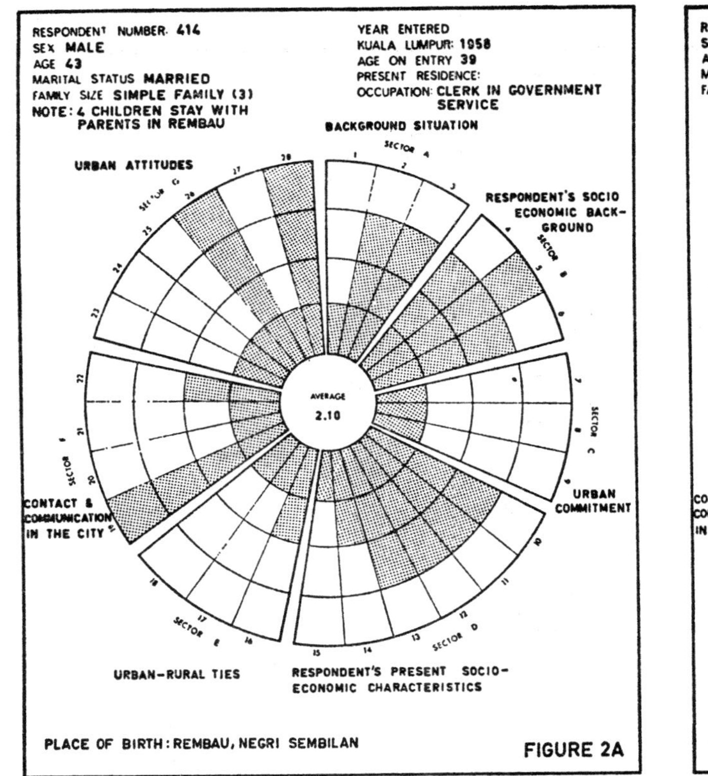

Figure 2 (A and B). Holograms of two individuals whose adaptation to the city is satisfactory

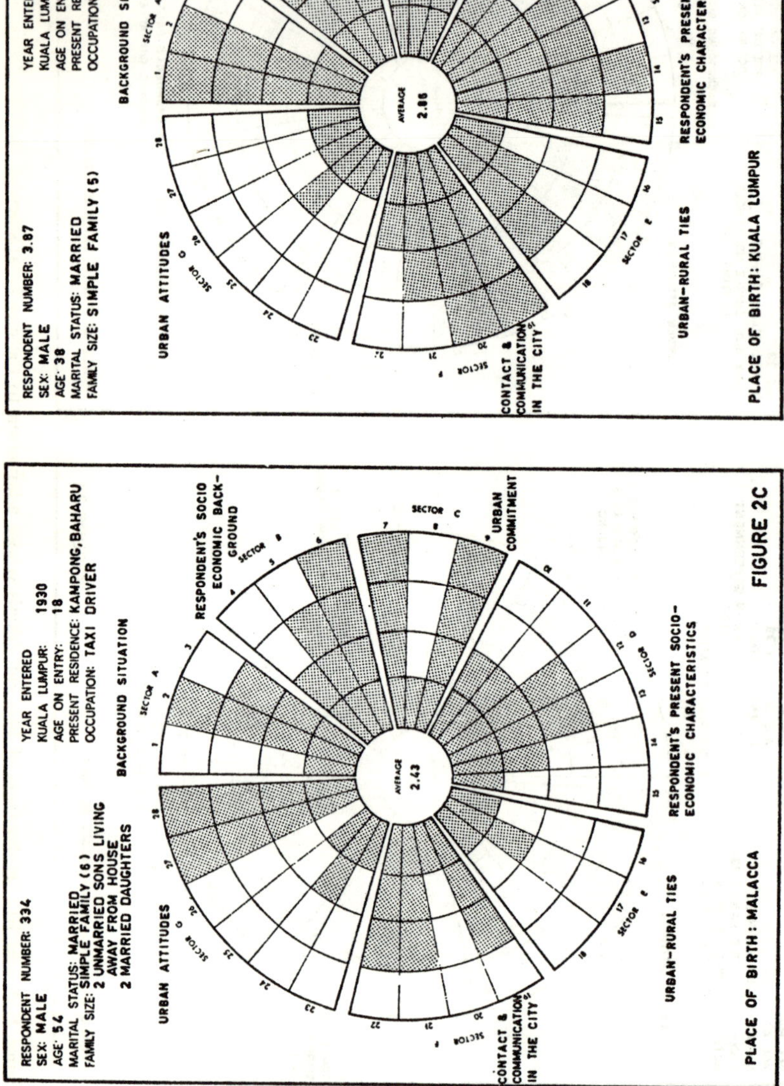

Figure 2 (C and D).   Holograms of two individuals whose adaptation to the city is satisfactory

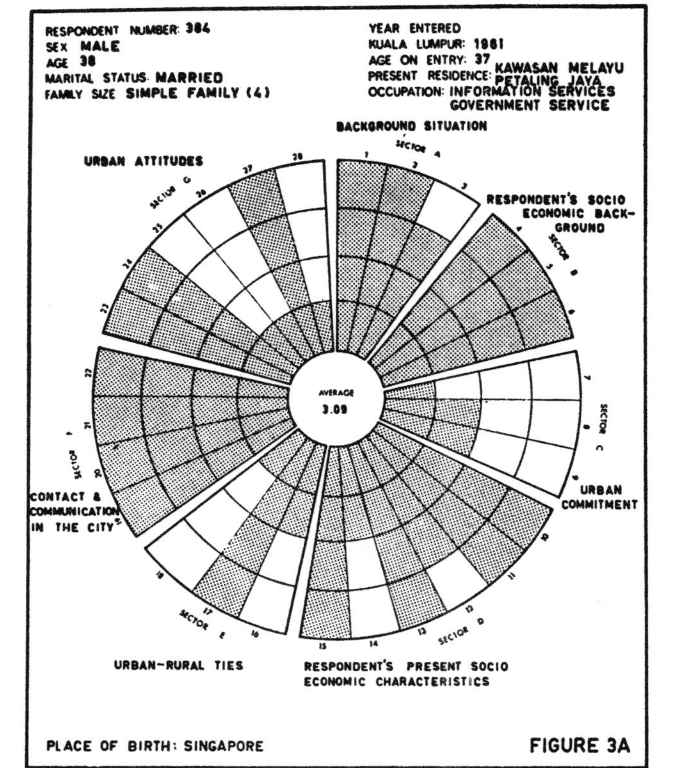

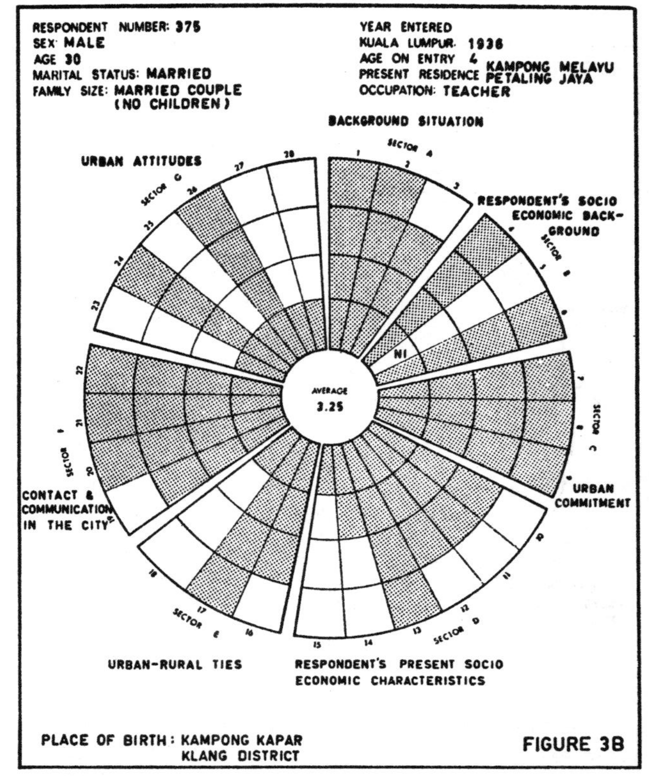

Figure 3 (A and B).   Holograms of two individuals whose adaptation to the city is better than satisfactory

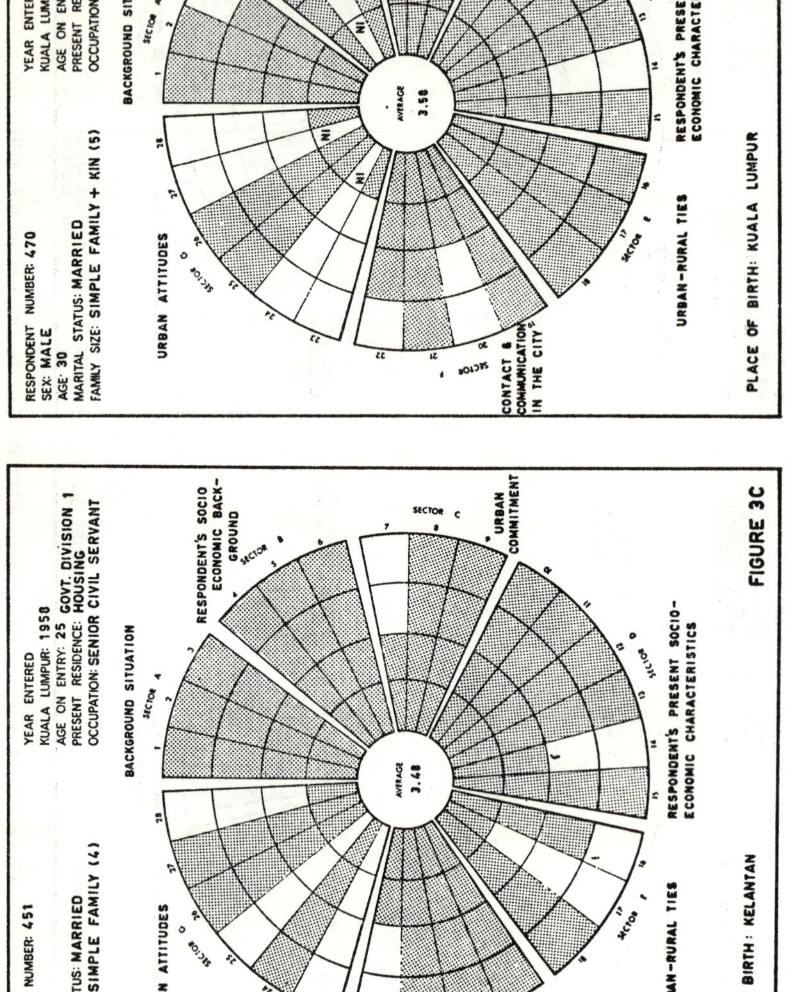

Figure 3 (C and D). Holograms of two individuals whose adaptation to the city is better than satisfactory

visual assessment of the structure of each individual's position to be ascertained, and in addition, allows a comparison at the individual level (not the group level) to be carried out. In the next section, I shall analyze each of these sectors of the urban indices.

It should be stressed that in presenting the data concerning each household head in this form, my aim is to illustrate the varied and often contradictory positions that an individual may assume when he or she lives in a city. Ness, writing about his interviews with government officials in Malaya, says:

Especially in an interview that stretches over more than an hour, and then continues over a "stengah" at the rest house or over cocktails at a party, people contradict themselves directly and indirectly, often more than once on the same subject. It is not that they lie or attempt to deceive the questioner, though this does happen. It is merely a reflection of the great human capacity for holding conflicting ideas with little strain (1967:x).

Indeed, it is clear that this great "human capacity for holding conflicting ideas" can be extended to an even broader capacity to adopt seemingly antithetical positions or postures. The advantage of the hologram is that it allows a more complex and holistic picture of the individual in the urban situation to emerge. He is not some passive adapter to an urban environment he cannot control. Thus we see an individual of complexity — there are no fewer images of the man who lives in a city than of the man who is a rural dweller. They are men; not urban men or rural men.

Some comment must be made about the limitations of the survey instrument as a means of collecting information for the ensuing holograms. The survey, to continue Bauman's analogy, is itself a photograph. Each questionnaire is delivered at a point in time and it records only a momentary slice of an individual's life. The reaction of the respondent may be distorted by the questioner's appearance; by his own immediate needs (at the end of a long tropical day: the need for food and sleep); by as many factors as one may conjure up. The photo may underexpose or overexpose — it is only a distorted moment of the individual's life. And these distorted moments we blow up into the reality of the total individual. The conclusion is obvious. The hologram, based on the survey, is only of limited value; and the author would have preferred to pursue the greater depth of the family studies as did Lewis in his significant work on Latin American families (1959).

INDIVIDUAL ANALYSIS: A HOLISTIC PICTURE

Despite these limitations the hologram does at least indicate that individuals do hold a complex and often conflicting set of LEVELS [positions] on a theoretical rural-urban continuum. What is more, it is the argument here that no single variable, least of all the single fact of residence in the city, will act as an adequate explanation of the individual's behavior in the city. Rather, each action (in Western theory characteristically described as an "urban-influenced" action) will depend on a whole constellation of variables, as well as the position of each individual within his total society.

Thus it is the constellation which counts, not the single influencing variable. For instance, even a comparatively simple decision such as sending remittances to a relative in the countryside may be influenced by many other factors than the mere possession of money. The danger of seeking an independent variable in human behavior is the tendency to oversimplify man's actions. And this, of course, is the greatest weakness of the body of Western urban theory which has grown up, postulating the city as an independent variable.

In this section I have chosen twelve Malays from Kuala Lumpur City and constructed holograms to illustrate this point. The method of selection is not random; rather it is an attempt to indicate the spread of type rather than to be representative. The procedure was as follows: the 560 means were ranked from the lowest to the highest mean and four means selected from each level, aiming at as wide a spread as possible. On this basis twelve individuals were chosen and holograms constructed.

Level One: Marginal Urban Adaptation: Four Case Studies

RESPONDENT 046 (HOLOGRAM I): MEAN 1.22   Respondent 046 (see Figure 1A) was ranked lowest of the completed holograms. A male of fifty-five, born in Malacca, he had been resident in Kuala Lumpur for twelve years; had been educated at Malay primary and worked as a farmer until the age of forty-three. In 1950 he left his farm in Malacca at the invitation of his son to join him in Kuala Lumpur. At the time he left for Kuala Lumpur he was unemployed, living on help from his nephew, and separated from his wife. In the twelve years since he arrived in Kuala Lumpur he has had three jobs. After four months of searching for a job, he found one as a laborer with a European firm. After that he was employed by the Central Electricity Board (again as a laborer). Finally, he took his present job as a laborer for the railway.

His lack of skills, Malay primary education, and low income did not help him in his general adaptation to the city. But he has taken some steps, notably purchasing a squatter house of fairly good quality in Kampong Haji Abdullah Hukum, which may lead him to settle more permanently in the city. Unfortunately, there is only limited information on his rural contacts but he has married again, a wife selected for him from his own district. He no longer owns any land in that district. (He comes from the Minangkabau area, where custom would prohibit his inheriting the land of his wife.)

Generally he seems undecided about Kuala Lumpur. He is uncertain as to whether he will stay there all his life for he prefers to work in his home area. In addition, he seems to take little advantage of the improved facilities of the city. He does not read newspapers or go to the cinema and knows very little about other areas of Malay settlement in Kuala Lumpur.

His attitudes toward such issues as traditional medicine versus Western medicine and the decline of religion in the city suggest no realization of the city as a breaking-down influence. He thinks that the *bomoh* "medicine man" (Winstedt, 1951) is unquestionably best for illness of the mind or the heart (in the romantic sense), or *kena sumpah* "spells", while Western medicine is more suitable for physical injury. His attendance at mosque has not declined through residence in the city. He is no more interested in politics since he moved to the city. His only positive assertion concerned the lack of friendliness of Kuala Lumpur Malays.

This respondent shows the lowest level of urban adaptation on our scale but (as this analysis shows) he has by no means totally resisted the city. It would appear that kin ties are probably one of the most important forces holding him in the city, just as they drew him there. As long as his son lives there, so will he. Meanwhile he has managed to co-exist with the city, if not fully participate in it.

RESPONDENT 265 (HOLOGRAM II): MEAN 1.63   Respondent 265 (see Figure 1 B) was the third lowest individual in terms of level of urban adaptation. Born in Parit Buntar in 1902, he had been living in a kampong four miles from Taiping for fifty-eight years, working a rubber "small holding." He had Malay primary education but no English education. Only recently arrived, he had come to Kuala Lumpur at the insistence of his brother-in-law in February, 1961. At the time he left for Kuala Lumpur he still worked his own small-holding, but felt he was growing too old to continue his work effectively.

In view of his recent arrival in Kuala Lumpur, it is perhaps not surprising that he is undecided how long he will stay. Certainly he is not enthusiastic to establish permanent residence, preferring to work in his home area. He still retains his land and home in his kampong, and presumably this offers some security if he desires to return.

He purchased a food-selling business in the Sunday Market three months after his arrival and is operating it with his brother-in-law. He claimed that his income was only $60 (Malayan) a month, but the interviewer commented this was very likely an underestimate. He travelled to Kuala Lumpur with his family, a daughter of eighteen at present teaching in a Malay school and a grandson of fourteen who is attending Secondary Continuation School (English) at Pasar Road. He rents a house for $36 a month, located behind the stalls, which is not elaborate but has adequate space and the basic amenities of electricity and water.

Relatively close ties are maintained with the rural home area. In the year that he has been in Kuala Lumpur he has returned to his home kampong three times for periods of up to twenty days, primarily to visit relatives and check on the condition of his rubber small holding. These trips back to the rural kampong are greatly facilitated by his self-employment. As his own boss, he can leave the business when he desires in his brother-in-law's hands. The example of this migrant shows the relative ease of circulatory migration between peasant and bazaar sectors of the economy. He does not remit any money to relatives in the countryside.

This migrant claims to have no time to read newspapers or attend the cinema. Instead, he must prepare food and sell it which takes all his spare moments.

His attitudes toward the urban environment seem to indicate a clear acceptance of what may be labeled the prevailing "rural" stereotypes. Yet the difference between attitude and action is quite marked. He is quite convinced that the people who live in the city are less religious, yet he attends mosque more frequently than he did in his rural kampong. However, he finds no marked differences between Malays in Kuala Lumpur and those of the kampong in terms of friendliness. The short period he has been in the city has neither increased his interest in politics nor changed his personality.

Like Respondent 046, he has entered the city at a much later age than most of the migrants — largely, it would appear, at the insistence of a relative. (But relatives' insistence aside, he still desires to return to his home.) His reaction to the city is on the whole not favorable. It is a place of work offering certain advantages for the education of his grandson and his own employment. His is a temporary and marginal adaptation.

RESPONDENT 002 (HOLOGRAM III): MEAN 1.85 Unlike the two earlier migrants, Respondent 002 (see Figure 1 C) arrived at the much younger age of twenty-five. He arrived in Kuala Lumpur almost a year ago with his wife and one child. Since his arrival a son, now three months old, was born. He rented a squatter hut for $20 a month in Kampong Sector almost immediately on arrival and was fortunate enough to acquire a job as a laborer in a sawmill within a few days.

His background is completely rural. He had worked as a farmer (rubber-tapper) in his home kampong close to Bandar Maharani (MUAR) in the same occupation as his father. No information was gained about his education, but it may be assumed he had Malay primary education for he occasionally reads the Malay paper, *Berita Harian*. He claims that at the time he left for Kuala Lumpur he was temporarily unemployed but still suggests that his main reason for coming to Kuala Lumpur was more for curiosity (to see Kuala Lumpur) than his desire to find a job. There was no mention of relatives in the city.

While this respondent prefers working in Kuala Lumpur (in part because of the "broader outlook"), he still intends to return to his home kampong. The location and general condition of his house is poor. The roof is thatched and there is no piped water, sewerage or electricity. His income of $165 per month does, however, provide him with enough money to purchase adequate meals and clothing for his family. He has bought a bicycle to travel to work.

He maintains close contact with his home kampong (where his wife's parents also live), having returned four times since his move to Kuala Lumpur. These were all short visits (duration three days) except for Hari Raya when he and his family stayed for one week. He does not remit money to his relatives largely because he says there is not enough for his own family.

He does not make great use of the improved communications media of the city, reads *Berita Harian* occasionally, but he never attends the cinema. His closest friend is a driver from the same kampong, but his knowledge of other Malay areas in Kuala Lumpur is limited to the two adjacent kampongs — Kampong Semerang and Kampong Baharu. He finds little difference in attitudes; for instance, religious behavior and friendliness are the same in countryside or city: "We are all Malays."

He does, however, feel that residence in the city has changed his attitudes. He is far more interested in politics than before he came to the city. ("The Alliance Party is best for the country," he says.) In addition he claims his personality has changed since he arrived in the city. He now says he has a "broader outlook on things."

This migrant, while spending only a short period of time in the city has adapted very quickly. He wanted to move to the city for the very reasons (to see and experience) which allow him more flexibility in his adaptation. The fact that he feels he has changed in the city does not, however, affect his commitment to reside there. He still will *balak-ka-kampong* "return to the kampong." His case stresses the many levels of adaptation which each migrant assumes.

RESPONDENT 293 (HOLOGRAM IV): MEAN 1.98   Respondent 293 (see Figure 1D) was born in Kampong Meru some five miles from Klang, twenty-five miles from Kuala Lumpur. He was one of a large number of migrants from Meru (of Javanese ancestry) who moved backward and forward between Kampong Meru and Kuala Lumpur in what is almost a classic form of circulatory migration.

He had only recently arrived in Kuala Lumpur (eight months' residence at the time of the survey). He had moved there partly at the invitation of his brother, and partly in search of a job. At the time of leaving for Kuala Lumpur he was unemployed, having lost his job as an attendant on a lorry running between Kuala Lumpur and Port Swettenham.

His earlier years had been spent in Kampong Meru, living with his mother and her family. His father visited generally on weekends from Kuala Lumpur, where he worked as a *tukang kebun* "gardener" for a European family. The migrant had been educated in Malay and left school at twelve to work at home. Since that date he had worked around home and as a lorry attendant for a Chinese firm. Thus while he had been working in Klang, an urban area, he had continued to reside in his rural kampong. When he first came to Kuala Lumpur to seek a job he did not bring his family, but once he had found a job as a gardener with a European family he acquired a house in a squatter area of Kampong Baharu and moved his family to Kuala Lumpur. Despite his short residence in the city, he prefers Kuala Lumpur to Kampong Meru and intends to stay in the city all his life.

His occupation as a gardener earns him an income below $100 (Malayan) a month, but as he has to pay no rent for his house (which he owns) nor for amenities, he claims the amount is enough to keep his family although he has received temporary financial aid from his brother. It is hardly surprising in view of the closeness of Meru to Kuala Lumpur (and its relatively easy access) that he and his family have returned home five times to see his parents since his arrival in Kuala Lumpur. The visits, however, are brief and rarely last more than a day. His wife comes from the same area so that it is possible for her to visit her relatives as well.

Although he has Malay primary education, the respondent does not read Malay newspapers or attend the cinema. He knows only one other area of Malay settlement and claims no Malay friends. His attitudes reflect generally the rural stereotypes apart from the fact that he believes Malays in Kuala Lumpur are more friendly and recognizes that the increased demands of the city and cost of food prevent his saving as much as he would desire.

Level Two: Satisfactory Coexistence: Four Case Studies

Most of the Malays interviewed in the study fell into this second level of adjustment to Kuala Lumpur (75 percent), a level which (it can be suggested) showed a satisfactory capacity to fit into the city's structure. Indeed, most of the city dwellers can be said to exist in this "balance" between the rural and urban poles.

RESPONDENT 414 (HOLOGRAM V): MEAN 2.10 Respondent 414 (see Figure 2A) is very similar to those migrants on Level One in that he has spent only a short time in Kuala Lumpur, and entered at an older age than most of the migrants. Born in 1919, he spent his early years in Rembau, despite the fact that his father, employed as a policeman, was away from home frequently.

This respondent has a history of ample experience with the urban situation. He was educated in a Malay primary school as well as English and continued with English at the secondary level. Immediately after he left school he joined the police force and later became a clerk working for the British Military Administration. Later he joined the administrative department of the Malayan Army where he as employed was a clerk.

It was in this position that he was transferred to Kuala Lumpur in 1958. During these earlier periods, he spent much of his time at Port Dickson Army Encampment and at Raub, which are small urban centers. Certainly in terms of the degree of "occupational urbanization" he was well equipped before his entry into Kuala Lumpur. Despite his five years' residence in Kuala Lumpur, he is by no means committed to the city. He intends to return to his home kampong as soon as he finishes working in Kuala Lumpur and prefers to work elsewhere. This view is almost certainly backed by the fact that his wife's parents and his own parents own land in the kampong to which he would like to return and work as a farmer.

His present socioeconomic position is comparatively secure. He earns an income of $310 a month working as a clerk on a Division-2 scale,

which is quite a high-status occupation in government service. He rents
an entire house for the comparatively low sum of $41 (Malayan) per
month but has made little effort to build up a supply of status amenities,
such as a refrigerator, which many other individuals in the same income
scale have made efforts to acquire. The majority of his children still live
in his home kampong and it is hardly surprising that he keeps very close
contact with his home area. He remits $50 a month to his parents for the
education and upkeep of his children, and attempts to visit the family in
Rembau as often as possible. Last year he managed four visits, the
longest of which was one week. These visits are conditioned by the
availability of leave.

As part of his job he says he reads the *Straits Times*, *Berita Harian*, and
the *Utusan Melayu* every day. He does not attend the cinema and has not,
as yet, acquired any close friend in the city. He has made no effort in his
five years of residence to establish the spatial dimensions of the Malay
community in Kuala Lumpur. Clearly he dislikes the urban environment,
feeling that in terms of most forces — a decline in religious values and the
unfriendliness of the Kuala Lumpur Malays — it has been a bad influence. As he says, the Malays in Kuala Lumpur are "less friendly."
"People in town mind their own business." Nevertheless, he feels that
Kuala Lumpur has changed him in terms of his personality for he has
widened his social contacts and made contact with other ethnic
groups.

This migrant, then, represents a classic example of the individual who
regards the city purely as a workplace, and not as a place of commitment.
To him it is a place to live because that is where his job has taken him, but
not a place to remain, and as soon as he finishes his government career he
will return to his home kampong and take up the life of a farmer which
he clearly prefers.

RESPONDENT 236 (HOLOGRAM VI): MEAN 2.34   Respondent 236 (see Figure
2B) represents a comparative rarity among the individuals interviewed in
the survey — a bachelor living by himself. Born in a kampong close to
Bentong, Pahang State, he spent most of his early years in his parents'
home where he helped his father on the small holding when he was not
in school. After he left school he came to Kuala Lumpur to search for
a job (unsuccessfully) with the intention of continuing his schooling. He
did, in fact, spend one year improving his English at secondary level.
During this time he stayed with his brother, a government servant who
lived in government-provided accommodation, close to the Stadium
Merdeka. However, when his brother was shifted from Kuala Lumpur,

he had to vacate this accommodation and he moved to the present room he rents in Kampong Baharu.

Apart from the desire to continue his education, he left his home kampong because he wanted to join his friends in Kuala Lumpur who had left the kampong already and to register at the employment exchange in the hope of finding an occupation. After one year's schooling he did find a job as a salesman, which he continued for nine months. He then took a job as a technician in the X-ray department of the General Hospital at Kuala Lumpur. This he has held for the past three years and three months.

Considering his comparative youth and short period in the city, he has managed to progress well. Still, as he comments, he finds it hard to save, and his expenses are quite high, particularly the $40 a month he pays for renting one room in the house where he stays. When that is compared with the $20 which families pay for an entire house in some of the squatter areas, it is clear why the out-movement of Malays from the crowded Kampong Baharu to newer squatter areas has occurred.

As yet he has not concerned himself with the purchase of many consumer durables. He does own a bicycle which was given to him by his father, and this is his main asset, apart from clothes. There was no information on whether he remitted money to his parents in his home kampong, but he did return up to four times a year, generally staying for about a week in order to see his parents and visit former friends. He took considerable advantage of the improved communications — mass media of the city — reading the English newspapers and weekly newspapers, but attended Malay films only irregularly.

He had a large number of friends, mostly residents in Kampong Baharu, many of whom he had known in his own kampong before he came to Kuala Lumpur. In general, his attitudes were the most clearly urban of any of the individuals so far discussed. While he did not comment on the effect of the city on the general degree of religious attendance, he felt that in his case he attended mosque less frequently than he had before.

It was harder to save in Kuala Lumpur because of the additional expenses. For instance, he mentioned that one used firewood in the kampong; in the city one generally used kerosene. In addition there were more amusements, hence more costs. Generally he felt that the Malays in the city were more friendly and that he had become much more interested in politics since he lived in the city. These characteristics all add up to the complex picture of an individual who, while he is in no way committed to permanent residence in the city, manages to get as full a life as his comparatively low income will allow him.

RESPONDENT 334 (HOLOGRAM VII): MEAN 2.43   Respondent 334 (see Figure 2C) represents an exceptionally interesting example of geographical mobility. Now fifty-four, he first entered Kuala Lumpur at age eighteen, but during the Japanese invasion returned to his home kampong in Malacca and came back to Kuala Lumpur at the end of the Second World War. He has been married twice, having divorced his first wife. He has had eight children by the two marriages — four of whom are still living with him and four who are living elsewhere. Of the latter, two of the boys are unmarried and working at the Malayan Teachers' College, where they have accommodation provided. Two of his daughters are married and living with their husbands in other parts of Malaya. Of the children still living with him, ranging in age from ten to seventeen, all are attending school. Three are girls attending English secondary school, and the youngest boy, aged ten, attends the Malay school in Princess Road.

The respondent was born in a kampong on the outskirts of Malacca where his father was engaged in the state government as a clerk. He was married young — before eighteen — to a girl from Singapore, and went to Singapore first to work with his father-in-law who was a seller of *song-koks* "hats." However, he held this job for only one and a half years before he came to Seremban and began work as a chauffeur for a European family. This job lasted for a short time only before he came to Kuala Lumpur and went to work as a chauffeur for other European families. Later he joined the Sri Jaya Transport Company (a Malay taxi and bus service) as a taxi driver and has been working in that occupation for the last twenty years.

Although he lives in a peri-urban kampong, his father had an urban job so that his experience with urban areas was considerable before he took his first city job. Yet despite the long period in Kuala Lumpur, he still does not intend to stay there all his life but hopes to return to Malacca where he has inherited a few acres of rubber-land. It is interesting to note that his wife owns a quarter-acre of land in Kampong Baharu on which they eventually intend to build a house for their children if the latter choose to stay in the city. If not, he will rent it when he returns to Malacca.

Generally, his socioeconomic status is better than many of the Malays in Kuala Lumpur. He earns over $200 a month and pays $48 per month rent. But the cost of his children's education and other expenses, particularly those related to his children, do not permit him to save. He has very close contact with his parents who are in the rural area, especially his mother, who is not well. He visits his ailing parents in his home kampong more than twice a month, bringing them medicine or food, and sometimes money.

In general, while in the city he has, considering his lack of English, taken good advantage of the availability of improved communications. He has made many friends, both at his work and in Kampong Baharu. His attitudes, however, remain persistently rural in that he views the city as a "disruptive" influence on religion and friendliness, although clearly he also regards it as a "positive" influence. He has become more interested in politics and feels that the city has changed him personally — not, it must be emphasized, in a particularly beneficial way. Thus, he argues that the large number of dependents and increasing number of expenses in the city are causing him excessive worry which he is sure he would not experience in his home kampong.

Nevertheless, he is very positive that his children will have as good an education as he can give them in the terms of his ambitions for them. He is thinking that his son should be educated enough to pursue a professional career in engineering. He hopes, too, that his daughters may take up teaching as a career.

Thus, except for the period of the Japanese invasion, this migrant has been resident in Kuala Lumpur for almost thirty years, yet he still looks forward to returning to the countryside and keeps very close contacts with his parents there. His problems are certainly sizable and have been exacerbated by his second marriage — additional expenses have been incurred because of the increased size of his family — and his realization of the need to provide his children with the best education possible. But, despite this awareness of the advantages of the city, he waits only to return to the countryside and his home kampong. For him the city is a workplace to which he has adapted, but in no sense has he committed himself for his entire life.

RESPONDENT 387 (HOLOGRAM VIII): MEAN 2.86   Since the indices measuring the levels of urban adaptation are heavily weighted in favor of urban residents, it is hardly surprising that the Kuala Lumpur-born are prominent in Level Three. However, as we pointed out in the text, the mere fact of birth within Kuala Lumpur does not automatically provide an individual with advantages for adaptation to the urban situation, nor does it necessarily mean that his contact with the rural areas is lacking.

This is well-illustrated by Respondent 387 (see Figure 2D), a Kuala Lumpur-born resident who has seldom been out of a city and yet retains close contact with his wife's rural kinfolk who reside in the country. This individual, born in 1924, lived in a kampong on the northern fringes of the city near Sentul Pasar. He spent the first twenty-three years of his life here with his father, helping on their rubber small holding.

But for the Japanese invasion he probably would not have remained so long with his parents. He did not leave them until he joined the police force at twenty-three. He was employed in the police force as a wireless operator four years before he was transferred out of Kuala Lumpur to Kuala Lipis and later to Banting in Kuala Langat District, Selangor State. He returned to Kuala Lumpur in 1955 where he took a position with the Statistics Department and later moved to the Registration Department as an interviewing officer. At the age of thirty-eight he is married to a woman from a district adjacent to Kuala Lumpur (Ulu Langat) and has raised a family of four.

He is firmly committed to remaining in Kuala Lumpur all his life but still maintains close links with his wife's relatives in the district of Ulu Langat, visiting them approximately once a month for periods of up to two days, and if possible, longer. Money is sent to his wife's parents regularly, though this is not a great amount. He is committed to permanent residence in Kuala Lumpur in other ways as well. For example, he has purchased a house in Kampong Dato Keramat on a fifteen-year repayment plan, at a rate of approximately $32 a month to the municipality.

He has also managed to acquire more status amenities than the majority of the other individuals interviewed. He owns a 1950 Morris which he uses to visit in Ulu Langat and for travel around Kuala Lumpur. He takes full advantage of communications available in Kuala Lumpur, reading both English and Malay newspapers (having studied both English and Malay at primary level), and he has a number of friends living in Kampong Dato Keramat. His attitudes are surprisingly imitative of the traditional rural viewpoints (as can be seen from Hologram VIII) mainly with respect to the friendliness of Malays, for he considers that there is much the same attitude between Kuala Lumpur Malays and those living outside. However, despite the fact that he is permanently stabilized in Kuala Lumpur, the web of kinship involves him in continuing contacts with rural areas, as does his occupational history. Thus he is well aware of the urban-rural differences that may exist in Malay attitudes, and clearly believes them to be of some importance.

Level Three: Urban Men? Four Case Studies

Finally, we will consider four case studies of Malays who fall into the upper level of adaptation.

RESPONDENT 384 (HOLOGRAM IX): MEAN 3.09   Respondent 384 (see Figure 3A) represents the Malay who has an excellent urban background which has given him ample experience with the urban situation. Born in Kampong Melayu, Singapore, he was educated at English secondary school, and passed his senior Cambridge examination. He was employed as a journalist by the *Straits Times* while in Singapore and as an information officer with an oil company in Brunei. Presently he is working with the Information Services of the Malayan government in an upper-civil service position. He is, however, a recent arrival in Kuala Lumpur, having spent just over a year there after being transferred from government employment in Singapore. His socioeconomic status is high. He earns over $500 a month in an upper civil service position and possesses a majority of the status symbols of the new elite — motor car, regrigerator, and radio-phonograph. In the last year he has visited relatives in Singapore four times but does not remit money to them. He reads all newspapers, attends the cinema regularly, and claims to have friends of all races, though his closest friend is a Malay, the editor of the *Berita Harian*. His attitudes generally reflect his urban background although he considers the Malays in Kuala Lumpur less friendly than those in Singapore.

Hologram IX shows clearly that he is not committed to permanent residence in Kuala Lumpur. He still owns land in Singapore and quite probably will return there, but at the moment he is undecided. This migrant, then, does not fit into any category of a rural migrant moving to the city. Rather, he is an interurban migrant, for he still retains his property and some of his personal friendships and kinship ties in the city of Singapore. He is a case of interurban loyalty with the web of kinship rather than one of preference for a rural or urban evironment.

RESPONDENT 375 (HOLOGRAM X): MEAN 3.25   Respondent 375 (see Figure 3B) should more correctly be regarded as Kuala Lumpur-born since he has lived in Kuala Lumpur since the age of four. His father was engaged in selling clothes and during his early years he lived in the family home at Kampong Baharu. Later they moved to a house on Klang Road (now the old Klang Road) not far from the present area of Kampong Petaling Bahagia. He was educated at English secondary school and later at the Malay Teachers' Training College and is presently a teacher.

He is firmly committed to future residence in Kuala Lumpur even though his wife, who comes from Kampong Kapar, Klang, to which his parents have returned, is also from the same area. At present he is earning an income in excess of $300 and living in a rented house for $60 a month in Kawasan Melayu (the Malay area of Petaling Java). He does not keep very close contact with his family, visiting them only two times a year, despite the fact that they are relatively accessible in terms of public transport. He does not remit money to them, and in fact, generally seems to have limited his contacts to a minimum.

He makes full use of the communications and other facets of the city, has a large number of friends, and is well aware of the many and diverse settlements of Malays in the city. His attitudes are a mixture — generally he is inclined to regard the city as a force that does change people (affecting religion, attitudes and friendliness), but he is of the opinion that it has effected little change in him. This may be because, having been resident there for so long, he sees the changes in his personality as principally a result of his general maturation.

RESPONDENT 451 (HOLOGRAM XI): MEAN 3.48   Social scientists doing research in the non-Western world make much of the concept of Westernization, often using it synonymously with "modernization" to mean an individual or group of individuals that has adopted the mores and value judgments of the supposedly advanced individuals of capitalist societies.[6] While the author thinks it is exceptionally hazardous to use this concept in the context of the non-Western world, if the concept is going to be utilized it might be applied to Respondent 451 (see Figure 3C).

Born the son of a doctor, he has had the classic education of the Malay elite — studying first at the Malay College at Kuala Kungsar and then moving to the United Kingdom, obtaining university degrees from Cambridge and Oxford. As the accompanying hologram shows, his whole background is one of constant experience with urban areas. He joined the Malayan civil service in 1958 after completing his degrees overseas, and since then has held an important post in a top government department.

For a Malay he has accomplished the rare feat of marrying a girl from another ethnic group whom he met when he was studying overseas. They have two children, both born in Kuala Lumpur, and employ two Chinese servants. He is, of course, in the top socioeconomic grade, earning an income in excess of $500 and his wife is working also, giving them a combined income of almost $1,600 per month. His contacts with his relatives in areas outside Kuala Lumpur are irregular, rarely exceeding two visits a year though he continues to send money regularly to his parents.

Not surprisingly, he makes considerable use of the media, and his

---

[6] For a discussion of some aspects of this concept see Hagen (1964); Hoselitz (1960); and Moore and Feldman (1960).

friendships in the city are wide, though he knows only a few areas of Malay settlement. Most of his friends, he claims, come from mixed ethnic groups. His attitudes reflect his urban background as well as his honesty, for he felt he could not comment on questions concerning religious attitudes in the city or for that matter, friendship, as he is not well enough acquainted with these two phenomena in Kuala Lumpur City.

This individual probably represents the most well-educated of any in the sample, as well as being a Malay who clearly understands the wider values and need for mixed ethnic harmony in the city and in the total society. He is firmly committed to residence in Kuala Lumpur as is indicated by the overall configuration of his hologram.

RESPONDENT 470 (HOLOGRAM XII): MEAN 3.58   This Kuala Lumpur-born Malay (see Figure 3D), employed in a senior government post, represents (as measured by the indices) a thoroughly urbanized individual. He came from a comparatively poor family in which his father was engaged as a chauffeur with only a limited education, but he has a remarkable education record, having studied at universities in China, Taiwan, and the United States for four years. He presently resides in government housing in Kuala Lumpur but he had made a substantial number of moves within Kuala Lumpur during his early years with his family. His father, when employed as a chauffeur for Europeans, generally lived in housing provided by them.

He is firmly committed to Kuala Lumpur and has no relatives living in the countryside or elsewhere. Although his attitudes are not completely urban he represents an urban individual who has had the maximum opportunity to achieve his present high post in government service. It is interesting that among the top-status individuals in the sample there are only two Kuala Lumpur-born, the majority of the others coming from other parts of Malaya. This, then, is an urban individual, totally committed to residence in Kuala Lumpur and to his future in the city.

CONCLUSION

In a way, this study represents a reversion to the older model of the rural-urban dichotomy criticized earlier. But there is a specific reason for this regression, namely, to point out that, allowing for the design of the analysis which utilizes the continuum between the "rural person" and the "urban person," the end result indicates that the majority of Malays (in terms of the continuum) are "rural persons" and "urban persons" at the same time. Some may have more urban characteristics than others, but this is in itself no surety that they will adopt "supposed" urban attitudes. In other words, the capacity of the individual to hold these seemingly antithetical positions, as assessed by the rural-urban continuum, invalidates its predictive qualities. The individual, even the most marginally provided for, is far more flexible in taking what he wants out of the urban situation than the model would allow, accepting the fact that this flexibility will be limited by the position of the individual within the broader structure of his society. Ultimately, the individual is the product of his society, not of his city.

APPENDIX: URBANIZATION INDICES

(Note: Each of the scores in these indices was expressed in quartiles and transferred to the appropriate ring of the hologram.)

Sector A: Background Situation

Sector A consists of three indices which give an indication of the individual's early influences and experience of the urban situation:

Index 1   URBAN RESIDENCE IN EARLY YEARS is measured as follows:
$$\frac{\text{Years spent in towns over 2,000 up to fifteenth birthday}}{\text{Number of years (14)}} \times 100$$
It was hypothesized that the greater number of years spent in the towns, the more likely it was that the individual would be able to adapt to the city.

Index 2   THE DISTANCE OF THE MAJOR PLACE OF RESIDENCE FROM THE LARGEST URBAN AREA IN THE STATE BEFORE THE INDIVIDUAL'S FIFTEENTH BIRTHDAY was considered to be important. It was hypothesized that the closer the residence to the larger urban center, the more likely the individual would be able to adapt to the city.

Index 3   FATHER'S OCCUPATION was measured to give an indication of the individual's likely entry into urban-centered occupations. It was hypothesized that the higher the status of father measured by income and occupation, the more likely that the individual would be able to adapt to the city.

Sector B: Respondent's Socioeconomic Background

Sector B is an attempt to measure the individual's socioeconomic background. Once again, ranked from "1" in ascending order to "4" in terms of what are considered to be the most advantageous individual assets to enable the individual to play a full and active role in the city. Three indices are used to measure these factors:

Index 4 RESPONDENT'S EDUCATION was ranked from higher education, level 4 (i.e. English secondary and attendance at higher-education institutions) to no education, level 1. Malay primary only was 2. Malay and English primary was 3.

Index 5 OCCUPATIONAL BACKGROUND was classified by levels as follows:
1. No previous employment apart from family labor on peasant farms
2. Unemployed or in daily employment possessing no skills (i.e. no occupational training)
3. Employed with some skills (generally with some training needed, such as chauffeurs)
4. Employed and possessing distinct occupational skills (e.g. civil servant, Division 1).

Index 6 URBAN EXPERIENCE BEFORE ENTERING KUALA LUMPUR was figured as follows:

$$\frac{\text{Years spent in towns over 2,000 up to fifteenth birthday}}{\text{Years after fifteenth birthday before entry to Kuala Lumpur}} \times 100$$

The ranking was from level 4 (75 to 100) to level 1 (0–24–9). It should be noted that Index 6 is not applicable to Kuala Lumpur-born with the exception of those who have been working outside Kuala Lumpur and returned.

Sector C: Urban Commitment

Sector C measures urban commitment. The importance of this index to much of the sociological work carried out in the underdeveloped world, particularly in Africa, should be noted. Three indices have been utilized:

Index 7 THE STABILIZATION INDEX measures the years in Kuala Lumpur since fifteen. The results were ranked as before.

$$\frac{\text{Years in Kuala Lumpur (metropolitan and peri-urban)}}{\text{Years since fifteen}} \times 100$$

Residence in Kuala Lumpur was defined broadly to include residence in the peri-urban fringes such as Kampong Pantai Halt.

Index 8 THE COMMITMENT OF THE INDIVIDUAL was measured in terms of his answer to question 128 which consisted of two parts:
Do you intend to stay in Kuala Lumpur all your life?
Yes / No / Don't know.
When you have finished working in Kuala Lumpur, will you go back to your home district?
Yes / No / Don't know.
The answers were based largely on the first part of the question. Thus "yes" was ranked as level 4; "no" as 1; and "don't know" as 2. In cases where there was doubt about the validity of the answer, the second question was used to clarify it.

Index 9 PREFERENCE FOR KUALA LUMPUR AS A LIVING PLACE was measured by question 123:
Do you prefer living in Kuala Lumpur more than your home district?
Yes / No / Don't know.

Sector D: Respondent's Present Socioeconomic Characteristics

Sector D is designed to measure the individual's socioeconomic characteristics. In terms of ranking the results, the assumption has been made that higher status occupations, higher incomes, house ownership, etc. provide the individual with advantages with respect to his capacity to cope with the city.

This is, of course, a debatable assumption, since individuals of many different socioeconomic grades may adapt well to the city; but in terms of their capacity to cope with the city and improve their position, their opportunities may be limited. Six indices were used in this sector:

Index 10 OCCUPATION was ranked into four categories following the ranking of Index 3.

Index 11 INCOME was subjectively ranked as follows, after an evaluation of the household incomes:
1. $99
2. $100 to $249
3. $290 to $499
4. $500 and over

Index 12 ECOLOGICAL SITUATION was defined as follows:
1. Fringe squatters
2. Inner-city squatters
3. Legal Malay settlements
4. Government housing (middle and upper grade) and private housing

Index 13 HOUSEHOLD AMENITIES were defined as follows:
1. Poor quality (no electricity, water or piped sanitation)
2. Better quality (piped water / no electricity or piped sanitation)
3. Legal Malay settlement amenities (water and electricity / no sanitation in some cases).
4. High quality (all amenities)

Index 14 HOUSE OWNERSHIP was classified as follows:
1. Staying with relatives
2. Tenant
3. Own house but not land on which situated
4. Own house and land

Index 15 POSSESSION OF STATUS AMENITIES was classified as follows:
1. None
2. Possess motor scooter or motorbike

3. Car or refrigerator
4. Car and refrigerator

Sector E: Urban Rural Ties

Sector E is designed to measure urban-rural ties. Three indices were chosen:

Index 16   NUMBER OF VISITS TO RURAL AREA PER YEAR:
1. Nine or more
2. Three to eight visits
3. Three visits
4. None

Index 17   REMITTANCE OF MONEY:
1. Regular
2. Irregular
3. Level 3 omitted
4. Do not remit

Index 18   MARITAL TIES:
1. Wife from home district; marriage arranged
2. Wife from home district; marriage not arranged
3. Wife from elsewhere; marriage arranged
4. Wife from elsewhere; marriage not arranged
It should be noted that this index is designed to measure the degree of social pressure operating. The interviewers were asked to clarify the meaning of "arrangement" (since few Malay ceremonies are not arranged) as meaning the selection of a mate by parents or kinfolk.

It is assumed that the man who chooses his wife from other areas (not on parental advice) is more emancipated than those who do not.

In all these indices, it is assumed that the closer the link with rural areas, the more likely this is to inhibit urban adaptation.

Sector F: Communications and Contact in the City

One of the most frequent assertions concerning urban residence is that it exposes the individual to new ideas and attitudes through increased availability of newspapers, films, association, etc. On the face of it, there seems little to debate with such an assertion, but does the undeniable existence of these aids mean that the individual will take advantage of them?

Sector F attempts to measure some of the broader indications of the individual's utilization of these communications media and the friendship patterns which grow up among the urban residents. Here some attempt was made to measure the role of work as a place in which friendships are made. Finally, an effort was made to measure the degree of community awareness by the knowledge of other Malay areas. (This was only of limited value.)

The following indices were devised:

Index 19   REGULARITY AND TYPE OF NEWSPAPER READING:
1.   Do not read newspapers
2.   Malay or English irregularly (i.e. not daily)
3.   Malay or English regularly (daily)
4.   English and Malay regularly (daily)

Index 20   REGULARITY AND TYPE OF CINEMA ATTENDANCE:
1.   Do not attend
2.   Malay or English irregularly
3.   Malay or English regularly
4.   English and Malay regularly (more than once a month)

The reason for the distinction between the "Malay OR English" and "Malay AND English" communication types is simply to indicate the breadth of contact with the communications media. Those who have contact with the two streams of language are assumed to have broader contact than those who do not.

Index 21   FRIENDSHIP PATTERNS was based on question 116, designed to ascertain the respondent's closest friend (assumed to be mentioned first on the list). It is divided as follows:
1.   None
2.   Kin
3.   Neighbors / other
4.   Workmate

Index 22   KNOWLEDGE OF OTHER MALAY AREAS IN KUALA LUMPUR:
1.   Do not know any
2.   Three or less
3.   Four to eight
4.   Nine or more

It might be argued that the ranking of this category could be reversed, based on the assertion that a greater knowledge of Malay areas represents some form of community awareness (ethnic strengthening) with regard to the supposed breakdown of ethnic identity often said to occur in the urban setting.

I do not hold to this position, arguing that the knowledge of a greater number of Malay areas shows greater awareness of the urban situation and hence should be ranked above the other indices.

Sector G: Urban Attitudes

Sector G is devoted to urban attitudes. In general, it attempts to measure the degree of acceptance of what may be regarded as rural stereotypes concerning the urban milieu. The assumption in ranking is that the more closely the individual comforms to the stereotype, the less urbanized he tends to be. Six indices were chosen:

Index 23   ATTITUDES TOWARDS RELIGION IN THE CITY were calculated from response to question 106:
Do you think that people who live in the city are less religious than those who live in the country?

True / Not true / Same / Don't know.
   The above query was ranked as follows:
1. True
2. Same
3. Level 3 omitted
4. Not true

Index 24   RELIGIOUS ATTENDANCE IN THE CITY was based on question 108:
Do you attend mosque more frequently, less frequently or the same as you did
in the kampong?
   The question was addressed only to the migrants and did not apply to the
Kuala Lumpur-born except when they had been away from the city and had
returned. It was ranked as follows on the assumption that the urban residence
tended to break down religious adherence – a stereotype assumption:
1. More
2. Same
3. Level 3 omitted
4. Less frequently

Index 25   MALAYS' FRIENDLINESS IN KUALA LUMPUR was based on question 115:
Are Malays in Kuala Lumpur more friendly or less friendly than Kampong
Malays?
More / Less / Same / Don't know.
   It was ranked in the following manner:
1. Less
2. Same
3. Level 3 omitted
4. More

Index 26   SAVING IN THE CITY was based on question 109:
Do you think that it is easier to save money, or harder to save money in Kuala
Lumpur than in the Kampong?
Easier / Harder / Same / Don't know.
   It was assumed that the rural stereotype was that money was easy to acquire
and save in the city. In fact, as the evidence shows, most residents felt it was
much harder.
   The ranking was as follows:
1. Easier
2. Same
3. Level 3 omitted
4. Harder

Index 27   INTEREST IN POLITICS IN THE CITY based on question 120:
Do you find you are more interested in Kuala Lumpur than you were before?
Yes / No / Don't know.
   It was ranked as follows:
1. No
2. Undecided
3. Level 3 omitted
4. Yes

Index 28   INDIVIDUAL CHANGE IN THE CITY based on question 121:
Since you came to Kuala Lumpur have you as a person changed?
Yes / No / Don't know.
   The answers were ranked as follows:
1. No
2. Don't know
3. Level 3 omitted
4. Yes

Again, the question was not applicable to the Kuala Lumpur-born except when they had been away from the city.

REFERENCES

ABU-LUGHOD, JANET
   1961   Migrant adjustment to city life: the Egyptian case. *American Journal of Sociology* 67:22–32.
BAUMAN, ZYGMUNT
   1967   Modern times, modern Marxism. *Social Research* 34:399–415.
BOGUE, DONALD J.
   1959   "Internal migration," in *The study of population: an inventory and appraisal.* Edited by Philip M. Hauser and Otis Dudley Duncan, 486–509. Chicago: University of Chicago Press.
BRUNER, EDWARD M.
   1961   Urbanization and ethnic identity in north Sumatra. *American Anthropologist* 63:508–521.
CHANDER, R.
   1972   *1970 Population and housing census of Malaysia-community groups.* Kuala Lumpur: Jabatan Perangkaan Malaysia.
CENTRE NATIONAL FRANÇAISE DE LA RECHERCHE SCIENTIFIQUE
   1959   *Étude sur les conditions de vie et les besoins de la population de Viet-Nam.* Paris.
EAMES, E.
   1954   Some aspects of urban migration from a village in north Central India. *Eastern Anthropologist* 8:13–26.
EPSTEIN, A. L.
   1967   Urbanization and social change in Africa. *Current Anthropology* 8:275–312.
GULLICK, J. M.
   1956   *The story of early Kuala Lumpur.* Singapore: Donald Moore.
HAGEN, EVERETT E.
   1964   *On the theory of social change.* London: Tavistock.
HAUSER, PHILIP M. *editor*
   1957   *Urbanization in Asia and the Far East.* Calcutta: UNESCO.
   1961   *Urbanization in Latin America.* Paris: UNESCO.
HOSELITZ, BERT F.
   1960   *Sociological aspects of economic growth.* Glencoe, Illinois: The Free Press.

LEWIS, OSCAR
1952 Urbanization without breakdown: a case study. *Scientific Monthly* 75:31–41.
1959 *Five families: Mexican case studies in the culture of poverty.* New York: Random House.

MANGIN, WILLIAM, *editor*
1970 *Peasants in cities: readings in the anthropology of urbanization.* Boston: Houghton Mifflin.

MAYER, P.
1962 *Townsmen or tribesmen: conservatism and the process of urbanization.* Capetown: Oxford University Press.

MCGEE, T. G.
1964 The rural-urban continuum debate, the pre-industrial city and rural-urban migration. *Pacific Viewpoint* 5:159–81.
1968 "Malays in Kuala Lumpur city." Unpublished doctoral dissertation. University of Wellington, Wellington, Victoria.
1971 *The urbanization process in the Third World.* London: G. Bell and Son.

MILBANK MEMORIAL FUND
1958 *Selected studies of migration since World War II.* New York: Milbank Memorial Fund.

MITCHELL, J. CLYDE
1966 "Theoretical orientations in African urban studies," in *The social anthropology of complex societies.* Edited by Michael Banton, 37-68. London: Tavistock.

MOORE, WILBERT E., ARNOLD S. FELDMAN, *editors*
1960 *Labor commitment and social change in developing areas.* New York: Social Science Research Council.

NELSON, JOAN
1970 The urban poor: disruption or political integration in Third-World cities. *World Politics* 22:393–413.

NESS, GAYL D.
1967 *Bureaucracy and rural development in Malaysia.* Berkeley and Los Angeles: University of California Press.

PROVENCHER, RONALD
1971 *Two Malay worlds: interaction in urban and rural settings.* Berkeley: Center for South and Southeast Asia Studies, University of California.

PRYOR, ROBIN J.
1971 *Internal migration and urbanization: an introduction and bibliography.* Townsville: James Cook University of North Queensland.

SIMMEL, GEORG
1957 "The metropolis and mental life," in *Cities and society.* Edited by Paul K. Hatt and A. J. Reiss. Glencoe, Illinois: The Free Press. (Article originally published in 1900).

THOMAS, D. S.
1938 *Research memorandum on migration differentials.* New York.

TURNER, JOHN F. C.
1967 Barriers and channels for housing development in modernizing countries. *Journal of the American Institute of Planners* 33:167–81.

TURNER, ROY, *editor*
 1962   *India's urban future*. Berkeley and Los Angeles: University of California Press.
TURSKI, RYSZURD
 1967   Town-country relations. *Polish Perspectives* 10:12–21.
WINSTEDT, RICHARD
 1951   *The Malay magician being shaman, saiva and sufi*. London: Routledge and Kegan Paul.
WIRTH, LOUIS
 1957   "Urbanism as a way of life," in *Cities and society*. Edited by Paul K. Hatt and A. J. Reiss. Glencoe, Illinois: The Free Press. (Article originally published in 1938).

Migration, Ethnicity, and Adaptation:
Bolivian Migrant Workers in
Northwest Argentina

SCOTT WHITEFORD, RICHARD N. ADAMS

On the basis of materials gathered on Bolivian migrants to northwest Argentina, we propose that migrants seek situations that permit participation in higher degrees of organization as circumstances permit. We argue (1) from a general axiom that human beings seek to improve their control over the environment; (2) that higher level organization provides better control than lower level organization; and (3) that consequently, when there are no contraints to the contrary, individuals will seek participation in a more complex organization. A secondary product of exploring this adaptive process of migrants is the realization that, in the case of migrant organizations in particular, ethnicity appears to govern membership during phases of less complex organization, whereas increased complexity of organization will be accompanied by a decrease in the importance of ethnicity as a criterion of participation.

The populations under study here initially were seasonal agricultural laborers who worked in the sugar cane harvests and whose dependency on the nuclear family was fundamental. Extended kinship and ethnicity provided additional bases for identification. Ethnicity here refers to cultural national antecedents.

The analysis will consist of comparing a typology of Bolivian migrant labor elaborated by Whiteford with a model of organization types (oper-

Fieldwork in northwest Argentina was carried out by Whiteford from April 1969 until November 1970 under a grant from the Ford Foundation. Full acknowledgements will appear in the dissertation currently in preparation. The present article evolved from discussion between the two authors. Whiteford prepared the first draft, Adams reworked it.

ating units) devised by Adams.[1] The typology of Bolivian labor was formulated as a means of descriptively differentiating adaptive situations evolved by the Bolivians and was done independently of Adams' model. Because of this, the application of the model has the advantage of providing a somewhat independent evaluation of the general thesis; but by the same token, Whiteford was not aware of the specific features of the model at the time of the fieldwork, and therefore the original data were not collected in order to be thus analyzed.

We will also explore the shifting of migrants from stable situations, with high complexity in terms of number of operating units, to situations of limited involvement during the most transient phases of wage migration. This situation is most disliked by the migrants and will be avoided entirely if possible, and where not, will generate strategies that help movement to situations of greater complexity. The latter is achieved when horizontal mobility, i.e. periodic migration, is reduced, and the increasingly complex organization is marked by greater ethnic heterogeneity.

BACKGROUND

The ethnographic material on which this study is based was gathered in the provinces of Salta and Jujuy in northwest Argentina. According to the 1960 census, there were 95,233 Bolivians in Argentina.[2] Of these, 43 percent were recorded in the province of Jujuy and 28.9 percent in the province of Salta. Both provinces border Bolivia and a major road runs through both of them connecting Bolivia and Argentina.

Bolivian migration to Argentina is a product of many forces and includes people from a wide range of socioeconomic backgrounds. Argentina has been a convenient haven for exiles from the multiple Bolivian revolutions, coups, and wars. Soldiers and generals alike have sought asylum in Argentina. The booming industry of the 1940's also drew Bolivians to the southern Argentine cities in search of work, but probably the biggest source of employment for recent Bolivian immigrants in northwest Argentina and Mendoza has been in agriculture, particularly in the harvesting of crops.

---

[1]   Whiteford's typology was first elaborated in Whiteford 1972. Adams' model appears in a preliminary form in Adams 1970, but the present discussion is taken from Adams 1973.

[2]   This figure underestimates the total Bolivian population in Argentina at this time, failing to take into account the large numbers of Bolivians without papers who would be reluctant to see census takers. By 1969 there had been more estimates ranging from 500,000 to 1,000,000 Bolivians in Argentina.

Many conditions in Bolivia combined to make it advantageous for some to migrate to Argentina: low Bolivian wages, a high exchange rate for the Argentine peso (a rate that has been gradually declining) political instability and the continual division by inheritance of many peasant holdings already too small to support a family adequately. In other cases rugged terrain, droughts, erosion, and the persistent shortening of fallow periods have led to a decrease in land productivity. All of these factors, combined with the glittering stories of Argentina, have prompted migration, often only seasonal at first, to Argentina (for a discussion of seasonal work and urbanization, see Whiteford 1972).

Life histories of present and former agricultural migrant workers who work or have worked in the *zafra*, the sugar harvest, form the basis of our descriptive data. The *zafra* has been an important source of employment for Bolivian workers, as the sugar plantations in Salta and Jujuy annually hire as many as 26,000 men between the months of May and September. These plantations are located in a region known as the Ramal, a fertile subtropical valley which runs through both Salta and Jujuy. This is the second most important sugar zone in Argentina, topped only by the province of Tucumán. In contrast to Tucumán, where there are thousands of peasant cane growers, six large plantations dominate the Ramal sugar production.

Originally, Mataco, Toba, and Chiriguano Indians provided the labor for the plantations but they proved to be too unmanageable and reportedly ate up to 10 percent of the sugar harvest. The plantations then turned to Argentine highland peasants. Because the *zafra* occurred during the winter months, peasant agricultural acitvity was precluded, and the men were free to work for the plantations. But like the Indians, the Argentines proved difficult to control, and protested wages and working conditions. Their attempts to form unions and conduct strikes prompted the plantations to look for another source of labor. Traditionally, small numbers of Bolivian workers had been hired by the plantations, and in an attempt to reduce labor problems the administrations made a concerted effort to recruit Bolivians as replacements for Argentines. *Contratistas* [recruiters] were sent to Bolivia and rewarded generously by the companies for each worker hired.

As discussed earlier, conditions in southern Bolivia encouraged migration to Argentina, and a further impetus was the dry season in some parts of southern Bolivia which coincided with the *zafra* period in Argentina. Although the *zafra* conditions did not live up to the glowing pictures painted by the recruiters, the pay was lucrative enough to draw thousands of Bolivians every year. Plantation administrators were pleased with Bolivian workers because they were willing to work long hard hours for low pay and did not become involved in union activity.

Once in Argentina, many Bolivian workers remained to seek post-*zafra* work. Some traveled as far as Buenos Aires, hundreds of miles away from the plantations, others went to the rich agricultural regions of Mendoza, Mar del Plata, and Río Negro to work harvesting fruit and vegetables, but many remained in Salta and Jujuy to work on the tobacco *fincas*, the vegetable farms, or in the towns of the region.

The urban migrants described here live in the city of Salta, the provincial capital and regional center, with a population of 176,130. Salta was founded in 1582 and once served as a trade link between the highland mines of Alto Peru and the mule-raising and agricultural regions of Córdoba and Tucumán. With independence, Salta lost access to the markets of Alto Peru and faced increased competition in the internal market for her agricultural produce. Today, Salta is again the center of a productive agricultural zone that produces sugar, wine, tobacco, beef, and vegetables for the domestic market and export.

LABOR TYPES ASSOCIATED WITH THE ZAFRA

A general typology of the migration patterns associated with the post-*zafra* period is presented to differentiate adaptive situations. Figure 1 indicates the basic work-living types and the most common pattern of movement from one category to another as reconstructed from life histories.[3]

Among the various adaptive patterns of agricultural workers in Bolivia, the most important are those of the INDEPENDENT PEASANTS and the RURAL SEMI-PROLETARIAT. Some workers had been independent peasant agriculturalists who either owned or rented land. Although Bolivian peasant agriculturalists were not the subject of direct study, data was gathered on former independent peasants who had been forced by the ecological deterioration of their own holdings, the parcelization of family lands, increasing family size, a scarcity of water for irrigation, deteriorating markets for their produce, or a combination of these factors to turn to the *zafra* for supplementary income to support their families.

By seeking outside work in Argentina, they become RURAL SEMI-PRO-LETARIAT, working four to five months of the year on the plantations

---

[3] Although the chart reflects the major patterns, there were exceptions. Furthermore, as the following material will indicate, people were not always able to move through the whole sequence but often remained in intermediary stages.

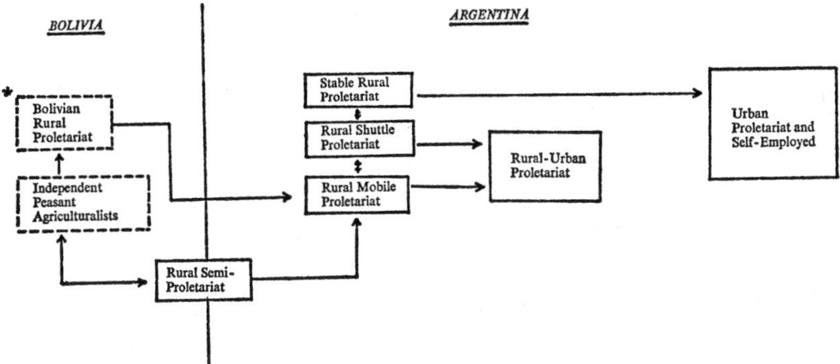

Figure 1.   Major inter-relationships of general proletariat types associated with the *zafra* in northwest Argentina

and returning to their farms after the *zafra*. The income resulting from their migration may be used to buy animals, household items, and more land. The rural semi-proletariat family is often integrated in the home community. The head of the family usually goes to the *zafra*. If the rest of the family joins him, some of the income is used to pay a relative for tending the animals, or even for preparing the land for cultivation, should the *zafra* extend into the planting season. In other cases, especially with older couples, the woman remains in Bolivia with the younger children and cares for the animals and fields, while the man goes to Argentina with the older children. In this case the older daughter helps in the fields with peeling and topping the cane and does the family cooking and laundry as well.

Bolivian peasants can also become RURAL PROLETARIAT IN BOLIVIA. Like the independent peasant farmer, the Bolivian rural proletarian was not a subject of this study, but some Bolivians who worked in the *zafra* had belonged in this category at one time. Many of this group had chosen to remain after the *zafra* to seek employment on Argentine farms. The most common pattern during the 1960's was to work on a tobacco farm in Salta or Jujuy; this is still prevalent, with the farms employing thousands of laborers during the two- to three-month harvest period. The farms are located in an elevated region which is within a hundred miles of the sugar zone, thus reducing travel costs for the worker who wishes to work on the farms after the *zafra*.

In Jujuy, harvest of the Virginia tobacco usually begins in early October, and in cases in which the *zafra* ends by mid-September, the *zafreros* are able to find employment on the farms within a few weeks.

The harvest of Virginia tobacco in parts of Salta does not begin until December, offering work for some of the *zafreros* who have worked in Jujuy harvests. It lasts until March or April, which leaves many workers without lodging or work until the *zafra* begins again in early June. Workers may sometimes join ongoing harvests on vegetable farms in the area. Others may take the long, arduous trip to Mendoza to seek work on fruit and vegetable farms, while still others may cultivate or plant the Criollo tobacco in Salta.

Almost nomadic, these workers and their families form the RURAL MOBILE PROLETARIAT, migrating to different farms with the changing of the seasons and the ripening of the crops. Unsure of where they will obtain their next job, the *zafra* is their only dependable source of employment. Insecure, at the mercy of the foremen and farm owners, and constantly migrating, the rural mobile proletariat has an extremely difficult time.

There are three major alternatives which rural mobile proletarians tend to use in shifting their migration patterns. They may become RURAL SHUTTLE PROLETARIAT, STABLE RURAL PROLETARIAT, or RURAL-URBAN PROLETARIAT. Of the three, the most common alternative is that of the rural shuttle proletariat. These make an agreement with a *mayordomo* [farm foreman] or an owner to return every post-*zafra* season to the same farm in Argentina. On the tobacco farms in Salta extra help is needed for planting the seed beds, transplanting, and cultivating. After the Virginia tobacco harvest, further work can be provided, possibly in the preparation of the Criollo tobacco, but more commonly in general farm activities left untended during the harvest. The rural shuttle proletariat family is often given permission to store their belongings at the farm while they are gone at the *zafra*. Although still inconvenient for the migrant and his family, the pattern offers greater security than that of the rural mobile proletariat. Needless to say, however, the farm and plantation owners are the real beneficiaries of the arrangement.

It is not uncommon for rural shuttle proletarians to tire of their situation and to seek more permanent rural employment, thereby becoming STABLE RURAL PROLETARIAT RESIDING IN ARGENTINA. In some cases rural mobile proletarians may also become "permanent workers," but this is more common for rural shuttle proletarians who have worked for a prolonged period on one farm. By becoming stable rural proletarians and giving up work in the *zafra*, migrants relinquish the higher harvest salaries for the security and convenience of farm work. A "good patron" is considered crucial if one is to make the change: a good patron is one who pays close to the minimum wage and more or less regularly.

Another alternative, open to both the rural shuttle proletariat and the rural mobile proletariat, is to move to the city. The RURAL-URBAN PRO-LETARIAT move to the city after the *zafra*, but return to the harvest the next year because it promises higher earnings and steadier employment than urban work. Following the *zafra*, the migrants once again return to the same or another city to search for work. Over time, many of the rural-urban proletarians in Salta managed to buy lots on the outskirts of the city, purchase building materials, and construct living quarters. Once they have a home in the city, families often divide up for the *zafra*. Parents are reluctant to take their children out of the city school, both for fear of disrupting their education and of exposing them to the unhealthy conditions of the work camp; also they do not like to leave their homes unoccupied. As with the rural semi-proletarians, older children who can work often accompany their father to the *zafra* while the mother and younger children stay behind in Salta.

In most cases, the rural-urban proletariat experience is transitory; migrants may abandon work in the *zafra* and either join the URBAN PROLETARIAT or become SELF-EMPLOYED URBANITES. This decision is usually not made until the migrant and his family feel that they are established in the urban environment. In a nonindustrial city like Salta, urban pro-letarians may depend on a multitude of short-term jobs in construction, brick making, and service businesses. Those who become self-employed may start their own store or may go into the building business on their own.

During the 1960's and before, the decision to break with the *zafra* was not irrevocable, but in 1970, because of great unemployment in northwest Argentina and increasing mechanization, some plantations decided to demand that the *contratistas* hire only men who had worked the year before in the *zafra*. Thus the break from the *zafra* meant that the urbanite had to feel relatively secure in the city.

OPERATING UNITS

Operating units have been suggested by Adams as a way of differentiating social organizations in terms of varieties of internal power organization. Power organization leads, in turn, to greater or lesser control over the environment, that is, to more effective and stable adaptation or less. An operating unit is:

a set of actors sharing a common adaptive pattern with respect to some portion of the environment.... [It] is a concept that permits us to compare all kinds of groups that survive. A central feature of the adaptation of an operating unit is its control over the environment, its technology (in the broadest sense) of handling or processing energy forms and flows. Adaptation involves changing these controls.... (Adams 1973:120–121).

For present purposes we will consider five types of units, discussed by Adams, in order from least to most powerful: identity, coordinate, consensus, majority, and corporate.

The least powerful operating unit is an IDENTITY UNIT. This consists of an aggregate of individuals or other kinds of units that share a common or parallel adaptive stance to the environment and, moreover, recognize this fact. However, beyond this simple identity, this identification of commonality, there is no coordinated behavior, no intentional interaction, no interdependence.

The identity unit has no intrinsic power by virtue of its organization beyond that individually held by its members. To actually increase the effectiveness of the adaptation of the unit, there must be some coaction, some coordination. For this, identity is a prerequisite. The COORDINATED UNIT is one wherein the component actors or units enjoy coordinate relationships, i.e. they are of roughly equivalent power with respect to each other, and through one or more of a variety of interests or commonalities, they interact, provide aid, etc., and generally establish a balanced reciprocal behavior.

Although the coordinated unit provides its various members with the advantages of the help of others, the unit as a whole, especially if it is a large one, is incapable of taking any extensive action on problems. It is principally a device whereby the individual's own abilities and capacities are enhanced through the collaboration (in these cases) or conflict with others. There is no centralized decision making in a coordinated unit, and its boundaries may be extremely ambiguous and shifting. Centralization of decision making reflects a major increase in the ability of a unit to cope with problems of the environment and, specifically, it allows the coordination of the members to be directed toward the solution of some problem in a way deemed to be for the common good. The minimal basis for this centralization is through the collective choice of the members, who allocate to some individual the right to make decisions; when this occurs, we have a CONSENSUS UNIT.

A unit of somewhat greater power is the MAJORITY UNIT. Whereas in the consensus unit members may withdraw support and leave when they so desire, in a majority unit the presence of a loyal majority provides the leader with what is equivalent to an independent source of power (composed of the power allocated to him). In a majority unit the leader can use the majority membership to coerce deviant members to fall into line. In situations in which maintaining order within the organization is necessary for effective action, the majority unit will prove more effective than the consensus unit.

Consensus and majority units are based fundamentally on power allocated to a leader by the members. Given this support, the leader, depending upon his own skill and ability, may use his backing to achieve things for the group as a whole. However, this kind of power base is no stronger than the collective power of the individual members, and when those members are wage laborers in a disadvantageous market, even their collective power may not amount to enough to solve some of their problems.

If a further increment of power can be added to that allocated by the membership to a leader, he may be able to accomplish even more. Usually when this happens, however, the amount of power that is being exercised by the leader grows beyond the administrative capacity of a single individual and thus the leader finds that he must delegate power back to selected members of the organization in order to get both internal and external tasks done. When this happens, there is so much power in the organization that we recognize a new type, the CORPORATE UNIT.

MIGRATORY STAGES AND OPERATING UNITS

We will now correlate the operating units just described with the labor types set forth earlier. In Table 1 the labor types have been ordered to suggest the general direction of migration from relatively stable Bolivian peasantry to relatively stable urban proletariat. Of course, individuals may follow any of the paths indicated in Figure 1. The different patterns of migrant participation in the operating units is discussed beginning with the identity unit and progressing in the direction of increased power to the corporate unit.

Identity Units

Migrants in all of the labor types participated in the most elementary operating unit: the identity unit. Here we are dealing with the Bolivian migrant who is ethnically distinct from most Argentines but whose relative identification differs from instance to instance. Among other

Table 1.   Presence or absence of different types of operating units in different labor types of migratory stages, with summaries of variations in adaptive circumstances

Labor types of migratory stages	Adaptive circumstances	Types of operating units (see also Table 2)				
		Identity	Coordinate	Consensus	Majority	Corporate
Bolivian peasantry (resident in Bolivia)	Peasant adaptation good so long as man-land ratio permits. This deteriorates, and forces community fragmentation, with families seeking work elsewhere	X	X	X	X	X
Rural semi-proletariat (resident in Bolivia and Argentian)	This is transitional, with peasant families retaining peasant residence part-time and mobile labor part-time. Success permits return to peasantry; failure forces shift to full-time mobility.	X	X	X	very slight	X
Rural mobile proletariat	This is the least secure and adequate condition. Individuals and families seek any more secure circumstances.	X	very slight	0	0	0
Rural shuttle proletariat	This ambi-rural condition gives some stability by more secure jobs, but residence is still uncertain. Income improves.	X	X	0	0	0
Rural stable proletariat	This provides single rural residence, but income is usually somewhat less than the rural shuttle proletariat receives.	X	X	0	0	0
Rural-urban proletariat	This provides superior residence, greater advantages for children, some alternative income sources, together with advantage of high *zafra* income.	X	X	X	very slight	very slight
Urban proletariat and self-employed	If work and income permits, this provides the greatest security and stability.	X	X	X	X	X

Bolivians, the identification has relative degrees of intensity: those from the same village or town, those from the same region. The Bolivian identification provides the migrant with a basis for seeking help in his initial stages of adaptation.

As the migrant's control over the environment improves, however, his relative identification based on ethnicity or common village antecedents is confronted by the fact that he is taking on more Argentine identification, and that this occurs as he becomes increasingly involved in more complex units that are themselves dependent upon the Argentine environment. Thus, although the migrant may never lose his Bolivian identification, he begins to take on other identities which, in turn, begin to provide a basis for entering into relationships in other kinds of operating units.

The Bolivians often arrive as individuals or in nuclear family units, occasionally with other dependents. These units collectively may be said to form an identity unit. Although each individual identifies with other individuals, the families recognize the presence of other families. Because the actual migrant unit varies from the single individual to the family unit, the totality may be seen as a massive extensive fragmented identity unit, characterized by parallel behavior but no coordinated activity.

Coordinate Units

The individual extended families that are found among the migrants are specific instances of the coordinated unit. This unit, of course, is important for the peasant farmer, as well as for the rural proletarian who is very dependent upon his employer for his work security. Yet in some cases, Bolivian families that have found permanent work on Argentine farms feel put upon by their relatives who would also like permanent or temporary work. The same seems to be true for the rural shuttle proletariat, although to a lesser degree because their situation is seen to be more precarious by both their relatives and themselves.

Bolivian urban proletariat in Salta see the extended family, a coordinate unit, as being of immense importance. Relatives are a key source of aid in obtaining employment, although, as we shall see later, not the only source. Extended families may share living facilities and in some situations pool resources to make investments.

The rural-urban proletariat are in many cases even more dependent upon the extended family to care for their children, belongings, and, perhaps, homes while they are working in the *zafra*. In some cases the mother stays in Salta while the father and older children go to the *zafra*. But the woman has an important role in the work team on the plantation, and if she is healthy and able to leave the children with relatives, she will often join her husband. The same is true for the rural semi-proletariat, who commonly depend on the extended family to take care of their land and animals in their absence. In a sample of fifty rural semi-proletarians, forty-three had livestock, and of these thirty-seven had extended kin taking care of their animals while they were at the *zafra*.

The only type of labor group wherein families do not even participate in a coordinate unit, with a few exceptions, is the rural mobile proletariat, who generally participate only in identity units. Those families who have been rural mobile proletariat for a long period have usually lost contact with their extended kin. There are many possible explanations for this. In some cases, the frequency of moving and the unpredictability of where their next move may take them can make these families difficult to find if they do not write each other.

Nuclear families are also split in this fashion. Parents often lose contact in other regions, because neither has a home base where they can be contacted. For some, the plantation serves as a home base, but families are often put in different work camps every year and the camps are often very isolated. Other families may work for one plantation one year and another the following year. Post-*zafra* work sites may be separated by great distances.

Another factor which influences intrafamily contact seems to be the family's resources. Families that have been highly mobile for long periods of time often do not have the resources or control over jobs, much less the living quarters, to lodge friends or relatives. They control so little of their environment that even the most elementary forms of organization do not evolve.

There are other factors too. In some cases kin live in areas distant from the migratory route of the mobile rural proletarians. Others do not have extended kin, which in turn may help account for their inability to develop a more stable niche in either the rural or urban environment.

Another form of coordinated unit important to some migrants, particularly in urban situations, are networks of "contacts," which are actively and openly developed. Contacts are friends who can be counted on to help in finding work. This is of extreme importance in a non-industrial community where most of the manual jobs are short-term. A good set of contacts is necessary to avoid prolonged periods of unemployment. For Bolivian migrants in Salta these contacts are almost always Bolivian, and often from the same region in Bolivia.

Contacts are less important in rural work because great distances between job sites limit the maintenance and reciprocal aspects. Furthermore, friends are not as necessary for rural workers to find jobs. Work conditions and pay varies between farms, and individuals may seek work on a farm where the patron is known for paying regularly and fairly. But obtaining work under these conditions does not require the maintenance of a network of contacts.

Consensus Units

The most important type of consensus unit among migrants is the voluntary association. Depending upon the village, Bolivian peasants may or may not participate, but they usually do. No Bolivian who is a full-time rural proletarian in Argentina seems to participate in any type of consensus unit. Although participation is not universal, many Bolivian urban proletarians in Salta do participate in varying degrees in a form of voluntary association – the fiesta complex.

The fiesta complex constitutes a series of large, annual fiestas celebrating the saint days of select Bolivian and Argentine saints. Invitations are sent exclusively to Bolivians or children of Bolivians. Sponsorship of individual fiestas changes each year and is restricted to individuals who have acquired sufficient wealth to be able to sustain the expense of preparations. Much of the preparation for the fiesta is shared with relatives and friends. The complex is an adaptive institution, supporting the Bolivians' self-identity as Bolivians in a foreign country. It also serves to acquaint migrants with the economic opportunities within the Bolivian population, and through Bolivian employees, with employment on Argentine firms. Thus for many Bolivians living in Salta, this is a very important type of network.

Another voluntary association in Salta is the Club Boliviano, but its members are mostly of a higher income level than the proletariat who work or worked in the *zafra*. Bolivian food is served, and national Bolivian holidays are celebrated in parties that are open to the public. These functions are occasionally attended by low-income Bolivians. To some extent the Club is interested in promoting the image of Bolivia and Bolivians in the community and has the support of the Bolivian consul.

Majority Units

In Salta, residents of each *villa* belong to a *villa* association – a majority unit – and these, in turn, are joined together in a federation which includes almost all of the *villas* as well as the *barrios*. There are no predominantly Bolivian *villas*, contrary to popular opinion in some Salta circles. In 1970 only one *villa* president was Bolivian and he was elected in a *villa* with a majority of Argentines. The residents of each *villa* elect a president who represents them at the federation meetings. He is a powerful figure in the *villa*, not only because he has been allocated power by *villa* members, but also because he is occasionally delegated power from the city government.

The *villa* associations have some influence with the city government. The president of the federation may have frequent visits with the mayor of the city, depending on the situation and the mayor. The associations petition for a wide variety of needs – paved streets, extension of city water pipes and electricity, child care centers, etc. They are important operating units utilized by urban residents to gain access to city services and facilities that otherwise might remain unavailable to them.

Because it was more common for the former *zafreros* who were urban proletarians to have their own lot and house than it was for the rural-urban proletariat, the former were more actively involved in the *villa* associations and the associations tended to represent their needs more fully. In contrast, rural mobile proletariats, who often lacked control over their housing situation, did not belong to any such associations. Rural proletariat also had no power in this area because they usually lived in housing provided by their patrons.

Corporate Units

Among the Bolivian migrants we can distinguish four kinds of corporate units. First, there are the national, provincial, and municipal governments, under which all residents are controlled. These are unavoidable and therefore do not enter into the choice procedures of the migrant, but they may be said to form part of his environment. Second, there are the corporate sugar plantations and other farms that employ the labor here under study. The laborers choose to work in these establishments, but in so doing they automatically place themselves within a corporate unit. However, it is not a corporate unit within which they have any allocative decision-making participation, and, as in the case of the government, it allows no real choice, but is implicit in the adaptive decision to work in the sugar cane harvest and is therefore environmental in nature.

Finally, there are two kinds of labor unions. The first is that which represents all sugar workers in the province of Jujuy and in which membership is obligatory, as monthly dues are extracted by the company from each worker's pay. Once again, membership in this form of corporate unit is implicit in *zafra* work, and so choice procedures are not open.

The second kind of union, however, is a variety open to workers during the post-*zafra* period. Urban proletarians who formerly worked in the *zafra* often belong to construction unions, bakers' unions, and a variety of other unions. Some rural-urban proletarians also belong to unions, especially construction unions, but they constitute a much smaller percentage than the urban proletariat. To a lesser degree, some rural proletarians belong to either one or two rural worker unions, FUSTCA (*Federación Única de Sindicatos de Trabajadores Campesinos y Afines*) and FATRE (*Federación Argentina de Trabajadores*). But neither the rural mobile proletarians nor the rural shuttle proletarians in this sample belong to post-*zafra* unions. Participation and membership in unions generally give workers greater control over their work environment. The inability to get work in unionized situations or to organize their own unions is a major problem for many of the workers.

TENDENCY TO MOVE TOWARDS ORGANIZATIONAL COMPLEXITY

We have examined the types of operating units relevant to the adaptation of migratory agricultural workers associated with the *zafra*. In this section we will examine the proposition, suggested by the ethnographic material, that people have a tendency to try to move toward situations of higher organizational power and complexity.

Table 1 suggests that certain migratory patterns have a higher probability of leading to one stage than another. For example, it is difficult for the rural mobile proletariats to accumulate sufficient capital to buy enough productive land to become independent peasant agriculturalists. It is easier for them to get work as permanent workers on farms or plantations. Based on open-ended interviews with hundreds of rural migratory workers, it appears that individuals in all of the stages have a strong preference for being independent peasant agriculturalists, preferably in their *pago*, or homeland. Independent peasant agriculturalists are both settled and working their own land instead of that of someone else; both things are deemed important. The one exception to this preference is among young men who used the opportunity to work in different parts of Argentina as a means of seeing the world.

General feelings often articulated among the stable rural proletariat and rural shuttle proletariat suggest a preference for agricultural work, but at the same time a dislike of being employed labor. In a sample of forty rural-urban proletarians in the city of Salta, a majority stated a preference for rural life if they had enough good land. In another sample of fifty rural semi-proletarians from southern Bolivia, eleven indicated they were probably moving to Argentina in the near future, but only because they could not support themselves on their land in Bolivia, even with the additional income of the *zafra*.

In general, the status of the rural semi-proletariat is one that is clung to by families unable to support themselves fully as independent peasant agriculturalists. In many cases, survival on their land can be maintained only with income from seasonal work. The *zafra* is regarded as a necessary evil. The sample of rural semi-proletarians showed that the *zafra* provided more than fifty per cent of their annual income.

If the migrant worker cannot become either an independent peasant agriculturalist or a rural semi-proletarian, his actions are colored by many factors, foremost of which are the size of his family and the age of his children. Life histories of migrant workers bear out the fact that the preference is generally to minimize multiple moves and to reduce insecurity. The first few years after arrival in Argentina, Bolivians who remain in Argentina during the post-*zafra* period move frequently. Over time, many either settle down in one area more or less permanently or become rural shuttle proletarians.

Of all of the stages, that of the rural mobile proletariat creates the most hardships for a man and his family. It is a stage that many workers have to pass through, and some never leave. A limited labor market, employers' avoidance of hiring people permanently, the seasonality of agricultural crops, the workers' scanty formal preparation, and limited resources combine to prevent many families for years from settling in one spot for more than three or four months at a time. The people caught in this process are extremely marginal, with very little control over their environment. They are also very atomistic, operating separately and participating in only the most elementary operating units.

The rural shuttle proletariat pattern is seen as a more secure alternative than the rural mobile proletariat pattern because it eliminates the waste of time, money, and energy allocated to finding work. Furthermore, in contrast to the stable rural proletariat, it makes it possible to continue working in the *zafra*, with the relatively high pay. Aside from the biannual moves, the major problem as seen by the workers is that they are at the mercy of the patron on the post-*zafra* farm, often accepting low pay and poor living conditions in exchange for the post-*zafra* security. Seldom do they receive the worker benefits required by law, such as the monthly allowances and milk for their children. Like the rural mobile proletariat, they do not belong to any powerful operating units.

Most rural shuttle proletarians tend to view their situation as transitional, or at least seem to hope it is. In a sample of twenty-one persons in this category who were asked about future plans, all but five suggested that they earned more at the *zafra* than they would if employed full-time on a farm, but they hoped eventually to become stable rural proletarians. The others hoped to return to family farms in Bolivia. Although the stable rural proletarians residing in Argentina have a position of security desired by many migrants, the security is usually only relative. Given the option, workers generally prefer large farms or plantations where unions (corporate units) exist and where government labor laws are adhered to.

In much of the literature on urbanization, push and pull factors have been suggested as the major reasons why rural migrants move to the city. Although the "bright light" theories of urban pull are probably applicable in many situations, in regions where rural employment exists as a viable alternative, it is often considered more practical than city life and work. For example, of the eleven rural semi-proletarians who were moving to Argentina, not one planned to move directly to an Argentine city, all choosing rural employment. Yet if they could have been assured of a good job in a city, the consideration might have been different.

Many migrants seem to feel more comfortable working as laborers on farms or plantations than with the prospect of moving to the city. The low level of formal education of the migrants is one factor responsible for this feeling. The mean number of years of schooling in a complete universe of two sugar plantation work camps totaling 456 men was 2.4 years. In a nonindustrial city like Salta, there is a large labor pool of unskilled workers from which employers fill a limited number of jobs; this allows them to maintain low wages, in some cases lower than those paid in rural areas during harvests. Although the rural migrant laborers may perceive permanent work on a plantation or farm as the most practical solution, there seems to be a general consensus that life in a city like Salta would be better than working on a farm, assuming a good job could be obtained. But the general impression is that such work is not available for people with their skills.

Yet some migrant workers do move to the city, almost on an experimental basis, with the hope of becoming established urban residents. In the sample of forty rural-urban proletarians living in Salta, all but three planned to become full-time urban residents eventually. They disliked the annual move to the *zafra*, but were unable to give it up because they had not become established in the city. The three who did not want to be urban residents hoped to go back to family farms in Bolivia once they had saved enough money; the farms were being run by their parents. This option did not exist for the others.

In a sample of Bolivians living in Salta who used to work in the *zafra*, all but the few skilled workers considered it easier to get permanent work in the country than in the city. With the exception of two men, however, they felt that life in the city was better than working as a rural proletarian because the worker had more options, could buy from more than one store, did not have to live in the housing of the patron, and could find more work in a smaller geographic area if he decided to leave his employer. They saw the rural-urban proletariat type as unsatisfactory because of the necessity of moving twice a year, but also as a stage that could develop into permanent urban living.

As urban proletarians or self-employed urbanites the Bolivians participate in a variety of operating unit types including consensus, majority, and corporate, which influence aspects of their environment ranging from housing to work conditions. The most powerful units are not ethnically homogeneous but include both Argentines and Bolivians who share common problems in the environment.

In summary, migrants seeking greater security attempt, although not always successfully, to move into environments in which they can participate in more formal and powerful operating units. In each situation the most powerful groups are ethnically heterogeneous.

CONCLUSIONS

The significance of this evident tendency to move into societal situations which permit greater degrees of organization has more to do with the evolutionary process than with questions of motivation. At the emotive level, we are probably observing a process of seeking greater security in job and residence, not some nebulous need for organization. At the evolutionary level, however, we are observing the process of natural selection and the survival of the fittest and, indeed, a microscopic and contemporary replaying of the shift from nomadism to agriculture that has been enacted so often by humanity in the past.

Table 2. Detail summaries of kinds of empirical operation units existing within each type of operating unit for each labor type

	Identity units	Coordinated units	Consensus units	Majority units	Nonobligatory corporate units
Bolivian peasantry *(in Bolivia)*	Bolivian; common territorial antecedents	Community and kin reciprocal relations, especially extended families	Participation in community affairs	Community and extended family social control	Bolivian community organization; fragmentation
Rural semi-proletariat *(in Bolivia / in Argentina)*	Ditto above New identification with migrants from Bolivia in Argentina	Ditto above Important reciprocal help among migrants in Argentina; dependence on migrant relatives	Ditto above None in Argentina	Ditto above None in Argentina	Ditto above None in Argentina
Rural mobile proletariat	Ditto above	Fragmentation suspends or destroys coordinate relations; kin contact lost over long time periods; nuclear families fragment	None	None	None
Rural shuttle proletariat	Ditto above, with identification as labor on specific farms	Increased stability enhances reciprocal dependence relations; re-emergence of extended family	None	None	None (except possible occasional ranch union membership; no supporting data)
Rural stable proletariat	Ditto above	Ditto above	None	None	Occasional rural union membership
Rural-urban proletariat	Ditto above; new identification as resident of specific Argentine urban locale	Ditto above; with increased dependence on extended family, especially during rural phase	Fiesta complex	Some participation in *Villa* Association if on owned urban lot	Some participation in urban labor unions
Urban proletariat and self-employed	Ditto above; with loss of migrant and rural identification	Ditto above; (but no further rural phase)	Fiesta complex Club Boliviana (Salta)	*Villa* Associations of lot owners	Labor unions in urban occupations

(Rows from Rural mobile proletariat through Urban proletariat and self-employed are grouped as "in Argentina.")

The fact of stable residence permits a higher degree of organization, just as the income possible permits a greater input of time and effort into the organizations. The ability to participate in progressively more highly organized units may or may not reflect some psychic need of the individual, but it clearly means that he is participating in a social unit that is more powerful and that can, as a consequence, protect him better and provide better for his individual survival prerequisites.

Survival of the individual consists of either fragmentation or unifying solidarity of social units, depending on what is appropriate. The break away from Bolivian peasantry takes place as a rational response to the fact that the peasant households can no longer survive in communities of households on increasingly diminishing inputs. The scattering takes place via the transition to the rural semi-proletariat. Even this, however, is not adequate for many families, and many move further to a condition of continuing rural mobility. This clearly is the least secure form of adaptation, and one that permits almost no organization beyond that of the migrants' households and whatever mutual help may come from familiarity with others in the same situation.

Circumstances, both periodic and catastrophic, then buffet the migrant laborer and his family, sifting and winnowing such that different alternatives are found among the varieties of rural proletariat situations. In Table 1, the "adaptive circumstances" are summarized for each of these labor types, and in Table 2, we detail and summarize the kinds of organizational units that were discovered in the course of Whiteford's investigation in northwest Argentina. It is quite clear, as Figure 1 indicates, that there is no return desired from the higher organized Argentine adaptations to the lower. The only return spoken of is the possibility of a return to Bolivia, to enjoy the same degree of success and organizational security that has been achieved in Argentina. But because this is seldom possible, the Bolivian is increasingly urbanized and enculturated into the Argentine context. He never loses his Bolivian identification, but he assumes new, additional identities in an increasing number of Argentine operating units, so that his ethnicity becomes increasingly diluted.

Unfortunately, the history of many Bolivian households makes it it clear that it is by no means a fixed conclusion that all will achieve urbanizing success, any more than it is certain that any evolving community will successfully improve its adaptational status, or that all its members will fare equally successfully. A great number of Bolivians continue in Argentina as rural mobile labor, with occasional periods of greater stability. They are the powerless, having neither the wherewithal to form or join superior organizational units nor, therefore, to benefit from the increased power that would be available to them were it possible to achieve such forms.

REFERENCES

ADAMS, RICHARD N.
  1970   *Crucifixion by power*. Austin: University of Texas Press.
  1973   "El poder: sus condiciones, evolución y estrategía." *Estudios Sociales Centroamericanos* 4:65–141.
WHITEFORD, SCOTT
  1972   "Bolivian migrant labor in Argentina: a second cybernetic case." Paper presented at the 71st meeting of the American Anthropological Association, Toronto, Canada.

Comments
The End of the Age of Innocence
in Migration Theory

JANET ABU-LUGHOD

Once upon a time we understood — or thought we did — the causes of migration, the uniformities and patterns of migratory movements, and the social and personal consequences of geographic mobility both for the movers and the units into which they moved. Whether described in terms of a mathematical "gravity flow" model on the geographic level, in terms of a "push-pull" model on the economic level, or in terms of a psychic cost "adaptation" model on the sociopsychological level, the resulting picture was reassuringly simple. Human beings, like iron filings, were impelled by forces beyond their conscious control and, like atoms stripped of their cultural and temporal diversity, were denied the creative capacity to innovate and shape the worlds from which and into which they moved.

All this is past; at least we may hope so. But in place of the satisfying closure offered by previous theories we find a treacherous morass of only dimly charted and far too complex terrain. The general "lay of the land" seems to be lost, leaving each researcher to explore in depth the six-foot plot allotted to him. Today's studies frequently err in the direction of straight ethnographies. Each recounts the "peculiar customs" of a unique band of migrants. Often there is little ability to distinguish just what is particularly unique about a given case, what is generic to a set of cases (and indeed what constitutes such a set), and what is, if not universal, at least somewhat usual or common to many types.

The purpose of theory should be to provide a sufficiently broad and systematic cognitive map of the migration process so that individual researchers can locate their findings within a larger framework of variables and processes. Once this has been provided, findings from individual studies can increasingly yield cumulatively meaningful results. This has not yet occurred in the field of migration, for our theory has lagged far behind the empirical work. The latter, however, has been impressive in the past decade; without it, in fact, we should scarcely find ourselves so desperately in need of theory revision.

Substantive work on migration, to which the present volume makes a significant contribution, has yielded a far greater degree of diversity than prior theoretical formulations could have anticipated. Diversities have been uncovered over time, thus allowing us to formulate a number of models of historic types of migration and to "unhitch," as it were, migration theory from modernization theory, an alliance which, while useful, was also blinding. Diversities have also been discovered across space. Culture areas have been found to vary greatly with respect to the pervasiveness, acceptability, selectivity, and mechanisms of adaptation to temporary and permanent population movements. Third, the monolithic category called "migrant" increasingly has had to be broken down into a complex array of subtypes, based upon the variety of forces operating to stimulate the move, upon the periodicity and degree of permanent commitment related to the move, and upon the location of migrants within the social structures of both sending and recipient units. Finally, paths to adjustment have turned out to be not only highly variable but not quite predictable, even within the same migrant type in the same culture area at the same point in time. Indeed, the concept of adaptation itself has often had to be rejected as a meaningful descriptive term, because we are no longer sure to what, indeed, migrants are required to adapt.

As these diversities have come to be expected, studies in migration have lost their defensive and argumentative tone. Authors seldom waste time now refuting existing theories, or feel the need to defend their work on the grounds that is provides a deviant case casting doubt on time-honored assumptions. In short, much deadwood has been cleared away, and far more aspects of the terrain have been delineated, albeit roughly. Migration theory appears ready to move ahead again.

The articles in this volume reflect in sensitive fashion the present state of the field. They represent, on one level, a highly eclectic mix — ranging from the broad historic-demographic national case study at one extreme to a set of personalized case histories at the other. Yet on another level the studies share certain basic assumptions which, while they remain largely unstated, indicate that the authors have operated under a common framework of theory which lies closer to the emerging paradigm than to the one which guided but also often restricted the field at an earlier time. We may be able to elicit this set of common assumptions, and, further, place each of the articles within a wider context if we examine the kinds of questions raised and answered in the studies that follow.

First, the articles share a basic respect for the continuities of migration over long periods of time and acknowledge therefore the need to examine any migration within the historic context of its occurrence. Brian du Toit's article on language and ethnicity as factors in African migration begins with the reminder that "the continuous movement of peoples has been one of the main characteristics of African society." The fascinating account of Balkan migration patterns by Joel Halpern illustrates with virtuosity and erudition that the roots of present population movements in that region lie firmly embedded in premodern patterns of migration, as do many of the adaptive mechanisms. Further, as he argues so convincingly, "motivations for mobility... are not simply conditioned by perceived economic opportunity... [but] are perceived through a cultural screen in which conditioned historic perspectives play a key role."

These historic perspectives constitute the essential data in the careful demographic analysis by Alfredo Lattes of international immigration and internal population redistribution in Argentina over the past century. Argentina constitutes a particularly crucial case because it has been, second only to the United States, the recipient of the largest number of international migrants and, with 60 percent of its population now in cities, has obviously undergone substantial rural-to-urban migration. Lattes traces these movements over time, allowing us to explore specific sociological questions concerning the effects of migration on the social structure and class cum-ethnic cleavages of an entire society.

Second, the articles all question, either implicitly or explicitly, the relevance to their non-Western foci of inquiry of the migration theory developed largely in the United States and Western Europe. Most ignore, or at least appear not to expect to find in their research sites, many of the phenomena — social and personal disorganization, the breakdown of family ties, the onset of impersonality — associated with migration in Western theories. They appear to accept the fact that cultural variations produce migrant types and migration patterns that are simply unaccounted for by accepted theory. T. G. McGee argues, for example, that only by substituting twenty-eight class and "modernization" variables in place of the "urbanism as a way of life" stereotype was he able to make sense and system of the data collected from 560 Malay household heads living in Kuala Lumpur, most of them migrants. His respondents held too many contradictory attitutes to be subsumed under a unidimensional set of concepts.

The basic, persistent, and strong force of kinship (and its extension, ethnicity) is assumed by all authors to operate in the migration process, and because they are looking for it, they find it. Halpern documents its importance in Yugoslav migrations, du Toit notes its pervasive role in African population movements, and Cardona and Simmons stress its recurrent appearance throughout Latin America. This latter point is specifically confirmed in the more detailed study of one Latin American example by Whiteford and Adams. In all fairness, it should be pointed out that once Western researchers were resensitized to the role of kinship through a rash of comparative studies, they also began to notice the operation of this force in more familiar examples.

Variations in migrant types and in alternative paths of migration are documented in all the articles in this volume. Up to this point, theory has focused largely on one central type, with variations viewed as deviant. That "type" was the rural migrant who left his village to live permanently in a large city quite removed geographically, culturally and in terms of easy communication from his place of origin. As cases are drawn from a wider range of societies at different levels of development and in different culture areas, however, this type has receded into the background, or at least has taken its proper place within a far larger array of possible types.

Persisting linkages between rural and urban areas are now stressed, rather than the discontinuities, and the temporary or periodic migrant now receives as much attention as the permanent mover. Du Toit's article classifies African migrants on the basis of periodicity, distinguishing among three types of temporary migrants (the weekly commuter, the seasonal but circular migrant, and the sojourner whose point of reference and future intent lie in the village despite years of residence in the city) and several subtypes of permanent migrants. McGee documents these variations in Kuala Lumpur and attempts to measure them through an index of urban commitment. In short, he takes as a variable what was previously assumed to be a constant.

Rural-to-urban migration is also viewed as only one of several possible types of migration. The other two are: urban-to-urban migration, now a common form in Western societies at advanced levels of urbanization, but also to be found in Yugoslavia which has been exporting workers to the industrial centers of western Europe; and rural-to-rural migration, the major focus of Whiteford and Adams' study of Bolivian farm workers used in Northwestern Argentina to help in the seasonal sugar harvest. This latter type of migration has traditionally been overlooked in migration theory. But in societies organized around non-industrial means of living, it obviously still plays an important role in generating population movement and yields a new set of potential paths for future migration as one of its consequences. Whiteford and Adams identify a number of these trajectories, some of which ultimately feed a more permanent stream of proletarian migration into urban-industrial centers.

There are two final similarities which characterize the approaches followed or recommended in the various articles included in this volume. Both are related to strategies for dealing with the greater complexities uncovered. First, migration is viewed as a complex, multi-staged decision-making PROCESS, rather than a single-time and irreversible decision or move. And second, the migrant is viewed as a coherent personality with a relatively unique set of characteristics that form a configuration or PATTERN which must be grasped if his adjustment is to be predicted; single dimensional traits cannot be expected to predict either decisions to move or adjustive mechanisms after the move.

The strongest plea for treating migration as a decision making process comes from Brian du Toit who argues persuasively against push-pull or indeed any other unidimensional system for explaining migration. He suggests that migrants must be viewed as social actors subject to complex sets of conflicting pressures and interests which indeed change over time and in the very act of decisionmaking. The typology set up by Whiteford and Adams in many ways illustrates the theoretical prescriptions of du Toit, but with an added caveat. They note that because migration is not a once and for all "decision" so much as it is a gradual weaning away from one set of identifications and one social system to another which cannot be fully anticipated, the migrant's path cannot be neatly predicted. Once on his way, he is buffeted by chance, catastrophe, etc. and is as much a temporizer in the interests of survival as he is a "decisionmaker." The latter term may be too dignified, implying as it does greater control over life than a migrant often has.

McGee makes an equally strong plea for treating the migrant not as some collection of random traits but as an organized "holistic" system of personal, socioeconomic, and situational variables which can best be grasped through his method of constructing migrant "profiles." The profiles incorporate wherever possible the migration history as well as the characteristics of the migrant at one point in time, thus allowing an analysis of migration trajectories as well as migrant types. What McGee does on the level of the individual Cardona and Simmons attempt on the aggregate level. In the process they generate a number of hypotheses derived from Latin American data which might be tested profitably in other locations. They posit a "migration history" and cycle in which motives, selectivity and adaptation mechanisms characteristic of large numbers of movers change in the long-term process of the cycle.

All of these innovations augur well for a quantum jump in the power and general applicability of the migration theory now being generated. To some extent, changes on the value level may be responsible for the shift in the perspectives that are generating these new approaches. In the older paradigm, stability was valued and migration was, if not quite feared, at least viewed as an aberration or "disorder." Migration was considered a problem, and the application of migration studies was often directly linked to "controlling migration," reducing its impact, "keeping 'em on the farm." This view seems to be rather thoroughly rejected in the articles which appear here. It may well be that our increased willingness to accept change has led to a renewed interest in the positive effects of one of the most universal and powerful forces for change ever known — the movement of peoples.

PART TWO

Adaptive Patterns

Types of Migratory Patterns to a Small Dominican City and to New York

NANCIE L. GONZÁLEZ

Santiago de los Caballeros, in the Dominican Republic, lies in a long, narrow valley called the Cibao. If one travels in a southeasterly direction, this valley continues as part of the very fertile intermontane basin called the Vega Real. A northwesterly direction leads to the dry, almost desert Northwest Line and the Haitian border. However, a southerly or northerly route very soon leads one into the cool mountain areas of the Cordillera Central to the south or the Cordillera Septentrional to the north (Unión Panamericana 1967 :7, Figures 1, 2).

The original research plan for this study was to observe the migratory process as peasants moved into Santiago and to observe the continued interaction, if any, with their home territory. In order to accomplish this, two research assistants, both graduate students in anthropology at the University of New Mexico, lived in a rural area which was undergoing heavy out-migration toward Santiago and elsewhere. As the principal researcher, I lived in the city itself, where I investigated institutions of the city and patterns of living among the various social segments there. The materials were collected primarily during the period from June 1967 to August 1968 in the city and environs of Santiago.

Observation soon showed that there was more than one pattern or life style amongst persons moving to Santiago. After carrying out a quantitative study on the social characteristics of the total number of migrants from the original rural area chosen for study, I decided to explore in depth the life histories of one group of siblings, some of whose members had moved during their lifetime into the city, leaving the others at home. This led to the discovery of a different set of migrant characteristics. I will contrast here what appeared to be two distinct means of coping with urban life and try to account for the differences between them. I will also attempt to show that the differences are in part attributable to different institutional structures in the rural areas from which the migrants came, and in part the result of the way in which the migrants are received in the city, including the effects of institutionalized racism.

My assistants lived in and studied a small rural community in the Cordillera Central. I will henceforth refer to this area and to the culture studied as of the Sierra. (In manuscripts of their own, my colleagues have referred to the community they studied as Hatillo, and I will also use this name when necessary [Geffroy and Geffroy 1970].) The rural area which I studied, using the quite different methodology outlined below, I will refer to as the Flatlands. Both were tobacco and subsistence crop communities lying only a few miles outside the city of Santiago, although in different directions.

In Hatillo, the economic base was subsistence agriculture supplemented by irregular cash cropping of peanuts, beans, maize, and tobacco. In addition, a few households also engaged in small scale cattle raising and dairying. Many households also carried on some handicraft in order to supplement the family income.

Historical evidence suggests that the people of the Sierra have been there since at least the turn of the seventeenth century (Geffroy and Geffroy 1970:3). We know that the earliest Spaniards, having found gold in the Sierra, built several forts in this area during the early part of the sixteenth century; however, it was not until after most of the Indians had been decimated and the Spanish population relocated from the northern coast to the interior in the early seventeenth century that there were many permanent settlers.

Judging by the physical appearance of the people today, the original Spanish settlement has been virtually endogamous since early times. The phenotype is one of the most Caucasoid to be found anywhere in the Republic, with many of the people having blondish hair and light blue or green eyes.

The Geffroys have described the landholding system, which they believe derives from the early Spanish custom of granting common lands to a group of persons, often relatives, who agreed not to partition the holdings either during their lifetimes or in later generations. Individuals inherited the right to use land within the common holding and the rights were often translated into shares, much as in a corporation. In time, the shareholders who had inherited their rights became known as members of a *sucesión* [succession].

At the present time, according to the Geffroys, the *sucesión* may agree to partitioning. This requires legal action, entailing the payment of fees to the government. Sometimes, too, informal arrangements among heirs as well as informal negotiations with strangers or outsiders take place as members of the *sucesión* begin to seek their fortunes elsewhere, either in another rural area, or more commonly, in a city of the Dominican Republic or in the United States.

The household structure, marriage, and kinship patterns seem related to the landholding patterns briefly described. Thus, legal marriage rates are higher here than in the country as a whole. Consensual unions do occur, but they are most often a prelude to actual marriage. Furthermore, it was not common for persons to contract more than one marriage during a lifetime except in the case of death of a spouse. It would appear that, although this particular area had never been ideal for agriculture, when population pressure was slight and when cattle keeping was more prevalent, a decent standard of living could be achieved. However, as population increased, with a resulting larger number of shareholders claiming rights to a particular common landholding, it became more difficult to make a living by traditional means. Still, the difficulty of "selling out" kept many of the persons, even after they had physically left the community, more closely tied to their ancestral home than might otherwise have been the case.

Before I discuss the life of the Sierran migrants in Santiago, let me give a brief description of the Flatlands pattern with which I will be contrasting that of the Sierra. Although historical records for this area are even more scarce than for the Sierra, local tradition suggests that the community was once part of a sugar plantation, probably growing some tobacco and other crops as well. The early historian, del Monte y Tejada, has indicated that the whole area under the jurisdiction of Santiago was engaged in this sort of cultivation and in herding livestock at that time (1890:91). A note in the local municipal archives strongly suggests that a French immigrant had a plantation in approximately the spot now occupied by the community we studied. It is also known that some of the larger plantation owners in this area had slaves up to the time of the Haitian invasion in 1805, and many retained them until Haiti conquered the eastern portion of the island in 1822.[1] It is probably

---

[1] During this early colonial period there were large landholdings in the southeastern portion of the area which were primarily exploited as cattle ranches. It was only in the later decades of the nineteenth century that these areas became increasingly devoted to sugar. There were a few small sugar mills in the south during the early sixteenth century, but these were abandoned at an early date. The plantations in the Cibao of which I am speaking here seem to have been devoted primarily to sugar and tobacco.

due to these historical facts that the present population of the Flatlands is predominately Negroid, in sharp contrast to that described for the Sierra. Although one finds an occasional light-skinned person, endogamy seems to have kept the population more Negroid than otherwise. Although the most common Dominican physical type is mulatto, the Flatlands stands out, along with a few other communities in the Cibao Valley, as being extraordinarily black in relation to its neighbors.

In the Flatlands I heard of no common lands such as those described by the Geffroys for the Sierra. In each generation siblings work land owned by their fathers or mothers, but the land is permanently subdivided upon the death of the parent-owner. Because all children, regardless of sex, inherit equally, this ultimately results in extreme fractionation of the land. In 1967 and 1968, when this study was being done, the average landholding in the Flatlands amounted to less than fifty *tareas* per sibling group, according to informant estimates. In the case of the particular family studied, the elderly grandmother, still alive, upon whom all the others depended for their "rights" to the land, had exactly thirteen *tareas*. As she had fifteen living adult children, most of whom at the time of the study had several offspring, it is clear that the third generation had little hope of remaining in the area unless they found another source of subsistence.

On the other hand, in each generation, upon the death of the oldest living landholder, it is common for some of the children to sell their rights or their "pieces" to one or several of their siblings. As there is the possibility of inheriting through both mother and father, landholdings are sometimes separated by some distance, which makes it impractical for them to be worked efficiently. In such cases, trades may be made, or sales will be effected so as to reconsolidate the lands. Nevertheless, notwithstanding these types of regulatory mechanisms, population expansion has made it impossible for all the inheritors to remain on the land. In this, the situation in the Flatlands is like that in the Sierra.

The use to which the land is put is also similar. That is, the plots are planted with subsistence items, but are reserved for a small cash crop of tobacco during four months of the years. Unlike the Sierra, cattle are not kept, although an occasional pig and an assortment of chickens and ducks are to be found. These tend to be used either for family food needs, or as a kind of savings account to be converted into cash when emergencies arise.

However, household and family organization tend to be quite unlike what has been described for the Sierra. Legal marriage is the exception rather than the norm, and there is a very clear and definite matrilinear bias in the household and family organization. Indeed, my informants, part of a set of six uterine siblings, all had different fathers. Nevertheless, several of them knew their fathers and maintained cordial relationships with them, although they had little contact with their fathers' other relatives. There were clear differences in the ways in which they related to the two parental sides. Their mother and her relatives were by far the more important, and although they might appeal to their fathers for financial assistance in loans and help in getting jobs, they had little hope to inherit land from them, even though some of the fathers did have landholdings.

A common mechanism used in the Flatlands for helping a woman raise her children is to send the latter, especially the boys, to the city at an early age in order to live with and serve middle or upper class families there. In the group of six siblings I studied, the two eldest boys had been sent to Santiago at the age of about eight years. The third child, a girl, was mentally retarded and still remains in the *campo*, where she is cared for by the larger extended family. The fourth child, also female, remained in the *campo* until the age of sixteen, when she went to Santiago to work as a domestic for an American family. She has now migrated to New York where she lives on welfare with her first illegitimate child, fathered by a Dominican in New York who is married to another woman. The fifth child, a son, is still in the *campo*, where he helps his mother raise subsistence crops and tobacco, using traditional techniques. He claims to prefer the countryside and would like to remain there if at all possible.

In addition to a very small parcel of his grandmother's land, he and his mother also farm a small plot on a sharecrop basis. This land belongs to a local resident and former common-law mate of the woman, who did not, however, father any of her children. The youngest child, a girl, now seventeen, for a long time lived in the household of the man just mentioned, cooking his food, washing his clothes, and being fed, clothed, and schooled by his bounty. Now a young adult, she has made it clear that she does not wish to remain in the countryside, and has made several attempts to leave the bosom of the extended family to seek her fortune in Santiago. However, she does not care for domestic work and is unskilled in other areas. Aside from prostitution, there seems to be little that she can do to earn a living if she does not find a man with whom she can set up housekeeping. She has already engaged in one such temporary mating, but no children resulted. Meanwhile, she moves back and forth between country and city, living for a time with one relative and then with another until she is ejected, usually because of her refusal to work and her extravangant, even flamboyant, behavior.

The oldest males, now in their late thirties, have remained in the city, although it is significant that the living patterns they have chosen differ. The oldest is fairly well adjusted to city life in every way. Indeed, he appears somewhat out of place when he and his wife visit the old family homestead, on an average of once a month. He is employed at a candy factory where he makes eighteen dollars a week. His wife is unemployed, although she does pick up odd jobs now and then through the church, with which she and her husband are closely affiliated since passing through the *Cursillo de Cristiandad*, a movement which is of considerable importance among some sectors of the Dominican population. This couple has been married both legally and in church, this being practically unique in the history of the man's family.

The woman had two children, both of whom died, by another man before she met her current husband. Since then she has never become pregnant. Wanting children very much, fearing that God was punishing them for their unmarried status, they prepared themselves according to the doctrine of the church and were married while I was in the field. As of this writing, some five years later, she has still not become pregnant. They now accept this fate, attributing it to physiological deficiencies rather than to an act of God. It is clear even to them that their present standard of living, poor as it is, would be far worse if they had a series of children to feed and clothe. They now have become adherents of the "doctrine" of family planning and give lectures on this at various functions sponsored by the Church. The dietary pattern, dress habits, and general way of life of this couple shows clearly their desire to be upwardly mobile. The wife spends a good deal of time doing fancy handwork, which she claims she cannot sell because she would have to ask so much money for it that there would be no customers. Instead, she gives the items as gifts to members of her family, and to various middle and upper class patrons – usually persons she has met through the church and who have been kind to her and her husband in one way or another.

The second oldest son also lives with his common-law wife and four children in the city. However, rather than live in the center of town as does his older brother, he has purchased a small plot of land in a so-called *urbanización* in a *barrio* which is literally marginal in its location to the city. It costs fifteen cents and takes about half an hour by public taxi to get from their *barrio* to the downtown area. However, on their plot they have built a small, four-room, wooden house with running water in the yard, plus a very small kitchen garden to one side. The husband occasionally rents a plot of land near the *barrio* where he plants tobacco. After the harvest and during the rest of the year he works for the tobacco processing plant in Santiago. His wife also works there, doing jobs which are almost exclusively delegated to women – sorting and grading the leaves, and sometimes stringing them for drying.

They are unable to gauge their exact weekly or monthly income, because it is variable with the season. The work for the tobacco company is not done on any regular contract basis, the workers being hired by the day as the company needs them. When both are working and when the operation is in full swing, they may earn up to the equivalent of six dollars and fifty cents daily between them. In such cases, the mother of one of them comes in from the nearby *campo* to care for the small children. It is noteworthy that the Flatlands area is within forty minutes walking distance of this marginal *barrio*. The journey to the Flatlands from the center of town where the elder brother lives costs one dollar and fifty cents to two dollars by special taxi and even then many taxis will not make the trip during the wet season for fear of becoming mired down on the country roads. Thus the second brother has much greater access to his natal environment than his older brother.[2]

The second brother and his family, by all outward appearances, have remained *campesinos*. Their house style is exactly like that in the Flatlands, the dress style of neither the man nor the woman has changed, and their food patterns seem to be identical to those of their country relatives.

Although this second son has at various times suggested to me that he "might" marry his common-law wife, it is not likely that he will do so in the near future. Neither is it likely that either will leave the other for another mate. In fact, the marital unions of both of these brothers seem to be remarkably stable, compared with the situation among their siblings and antecedents in the countryside. I suggest that in both of these cases the urban environment has proven to be an economic improvement over that in the countryside, and that they have worked out a reasonable life style which allows them to cope with the problems of poverty within the confines of monogamy. It is also significant that their younger brother, still in the *campo*, has fathered at least one child out of matrimony with a woman who does not live in his house. As already noted, their

---

[2] The taxi ride from the marginal *barrio* to the center of town cost fifteen cents. It is true that the inner city brother might have taken a taxi to the *barrio* and then walked. However, the route by foot passed through many fields, muddy paths, and included the fording of two or three streams. The type of clothing worn by this brother did not lend itself to making such journeys, particularly if he and his wife were also burdened down with presents of food and other items, as they frequently were. The taxis charged more because they had to take a circuitous route, and also ran the danger of getting stuck in the mud, as indicated above.

sister in New York has one illegitimate child, and although she states that she has no intention of adding to this number, her chances of remaining as she is seem slight. The youngest girl has already passed through one mating experience and will undoubtedly have several others before she settles down, if ever, with one mate. She is likely to keep searching for a suitable man who can support her, and end by having several illegitimate children by different fathers, as occurred in the case of her mother.

Now let us briefly examine the kinds of urban living patterns typical of migrants from the Sierra. Using names given me by the Geffroys, following their census of the rural community, I conducted a survey of all the Hatillo migrants, asking questions about household structure, education, income and expenditures, and marriage and family patterns. Some of the results of this may be found in González (1973). I will briefly recapitulate some of the data reported there.

The Sierra migrants were relatively well educated: 31 percent had gone to school for more than six years, although only 20 percent had actually completed the sixth grade and only 11 percent had never gone to school. These figures become more meaningful when they are compared with estimates for the Dominican population as a whole. According to reports of the 1970 census, 53 percent of the population fifteen years of age and over have had three years of instruction or less and 29 percent have never gone to school. The Flatlands migrants also appeared to be typical in terms of the countrywide data, although two of the six siblings had completed the sixth grade, and the others had attended school for only a year or two. However, it should be recalled that the two oldest boys had been placed with city families at an early age, where they acquired their education.

The Sierra migrants showed patterns of relative marital stability when compared with countrywide data. Only fifteen of the ninety-three adults in the sample had had other unions prior to their present arrangements, although 49 percent reported that they were either single or living in common-law union. The Geffroys (1970) believe, however, that the marital patterns of these city migrants indicate a trend towards decreasing rates of legitimacy in marriage, and a probable rise in the number of secondary and tertiary marriages when compared with rural custom.

Thirty percent of the Sierra migrants claimed that they still owned land in the rural zone, but this should be understood in relation to the previous discussion concerning landholding patterns. Clearly, many of these people do not intend to return to their country lands except to visit, and sooner or later they will probably dispose of them as the *sucesión* splits up. However, if things go poorly in the city, their rural holdings and position in the *sucesión* give them some security. The Flatlands migrants, on the other hand, had NO hope of returning to the rural area, for they realized that their chances of inheriting a usable plot of land were nil. The second son did engage in agriculture, but as a sporadic, rather than regular, commercial activity, and the youngest son, still with his mother, may end by consolidating a few parcels of siblings' shares if he is able to raise the money through one means or another. He may also simply continue working as a sharecropper for the rest of his life.

Several of the Sierran migrant families lived in fairly affluent, middle class neighborhoods. Although a few lived in *barrios* marked by extreme poverty, the people themselves (and my observations of them) indicate that they were doing relatively well in the city. On the other hand, many of these people lived fairly well in the countryside too. Their higher levels of education enabled them to seek and find a variety of wage-paying jobs in the city and some of them had opened small businesses which gave them considerably more income than they could ever have hoped for in the countryside.

The statistical materials available from the Hatillo migrants study in Santiago showed that of the thirty-four males, thirty-one, or 91.2 percent, were employed at the time of the survey. Of these thirty-one employed, four declined to give figures on their incomes. However, of the remaining twenty-seven, thirteen, or 48 percent, earned from two to sixteen dollars weekly. Another ten (37 percent) earned from seventeen to sixty dollars weekly. Four (15 percent) reported earning between 147 and 380 pesos per week. I should note that the latter figures are extraordinary for the Dominican Republic. To give the reader an idea of what these mean, a graduate sociologist, with a master's degree in that field from an American University, employed in Santo Domingo, earns 400 pesos a month.[3]

The picture for women is quite different, and not as clear-cut in analysis. Seventeen females reported that they were employed. Twenty-eight females reported themselves unemployed, but it is unclear whether these women, all of whom were acting as housewives, were actively seeking work, or whether they merely would have accepted employment if it had appeared. The ideal situation for this group is that the married woman remain in the home as a housewife. On the other hand, many

---

[3] At the time of the research and even now the peso is officially evaluated as the equivalent to the dollar. However, a black market has long existed by means of which a clever person can secure from 10 to 18 percent more for American dollars. This is one reason why the remittances from the United States are even more valuable than it would appear on the face.

women carry out both their domestic duties and work either part-time or full-time inside or outside the home. Some of them are dressmakers, or hairdressers, or make things at home to sell. Therefore, this figure of unemployment is not comparable to that for the men. Of the seventeen women who reported themselves to be employed, only fifteen gave information on income. Eleven earned between two and sixteen dollars per week and four earned from seventeen to sixty dollars per week. No woman earned more than sixty dollars per week.

Figures concerning present or past unemployment are also revealing for this sample. Ninety-five percent of the men claimed that they had never been unemployed for as long as a month. Ninety-one percent of the women claimed the same thing. One man claimed that he had been unemployed for three months and one for as long as eleven months. Of the women, on the other hand, one reported she had been unemployed for eight months, one for twelve months, one for twenty-four months, and two for ninety-nine or more months. It seems likely that the last four women, at least, were not actively seeking work, and it is also probable that many of the remaining women who claimed never to have been unemployed were actually housewives. I feel that the figures for female unemployment in this survey are very unsatisfactory. I produce them here merely to point up some of the problems in securing this kind of information in urban areas.

On the other hand, the Flatlands migrants (and on this and other matters I rely not only upon the six siblings and their experiences, but also upon what they and their neighbors told me of other migrants from the Flatlands) have little education and their opportunities in the city are fewer. Employment is irregular and not highly remunerative.

There are two additional factors, which I cannot document as clearly as I would like, but which I nevertheless believe are important in understanding the differences between the two sets of migrants described in this paper. The first has to do with the fact that many Sierrans have gone beyond Santiago to Santo Domingo and even to New York City to seek their fortunes. Many of these send remittances to their relatives in the *campo* as well as in the city of Santiago. Indeed, even though not receiving remittances, nearly every family in the rural community studied had at least one relative in New York City or elsewhere in the United States to whom they could turn if they themselves decided to migrate. I have described these migratory patterns elsewhere (Gonzalez 1970), and a recent doctoral dissertation (Hendricks 1971) provides additional data on their way of life in New York.

It has been well documented that migrants crossing international or even regional borders tend to follow relatives, being helped over the initial difficulties by kinsmen who take them into their homes, teach them proper patterns of behavior in the new environment, and find them jobs. In this regard, I think it is significant that when the Flatlands woman, now in New York, first sought a visa for the United States, she had absolutely no idea of how to go about it. She counts not a single relative in all of New York, and only one, an aunt, living in Santo Domingo. Nevertheless, as I was able to help her get a residential visa for the United States, she searched for someone from the Flatlands who might take her in upon her arrival in New York. After waiting three years, during which time she lived elsewhere in the United States, she finally heard of a woman from the other side of the community who offered to let her live in her house until she could become established. It turned out that this woman ran a boarding house in New York City, and although the family of the young migrant had assumed that she would care for their daughter and sister as a friend and neighbor, this turned out not to be the case. Indeed, the young woman today in part blames her former landlady for her pregnancy and consequent "disgrace" in having an illegitimate child, as the landlady was "not careful" about the comings and goings in her house.[4]

Having now spent a total of five years in the United States, three of them in New York, this young woman is well versed in the coping mechanisms used by Latin immigrants to this country. However, she has not been able to arrange for any of her siblings or other relatives to come to New York. Apparently it takes a larger cooperating group to assist would-be migrants to make the initial arrangements, whether they be legal or illegal. My informant has still not given up hope, however, and continually speaks about bringing her mother to help her care for her child so that she may get off the welfare rolls and return to work in the garment industry.

A few years ago, when I did research on the problem, Dominicans were not heavily represented on welfare rolls in the United States. My informant from the Flatlands now estimates that 70 percent of all Dominicans in New York are receiving some kind of governmental assistance. Although her estimate is certainly not to be taken as quantitative data,

---

[4] It is important to note that this informant was extremely eager to have this child, even though it was to be illegitimate. Furthermore, she wanted to bear it in the United States so that it would be an American citizen. Her entire family considers her to be quite fortunate in this regard, even though there was a certain amount of chagrin expressed when the father of the child abandoned the mother completely.

it does say something about her own personal network in New York City. I have not at this time the kind of evidence needed to prove it, but I suggest that those Dominicans on welfare in this country will generally NOT be Sierrans or other Dominicans with similar cultural and social backgrounds, or (and this is not an independent variable) those who have extensive kinship networks in New York.

In explaining why these patterns should so differ, and why the Flatlands people have not been able to establish themselves financially as successful urban residents in the same way as those from the Sierra, I believe that the racial factor cannot be ignored. In recent years it has become fashionable among social scientists as well as among politicians to pretend that racial differences are not important, or indeed are nonexistent. The Dominican Republic prides itself, in contrast to the United States, as its citizens believe, on having no racial prejudice. Nevertheless, it cannot be purely by chance that the majority of the lower class is dark-skinned, while those in the middle and upper classes tend to be lighter. In short, the pattern is very similar to what is found in the United States and elsewhere in Latin America.

It is particularly illuminating that in a study on poverty in another Dominican village not far from Santiago, Susan E. Brown (1973) found that darker-skinned women tended more often to live in free unions than their lighter-skinned neighbors, and that they were viewed by the rest of the community as being poorer, even though Dr. Brown was able to document that their living patterns were actually more adequate in terms of providing good nutrition, good housing, and a lower infant and child mortality rate.

I suggest that in the Dominican Republic and in the United States the darker-skinned migrants will have MORE DIFFICULTY in making the necessary adjustments, and in perpetuating the migratory pattern amongst their relatives. I do not suggest that this is due to any inherent deficiency in their genetic composition; indeed I specifically reject any such suggestion. On the other hand, I do suggest that the attitudes of the larger society in both the Dominican Republic and in the United States make it more difficult for these persons to succeed by not allowing them full access to educational and employment opportunities. Indeed, their situation falls into the self-fulfilling prophecy category in that their lack of success is then used as evidence that they cannot perform and they are therefore not EXPECTED to behave as do whites. The moral imperatives which weigh so heavily upon lighter-skinned persons with different culture are often but hollow words to the blacks. Here again, I must refer to Susan Brown's work in a village containing both blacks and whites.

Even though some of the white women were living in extreme poverty and coping less well than the blacks, they placed such a high value upon monogamy, marital legitimacy, and fidelity that they were rendered unable to engage in the more viable serial mating patterns of their darker-skinned neighbors.

On the other hand, all Dominicans, as is the case in most Western Christian nations, including our own, recognize that the societal norms include marriage sanctioned by the church and state. Indeed, they prefer this whenever possible, but many do not really EXPECT it to be possible for themselves. Such persons also know, through experience and through the examples of their parents and even grandparents, that the world will not come tumbling down upon them if they mate more than once, even several times. In this sense, as in some of the studies of divorce in the United States, for example, it might be said that illegitimacy runs "in families," not because of any genetic, psychological disposition, but merely because one adopts the living patterns, attitudinal sets, and philosophical bases of one's own family.

True, breaks with tradition occur, and in both directions. Thus, in the case of Jorge and Angela, the eldest couple in my group of sibling in-informants, their desire to become part of the middle class is apparent in many aspects of their life today, including their decision to be married in the church. The other side of the coin, as Susan Brown has demonstrated, is that in recent years a few of the white women in her village whose ancestors would have frowned upon serial mating have resorted to this as a means of coping with their poverty (Brown 1973). We know far too little of how these changes take place, but study after study of migration or of migratory patterns indicate that extreme changes in life style often accompany the move to a new location.

It is also possible in many cases, as I have tried to show here, to migrate to a city and end by living very much as one might have before the move. This is reflected not only in the case of the second Flatlands couple, living in a marginal *barrio* of Santiago much as do country relatives, but also in the case of the young woman in New York City who is following, unwittingly perhaps, in the footsteps of her own mother when it comes to marital patterns. Unlike her mother, however, United States welfare in the form of Aid to Dependent Children, has given her the freedom to decline new temporary male partners – at least for the time being. Whether other societal pressures will urge her into another sexual relationship and another pregnancy remains to be seen.

Many have suggested, when discussing Puerto Rican migration to New York, that color differences become far more apparent in the States than they might have been at home. I am not sure that I agree that the differences are so great. However, what does seem clear to me is that the darker-skinned Dominicans (and probably Puerto Ricans) tend not to associate themselves with American blacks or even with West Indian blacks living in the United States. Rather, they are drawn to other Dominicans or at least to other Caribbean Hispanos. The latter groups are only recently beginning to form ethnic pressure groups capable of improving the conditions under which many of them live in the United States. In some places, such as in parts of New York City and Boston, local neighborhood interest groups have sprung up and are beginning to make themselves heard. It is my impression, although I cannot document it, that the leaders of such groups from the Spanish-speaking countries involved tend to be the lighter-skinned migrants. Black Americans also have pressure groups, but because black Spanish-speaking persons tend not to align themselves with these, the black Spanish-speaking individual is left without effective representation at higher levels of socio-economic integration.

In summary, I am suggesting that the attitudes toward racial characteristics held by the leaders of the larger society in many ways condition the circumstances under which the darker-skinned migrant is allowed to move. Furthermore, this racial bias is frequently unrecognized because of the tendency to submerge race into culture on the one hand, or to deny its existence on the other. In the long run, of course, such circumstances prevent the darker-skinned person from benefitting by the move the way the lighter-skinned person does. This, in turn, sometimes leads the lay person and, unfortunately, some scientists as well, to suggest that the darker-skinned are somehow inferior – either through lack of intelligence or through some other psychological characteristics which prevent them from operating as they "should" in the new environment.

My concluding note is that migration of peoples from one country to another should be examined not only in terms of the macro-socio-economic conditions, but also in terms of the micro-environments between which they move. In some ways these micro-environments may be very different, and in other ways they may turn out to be quite similar to those of the home territory. In either case, I urge that greater attention be paid to these matters in understanding the patterns by means of which different categories of persons cope with the stresses and strains said to accompany the migratory process. The data presented here are offered as an example of how cultural and social definitions of race may mold the urban migrant in different ways, depending in part upon his background, and in part upon configurations of the new environment. The net effect is that social patterns of Dominican migrants to Santiago and to New York City tend to resemble those in the country areas from which they come more than they resemble those of each other after migration has taken place. Being in the city, *per se*, is not a sufficiently strong socializing force to create homogeneity.

REFERENCES

BROWN, SUSAN E.
 1973 *Women and their mates: coping with poverty in the Dominican Republic.* Andover: Warner Publications.

DEL MONTE Y TEJADA, ANTONIO
 1890 *Historia de Santo Domingo* (four volumes). Santo Domingo: Hermanos García.

GEFFROY, JOHN, MARGARET VÁZQUEZ GEFFROY
 1970 "The Hato system: backgrounds of a Dominican peasantry". Paper given at meetings of the Society for Applied Anthropology, Boulder, Colorado.

GONZALEZ, NANCIE L.
 1970 Peasants' progress: Dominicans in New York. *Caribbean Studies* 10(3):154–171.
 1973 "Santiago: city of gentlemen," in *Anthropologists in cities.* Edited by George Foster and R. Kumper. Boston: Little, Brown.

HENDRICKS, GLEN
 1971 "Dominicans in New York," Ph. D. dissertation, Columbia University Teachers' College.

UNIÓN PANAMERICANA
 1967 *Reconocimiento y evaluación de los recursos naturales de la República Dominicana.* Washington, D.C.

Social Factors in Migration: The Case of Tzintzuntzeños in Mexico City

ROBERT V. KEMPER

> The aspect of urbanism in Latin America which has been of primary interest to the anthropologist is migration and migrant adjustment. He first became concerned with urbanization through following the peasant to the city.
>
> JUDITH GOODE[1]

During the two decades since Lewis' pioneering fieldwork in Mexico City, in which he suggested that Tepoztlán migrants undergo "urbanization without breakdown" (1952), anthropologists have devoted considerable attention to cityward migration in Latin America. The causes and patterns of migration, its effects on communities of origin and destination, the characteristics of the migrants, and the psychological and economic aspects of their urban adaptation have all been investigated. However, the special emphasis which anthropologists have given to analyzing migrant SOCIAL adaptation reflects a long-standing professional preoccupation with kinship, family life, and social organization and also recognizes the proliferation of social mechanisms by which former peasants cope with urban life.

In the process, formal and informal associations have received particular attention, in large measure as a result of fieldwork carried out in Peru on squatter settlement organizations (Mangin and Turner 1968), regional

Fieldwork in Mexico City was supported by a National Institute of General Medical Sciences Training Grant (Number GM-1224), administered by the Department of Anthropology, University of California, Berkeley.
[1] In: Latin American urbanism and corporate groups, page 152.

associations (Mangin 1959; Doughty 1969), occupational groups (Bradfield 1963), and recreational clubs (Milliones 1970; Escobar 1969). Of course, these sodalities are not mutually exclusive; for example, Doughty (1969:961–969) reports that regional associations often sponsor dances and soccer teams.

But the Peruvian experience cannot be extrapolated uncritically throughout Latin America because differences in "local circumstances, economic development, [and] European influence" (Goode 1970:163) persist among nations and within regions of specific countries. Furthermore, the degree of Indian participation in rural-urban migration also influences the presence of self-help associations (Frank 1970:223). Indian populations with a rural heritage of corporate groups frequently develop new associations in the urban setting, whereas *mestizo* populations without such a background seldom establish or utilize urban voluntary associations. Thus, ethnicity is often a crucial determinant of the specific social mechanisms which peasant migrants select to confront urban life.

The case of Mexico is illustrative. A survey of recent migration and urbanization studies reveals that voluntary associations are significant mechanisms of social adaptation among ethnic groups in southern Mexico (see, for example, Colby and van den Berghe 1961; Folan 1962; D. Foster 1971; King 1967). In contrast, membership in formal associations was relatively unimportant among populations in non-"Indian" regions of Mexico (see, for example, Lewis 1952, 1959; Dotson 1953; Browning and Feindt 1971).

THE CASE OF TZINTZUNTZAN MIGRANTS

Thus, on two counts I was wrong to expect that migrants from the village of Tzintzuntzan, Michoacán (located 375 kilometers west of Mexico City, on the shores of Lake Pátzcuaro) would possess a village-based association such as those reported for *serrano* migrants in Lima. First, Tzintzuntzan's population is predominantly *mestizo*, with less than 10 percent of the villagers defined (by "self" and by "others") as Tarascan Indians. Second, I knew from Foster's longitudinal research (1948, 1967) in the community that corporate kinship groups are unimportant and that formal associations (e.g. the *mayordomía* system) have lost most of their traditional significance. Only later in the fieldwork did I recognize that successful social adaptation of Tzintzuntzeños in Mexico City instead depended on the propitious conjunction of a migrant's personal characteristics and on the urban environment's structural features.

I will describe here the urban social adaptation of Tzintzuntzan peasants in terms of: (1) their utilization of friendship and kinship ties in migrating to Mexico City; (2) their geographical mobility within the metropolis; and, (3) their relations with fellow Tzintzuntzan migrants in the capital.

During the time of my field work in 1969–1970, at least 483 persons were affiliated with Tzintzuntzan migrant households in Mexico City. The distribution was: permanent migrants, 246; part-time migrants, 38; spouses born outside Tzintzuntzan, 39; children born in Mexico City, 116; children born elsewhere, 24; non-Tzintzuntzan relatives, 10; and non-Tzintzuntzan friends, 10. I discovered the neighborhood location for

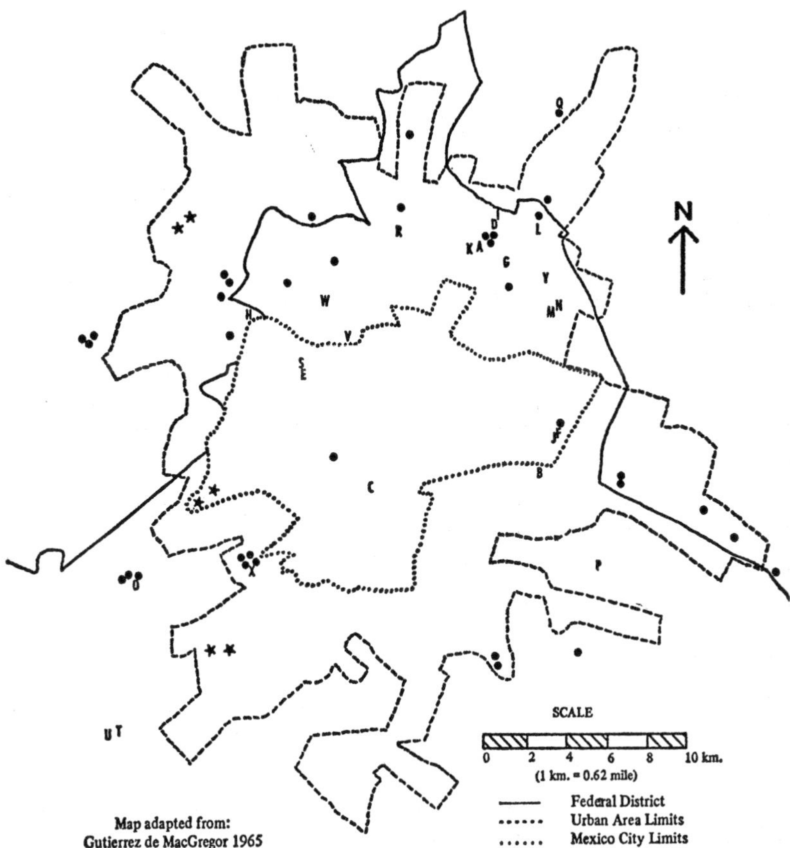

Map. Location of Tzintzuntzan Migrant Households in Mexico City: 1970.

sixty-seven and gathered detailed census and interview data for fifty-one of the seventy-four households in which the Tzintzuntzan migrants resided. Because I have described elsewhere the general approach and specific technical procedures employed in the field work (Kemper i.p.), I shall only mention here that the research yielded data based on personal interviews, casual conversations, detailed questionnaires, household census data, migrant life histories, family budgets, and psychological tests. In addition to these sources of information, the arguments presented here depend on a series of "social relations" interview schedules (N = 39) administered to a heterogeneous sample of adult migrants. This interview schedule was designed to examine the structure and content of migrant social ties and visiting patterns over a twelve-month period. The responses to this interview schedule suggest that some variant of "social network analysis" may be very useful for understanding the migrants' situation in Mexico City. I shall return to this point later.

FRIENDSHIP AND KINSHIP TIES: MIGRATION FROM TZINTZUNTZAN TO MEXICO CITY

Leonides Z. arrived in Mexico City in 1964 at age twenty-three, through the invitation of his uncle José, with whom he lived *arrimado* 'up close to', or 'as a guest', for more than a year. Leonides did not find work immediately but eventually became a laborer in an aluminium construction firm, where he worked for a year before landing a better job at which he is still employed.

The combined pressures of rapid population growth, occupational aspirations, the desire for improved living standards, and better education do not provoke all Tzintzuntzeños to abandon their native community for the glitter and glory of the metropolis. Nor does greater awareness of the outside world, through better access to radio, television, newspapers, and mass transportation, necessarily "cause" migration. Often, as the case of Leonides Z. illustrates, an additional factor — access to friends and kinsmen already settled in Mexico City — tips the balance in favor of a move to the capital. Because potential migrants are well aware that they will need help in order to locate housing and employment when they arrive in the metropolis, ties to previous migrants provide a substantial motivation at least TO ATTEMPT migration to Mexico City. The Tzintzuntzeños are not unique in assaying their situation in these terms; the importance of rural-urban social ties to the decision to migrate is fairly well-established for Latin America, as demonstrated by the studies of Germani (1961:213) in Buenos Aires, Herrick (1965:91) in Santiago de

Chile, Browning (1971:297) in Monterrey, and Butterworth (1962:261) in Mexico City.

SETTLING IN MEXICO CITY: THE IMPORTANCE OF SOCIAL TIES

When Aristeo R. could no longer go to California as a *bracero* 'farm laborer', he searched out a friend in Mexico City with whom he stayed for a year, while his family remained in Tzintzuntzan. Now, Aristeo often jokes about having slept with the dogs in the patio for a whole year, but he is thankful that his friend took him in when he was so desperate. His friend also arranged for Aristeo to hire on as a laborer at a metals factory where the friend was a tenured truck-driver (and a good friend of the boss). After he got the job, Aristeo brought his family to the city from Tzintzuntzan. They have been together in the city for three years and now live near the factory and close to the friend's home.

As Aristeo's case history illustrates, relations with ex-Tzintzuntzan villagers now settled in Mexico City not only influence the initial decision to move to the capital but also affect a migrant's chances for survival. The role of friends and relatives determines the circumstances of a migrant's initial urban adjustment in several ways, particularly with regard to socioeconomic status, location in the city, and job category. Furthermore, the utilization of personal connections lowers the economic and psychic "costs" of departing the village for a "new world." Such social networks thus convert individual migration into a continuing process with a constantly shifting set of actors, each new migrant profiting from the experiences, pleasant and unpleasant, of those who preceded him to Mexico City.

Very few Tzintzuntzeños — less than ten percent of more than 200 migrants for whom I have data — have settled in the capital without the aid of friends or relatives. In fact, most villagers have several potential links that can be activated in the migration process. The manner in which these links are utilized to ensure success in the city is best illustrated in the domains of housing and employment.

Housing

Upon arrival in Mexico City, most Tzintzuntzeños live *arrimado* with relatives or friends, to whom they seldom give money in exchange for room or board. Of course, new arrivals incur obligations, which they may have to fulfill at some undetermined future date; but these are normally considered social rather than pecuniary, and are thus weighed on the balance scale of traditional reciprocity rather than calculated in the coin of urban economics.

The *arrimado* relationship between a new arrival and a settled migrant confirms upon Tzintzuntzeños their initial socioeconomic status. Although the village status system is not homologous with that operating in Mexico City, the migrants have a preference for horizontal social ties; thus individuals at similar steps on the respective rural and urban socio-economic ladders are brought together. For instance, a migrant from a relatively affluent village family will move in with an urban middle class family, the level to which the most successful Tzintzuntzan migrants have climbed, while poorer migrants will settle into the homes of working class Tzintzuntzeños in the city. Thus, affluence assimilates affluence, poverty perpetuates poverty.

Although *arrimado* relations develop between relative equals, a signifi-cant measure of short-term INEQUALITY is inherent in this system. Because the established migrants have access to a valuable store of information about city life, new arrivals become their temporary dependents or "clients." This condition usually persists until the newcomer gets a steady job, finds separate quarters, and brings his own family (if any) to Mexico City. This process may take only a few weeks, but more often requires several months, and on some occasions a year or longer is needed to pass through an *arrimado* relationship.

Residential choice is usually significantly influenced by knowledge gained from a migrant's predecessors to the capital. They often counsel new arrivals on where to find inexpensive housing in neighborhoods relatively free from crime, drunkenness, and other social pathologies. As a result, a recent arrival's first separate residence, often a one-room rented apartment, tends to be located in the immediate vicinity of other migrants or in neighborhoods where Tzintzuntzeños previously have lived. The following case history provides a clear-cut example of this settlement pattern.

Upon arrival in Mexico City, Gabriel P. moved in with his older brother, who was himself staying with two ex-villagers. Gabriel lived there for seven months, then after getting a steady job at a nearby factory, he shared a room down the street with his brother. Gabriel then married a girl he had known in Tzintzuntzan and brought her to Mexico City. After a time, they moved around the corner, and then (after their first child was born) moved into a two-room apartment across the street. These short-distance moves permitted Gabriel to stay close to his brother and his friends, all three of whom still reside in this same neigh-borhood and visit each other regularly.

Employment

In addition to providing temporary lodging for recent arrivals, the more experienced migrants intercede as *palancas* 'levers' or *enchufes* 'plug-ins' to help obtain employment for their fellow Tzintzuntzeños. To the new arrival the *palanca* is treated as an extension of the familiar patron-client ties which he manipulated in Tzintzuntzan (cf. Foster 1967:241–242), in the sense that the senior migrant serves as a culture broker between rural and urban behavioral norms. In contrast, those migrants who perform as *palancas* view the relationship from a different perspective: they gain prestige in exchange for their expert manipulation of the real urban patrons — i.e. their job supervisors and union bosses who actually hand out the jobs. Thus, the *palanca* is neither rural nor urban, but instead represents a widespread Mexican social mechanism which is easily understood and analyzed in terms of village or city standards. As Simmons, Hanson, and Potter (1967:19) have observed, "person to person communication about job opportunities is certainly a traditional mode of search for rural people... and it is the most frequently successful mode of search in the city for unskilled workers." Because most Tzintzuntzeños enter the urban labor market with few, if any, special marketable skills, their reliance on personal *palancas* is understandable. In fact, of twenty-two adult males for whom I have this information, 82 percent had recourse only to friends and relatives in their job search; only 14 percent made use of "formal" resources like labor unions, civil service, or newspaper advertisements; and only 4 percent found work alone, by the method disparaged as *navegando* ['navigating', but in the sense of 'wandering']. Contrast the following case history with those where the *palanca* system functioned:

When Alberto A. arrived in Mexico City, he really didn't know anyone who could help him. So, he lived in the streets for a month while looking for work. He lived on soup and tacos and had little money. Some days he had only one meal. Finally, he found a job.

GEOGRAPHICAL MOBILITY AND URBAN SOCIAL RELATIONS

The few Tzintzuntzan migrants who arrived in Mexico City before 1960 tended to settle in low-rent working-class zones north of the central business district. Later, they prospered in their work and searched for housing in unoccupied peripheral lands while population pressure raised rents and worsened living conditions in the central city. This centrifugal movement also corresponded to increased employment opportunities in the rapidly growing northern and northeastern sectors of the metropolitan area, where nearly all major industries are concentrated. Few Tzintzunt-zeños have participated directly in land invasion schemes in Mexico City, although a few purchased "title" to land sold by the original squatters rather than buying property in a legal subdivision.

In contrast, recent migrants usually proceed directly from Tzintzuntzan to the city's outskirts where they settle initially with friends or relatives and then subsequently search for separate apartments. The high rents and cramped living conditions in the central city and the difficulty of obtaining transportation to distant factories, on the one hand, and access to previous arrivals' hospitality, on the other, combine to alter the earlier pattern of contact with the urban environment.

The change has important consequences for urban adaptation: while relationships between residents of traditional wards in the central city tend to be almost as frequent and intense as those in "closed" rural communities (Lewis 1965:495), slum dwellers are effectively isolated from Mexico City's factory employment opportunities, concentrated on the urban periphery. Thus, Tzintzuntzeños now arriving in the capital benefit economically by moving directly to the periphery, although their social relationships beyond the immediate household may be minimal until they are more permanently settled. In his studies in the city of Oaxaca, Chance (1971:141) observed a similar degree of limited social interaction among "suburban" families.

Parallel findings have been reported for Guatemala City. Based on a study of the populations of two low-income neighborhoods, Roberts (1970:349–350) concluded:

Geographical mobility between city and countryside is matched by geographical mobility within the city. The rapid expansion of the population has radically altered the urban residential distribution. Expansion has far outrun the available supply of urban housing. This has meant increasing densities in older neighborhoods, the spread of the city into outlying rural areas, and the proliferation of shanty towns.... Low-income families change residence frequently in the course of their life cycle, searching for the accommodation whose price, size, and location best suit their needs for the moment. The expansion of the city thus means geographical discontinuity in which neighborhood-based social relations are frequently being disrupted.

The distribution of Tzintzuntzan migrant households in the Mexico City metropolitan area (in June 1970, near the end of the period of fieldwork) is shown on the attached Map. The sixty-seven households for which I have neighborhood information are spread among forty-one urban *colonias*. The most striking features of their geographical distribution are (1) the absence of households from the traditional *herradura de tugurios* 'horseshoe of slums', (2) the concentration of households in peripheral working-class neighborhoods, and (3) the frequent formation of small, extended family "enclaves" in particular *colonias*.

The uneven geographic distribution of Tzintzuntzeños in Mexico City also reflects their entry near the lower end, but NOT at the bottom, of the urban socioeconomic hierarchy. This helps explain their tendency to cluster in working-class neighborhoods and to avoid the poverty-ridden conditions in the city's slums.

While geographical separation in Mexico City destroys much of the migrants' traditional sense of "community" identification, propinquity *per se* does not induce interaction among migrants who lack kinship ties, are of unequal socioeconomic status, and have been in the city for different lengths of time. An example may illustrate:

Five migrant households are located in one neighborhood in the city's northeast sector. Three are located on the same block and contain young migrants who share kinship ties, common occupations, and similar short-term exposure to the city. The other two households are located just three blocks away. These are related to each other by kinship ties, occupational category, and long-term urban residence. Although the two groups are aware of each other's presence in the same neighborhood, interaction between them is virtually nonexistent. In other words, in the single neighborhood are two, NOT one, migrant enclaves.

An important adjunct of geographical separation is the virtual absence of automobiles and telephones among Tzintzuntzan migrants in the city. Unable to contact each other except after time-consuming bus rides, it is not surprising that migrants view distance as a major hindrance to retaining high levels of social interaction with their fellow villagers now settled in the capital. Personal visits are the principal means for conducting social intercourse, but the great distances, sometimes requiring bus trips of two hours and several transfers, combine with the absence of alternative means of communication to severely limit its frequency and intensity. In such conditions, it is little wonder that the migrants feel that the nuclear household and the extended family enclave are more dependable sources of social interaction and economic security than their fellow Tzintzuntzeños in the capital. The lack of interaction is often so extensive that former friends lose contact with each other, and visit only on the rare occasions that they happen to see each other back in Tzintzuntzan during a holiday trip.

MIGRANT SOCIAL RELATIONS IN THE ABSENCE OF A VOLUNTARY ASSOCIATION

The absence of a formal or informal Tzintzuntzan migrant association provides several important clues to their participation in urban life: first, migrant social integration must rest solely on kinship, friendship, or *compadrazgo* 'ritual godparent' ties, often established in the village before migration; second, limited migrant social interaction encourages an outward search for potential urban contacts; and finally, urban adaptation requires a pragmatic analysis of social options rather than an extension of initial dependence on the migrants with greater urban exposure.

As the *arrimado* and *palanca* relationships demonstrate, Tzintzuntzeños in the capital base their social ties on individualistic criteria in which mutual expectations and obligations exist within a system of multi-purpose reciprocity. Foster (1967:212–243) has described in detail the way in which Tzintzuntzan peasants organize social relationships according to the "dyadic contract model." Once settled in the city, the obstacles to continuous social interaction imposed by geographical separation permit Tzintzuntzeños a wider choice of friends with whom they can activate reciprocal relations.

These dyadic social relations provide Tzintzuntzan migrants with sufficient emotional and economic stability so that urban adaptation proceeds without "breakdown." Tzintzuntzeños do not fit the category of "marginal" migrants unwilling or unable to participate fully in the urban social system. On the contrary, the relative weakness of social ties within the migrant population emphasizes the strength of the migrant family and permits easy extension of personal networks into other sectors of the society. To paraphrase Germani (1967:179), the maintenance of strong ties with fellow migrants may ease the initial ADJUSTMENT of new arrivals in the city but need not facilitate their ADAPTATION to urban culture. In the case of the Tzintzuntzan migrants, they utilize ties with those who have preceded them to Mexico City to gain a foothold on a job and a place to live, but after a few months, this dependence usually fades away to be replaced by a search for "outside" patrons, who are correctly perceived to have more access to power than one's fellow migrants.

Under these urban conditions, I found that the insights of social network analysis proved particularly helpful in understanding the totality of migrant social relations without losing sight of the significant differences that exist among individual Tzintzuntzeños in Mexico City. Furthermore, examination of personal networks, based on reciprocal dyadic contracts, shows how Tzintzuntzeños shift from a restricted view of the urban social system to a broadly based participation in social alliances related to occupational and eventually neighborhood commitments. Thus, the "urbanization" of migrant social relations — i.e. the shift from dependence on fellow migrants to a search for ties with other, often more powerful, urban allies — is crucial to their strategies for upward socioeconomic mobility.

In an effort to measure the degree and type of social interaction among Tzintzuntzan migrants in Mexico City, I asked a heterogeneous sample of thirty-nine adults, living in twenty-five households, to report on their relations with 141 other adult migrants between July 1969 and July 1970. (Subsequent census analysis showed that 160 adult Tzintzuntzeños lived in Mexico City during some part of this period. However, I believe that the sample included here is still representative enough for analytical purposes.)

Table 1 lists migrant responses according to type of relationship and Table 2 gives the frequency of migrant visits. Even a cursory examination of these tables demonstrates that knowledge of other migrants varies tremendously and that friendship, kinship, and *compadrazgo* ties are infrequent. If the statistical mean score represents a "typical" migrant, then such an individual would know (i.e. recognize the name of, in most cases) some fifty-three other migrants, would be related to seven, be friends with another six, and perhaps be *compadre* of one more. An analysis of the migrant visiting patterns shows that a "typical" migrant would have visited or been visited by only nine migrants outside his immediate household and would have seen only two or three fellow migrants frequently or regularly.

To proceed from a collection of personal networks to a description of the "total network" of Tzintzuntzan migrants in Mexico City, it would have been necessary to question every migrant about his social relations with all the others. Because this proved impracticable in the field, I shall limit my discussion to those twenty-five migrant households in which the theirty-nine respondents lived at the time of the interviews. I combined these personal links into "household networks" in order to gain a clearer perspective of migrant social relations.

Tzintzuntzan migrants in Mexico City almost always see each other in one of their homes. Nevertheless, the migrants consider their relationships to be individualistic and not binding on other family members. Thus, my analysis of households represents a second-level abstraction from social reality. This approach is justified because the conceptual problems of dealing with a thirty-nine by thirty-nine matrix are reduced and because

Table 1.   Social relations among Tzintzuntzan migrants in Mexico City

| | Respondents | | | | | |
Individual	Household	Not know	Knows	Friend	Relative	Compadre
1	R	110	18	2	11	0
2	A	50	28	56	7	0
3	C	116	12	5	8	0
4	B	90	34	5	10	1
5	C	54	64	10	11	2
6	C	107	16	10	8	0
7	I	117	12	6	6	0
8	D	125	4	3	8	1
9	Q	47	86	3	4	1
10	E	85	45	5	6	0
11	F	13	114	4	7	3
12	G	127	13	0	1	0
13	G	132	2	6	1	0
14	H	42	94	0	5	0
15	A	103	19	7	10	2
16	E	53	73	5	9	1
17	E	16	116	1	8	0
18	S	99	38	1	3	0
19	I	129	8	1	2	1
20	J	24	109	1	7	0
21	H	36	84	13	8	0
22	X	60	70	0	11	0
23	U	139	1	0	1	0
24	W	37	101	0	3	0
25	Y	75	64	0	1	1
26	V	50	86	0	5	0
27	P	75	44	5	14	2
28	J	33	105	2	1	0
29	J	50	86	3	2	0
30	K	47	64	22	8	0
31	K	64	62	11	4	0
32	T	74	44	13	10	0
33	K	113	12	4	11	1
34	L	95	35	2	8	1
35	B	62	58	4	15	2
36	M	82	52	0	7	0
37	N	82	54	0	5	0
38	O	71	57	8	3	2
39	F	29	100	0	11	1
	Mean:	74.7	53.4	5.6	6.7	0.6
	Ranges:					
	Low	13	1	0	1	0
	High	139	116	56	15	3

my data on socioeconomic status and related parameters is derived from household census schedules.

Although the network approach utilized here relies on analysis of

Table 2. Visiting patterns among Tzintzuntzan migrants in Mexico City

Respondents		None	Seldom (1–6/yr)	Frequent (7–24/yr)	Regular (25 +/yr)	Live with
Individual	Household					
1	R	137	4	0	0	0
2	A	134	2	4	0	1
3	C	123	12	4	0	2
4	B	121	15	0	4	1
5	C	124	10	2	3	2
6	C	122	7	6	4	2
7	I	133	6	0	2	0
8	D	130	9	1	1	0
9	Q	134	2	1	4	0
10	E	130	8	1	0	2
11	F	121	17	0	2	1
12	G	138	2	0	0	1
13	G	132	8	0	0	1
14	H	121	10	8	0	2
15	A	133	7	0	0	1
16	E	128	5	0	6	2
17	E	132	6	0	0	3
18	S	137	1	0	2	1
19	I	137	2	0	2	0
20	J	126	11	0	2	2
21	H	134	5	0	0	2
22	X	136	2	0	2	1
23	U	139	0	0	1	1
24	W	136	5	0	0	0
25	Y	140	0	0	1	0
26	V	136	3	0	1	1
27	P	133	6	2	0	0
28	J	107	31	0	2	1
29	J	128	9	0	2	2
30	K	117	21	1	0	2
31	K	127	5	3	4	2
32	T	138	2	1	0	0
33	K	131	7	0	0	2
34	L	137	2	1	0	1
35	B	123	12	2	3	1
36	M	137	1	0	1	2
37	N	137	1	0	3	0
38	O	133	7	1	0	0
39	F	134	3	0	3	1
	Mean:	130.6	6.9	1.0	1.4	1.1
	Ranges:					
	Low	107	0	0	0	0
	High	140	31	8	6	3

relatively short-term social ties, I want to emphasize that I do not conceive
of migrant social relations as forming a static pattern in any way. As
Gulliver (1971:352) has cautioned, this procedure of lifting "something

like THE social network... out of the continuum of social life by analytical procedures and for analytical convenience... introduces a danger that needs to be recognized and guarded against." But in the absence of any association or community units of analysis the social network approach gives a good heuristic approximation of Tzintzuntzeño social adaptation to life in Mexico City.

Table 3 is a matrix of visiting patterns among twenty-five Tzintzuntzan migrant households for the period between July 1969 and June 1970. I have followed Gulliver's (1971:279) suggestion that visiting is "a good indication of an active relationship." Only sixty-four links of a theoretical maximum of 300 (i.e. n[n-1]/2, where n = 25) were active during this

Table 3.   Visiting patterns for twenty-five Tzintzuntan migrant households in Mexico City: July 1969 – June 1970

	A	B	C	D	E	F	G	H	I	J	K	L	M	N	O	P	Q	R	S	T	U	V	W	X	Y	Total
A	-	w	s	w	-	w	w	-	-	-	s	s	-	-	-	-	-	-	-	-	-	-	-	-	-	7
B		-	s	w	-	-	w	-	w	w	w	-	w	w	-	-	w	w	w	-	-	-	w	-	-	12
C			-	-	-	-	s	-	-	w	s	-	-	-	-	-	-	-	-	s	-	-	-	w	-	5
D				-	-	-	-	-	s	w	w	w	-	-	-	-	s	-	-	-	-	-	-	-	-	5
E					-	w	-	s	-	w	w	-	-	-	-	-	-	-	s	-	-	w	w	-	-	7
F						-	-	w	w	s	w	-	-	-	w	s	-	-	w	-	-	-	-	-	-	7
G							-	-	-	-	w	-	-	-	-	-	-	-	-	-	-	-	-	-	-	1
H								-	-	w	-	-	-	-	-	-	-	-	-	-	-	-	w	-	-	2
I									-	w	w	-	-	-	-	-	w	-	-	-	-	-	-	-	-	3
J										-	w	-	-	-	w	w	-	-	w	-	-	-	-	-	-	4
K											-	-	-	-	-	-	-	-	-	-	w	-	-	w	-	2
L												-	-	-	-	-	-	-	-	-	-	-	-	-	-	0
M													-	s	w	-	-	-	-	-	-	-	-	-	-	2
N														-	w	-	-	-	-	-	-	-	-	-	-	1
O															-	-	-	-	-	-	-	-	-	w	-	1
P																-	-	-	-	-	-	-	-	-	-	0
Q																	-	-	-	-	-	-	-	-	-	0
R																		-	-	-	-	-	-	-	-	0
S																			-	-	-	w	w	-	-	2
T																				-	s	-	-	w	-	2
U																					-	-	-	s	-	1
V																						-	-	-	-	0
W																							-	-	-	0
X																								-	-	0
Y																									-	0
Total	0	1	2	2	0	2	3	2	3	7	9	2	1	2	4	2	3	1	4	1	2	2	4	5	0	64

Symbols
"–"   no visit
"w"   weak link
"s"   strong link

Note: To obtain the total number of visits made/received by any household, add the total at end of the appropriate column and row; e.g. the total number of visits made/received by household "J" = 7 + 4 = 11.

A STRONG link is operationally defined as seven or more visits between any pair of households during the twelve-month period surveyed; a WEAK link means six or less visits in the twelve-month period.

period. And only fifteen of these involved "strong" ties, which I have operationally defined as more than six visits in twelve months. The average number of different households visited was only five, and only 24 percent of the households maintained strong ties with another household. At one extreme, household "Y" had no links with any other households; at the other extreme, household "B" had ties with thirteen others.

Active social relations between these migrant households depend on status homogeneity, not status heterogeneity. That is, households of similar socioeconomic status and similar lengths of urban residence are more likely to maintain social ties, especially strong links, than are households in dissimilar categories. Even the *arrimado* and *palanca* mechanisms for initial social adjustment to city life do not truly violate this principle; they occur among persons who define themselves as RELATIVE equals. Middle-class migrants assist relatively affluent villagers, while working-class migrants help poorer villagers.

Status homogeneity, defined in terms of income levels and living standards, explains 67 percent (ten of the fifteen) of the strong ties, and 57 percent (twenty-eight of the forty-nine) of the weak ties between the migrant households surveyed. When defined in terms of length of urban residence, status homogeneity explains 67 percent of the strong links and 53 percent of the weak links between the migrant households. Thus, it is a better predictor of strong social relations than of weak social ties.

Two central features of these social ties merit attention. First, long-term residents seldom visit recent arrivals (except kinsmen). As one migrant who had lived in Mexico City since the mid-1940s remarked, "I don't know very many of the young Tzintzuntzeños in the city; when I lived in Tzintzuntzan, most were still children, and some were not yet born." Second, the social relations of long-term migrants are partitioned by socioeconomic status. Those who have achieved significant upward mobility and consider themselves to be professionals rather than workers, rarely visit with less affluent migrants. As another migrant declared, "I used to visit with some of the poor migrants, but we have nothing in common anymore. They only want to drink and pass the time; there was nothing for me in the relationship, and I always felt uncomfortable."

The principle of status homogeneity also operates in the kinship domain. Among the twenty-five migrant households, there are only thirty kinship-related pairs. Of these, eighteen maintain visiting relationships, with eight strong links and ten weak links. However, in only one case do two kinship-related households with dissimilar socioeconomic statuses maintain a strong link — and they are both recent arrivals. Thus, as Toomey (1970:269) states, "for kin to be contacted frequently and to constitute an influential reference group, they must meet other criteria than the merely ascriptive ties of kinship."

To recapitulate, evidence on socioeconomic status, length of urban residence, and kinship relations indicates that homogeneity rather than hetereogeneity is the rule for most active links between Tzintzuntzan migrant households. Why is this the case? I believe that the answer has both an economic and a psychological referent.

First, migrants recognize that in order to improve their status in the city, they must eventually establish contacts beyond the migrant group. Rather than remain clients of other Tzintzuntzeños, they seek patrons on the job, in the unions, in the government, and in other sectors where opportunity may arise. These patron-client ties are often formalized through the institution of *compadrazgo* 'ritual godparenthood'. A survey of 111 cases of baptismal *compadrazgo* revealed that Tzintzuntzan migrants not only choose relatives as *compadres* infrequently (26 percent versus 33 percent in the village sample collected by Foster (1969)), but they also choose nonmigrants in 69 percent of the cases. Furthermore, *compadres* chosen outside of the Tzintzuntzan migrant group are much more likely to be patrons than equals. In the long run, Tzintzuntzeños limit their demands upon their fellow migrants to persons in positions similar to their own. In this sense, the Tzintzuntzan migrants behave much like the residents of working-class neighborhoods studied by Roberts (1970:378) in Guatemala City:

In their personal dealings, most heads of family emphasize that it is desirable to maintain reciprocity in social relations. Most stated that they preferred to borrow money either from those to whom they also lent or under some system of interest payment where the debt relation is a commercial one. Some neighbors commented that they were no longer able to visit certain relatives, since these relatives were rich and they could not hope to return any favors received.

Status homogeneity also has a psychological aspect. Successful migrants, and those who are defined by others as successful even though they may be fairly poor in absolute terms, feel that *envidia* 'envy' is a major reason for the discontinuity of social relations between working-class and professional migrants in the capital. One middle-class informant divided the migrant population into two sectors — *los inferiores* and *los superiores* — on the basis of whether a person earned a living by using his hands or his head. Another felt that the reason no migrant mutual aid society existed was because *los maleducados* ['the uneducated', with the sense of uncultured] fail to appreciate how such an organization would improve their circumstances. This informant neglects to mention the price that they would have to pay in patron-client relations!

The psychological aspects of status homogeneity even influence relations among kinsmen. Thus, one informant explained that he and his brother both live in Mexico City but never visit each other. He claims that his brother is envious of his success in Mexico City. Because the necessary basis of reciprocity is missing, the two brothers avoid one another. This psychological tension also persists between migrants and villagers. For example:

Gabriel P. is reluctant to have friends who live in Tzintzuntzan visit his apartment in Mexico City. He would prefer to visit them in the village, as he did during Holy Week. His reason is that Tzintzuntzeños criticize his lifestyle — or might do so. He fears that his *compadres*, for instance, will think he lives well and then ask him for economic assistance.

This case illustrates how friendship, and even the supposedly sacred *compadrazgo* relationship, tends to be defined in instrumental rather than emotional terms by the Tzintzuntzeños in Mexico City. As Wolf (1966: 12) has pointed out:

Instrumental friendship may not have been entered into for the purpose of attaining access to resources — natural and social — but the striving for such access becomes vital in it.... In contrast to emotional friendship, which is associated with closure of the social circle, instrumental friendship reaches beyond the boundaries of existing sets, and seeks to establish beachheads in new sets.

CONCLUSION

I have examined here the social adaptation of Tzintzuntzan migrants in Mexico City from three perspectives: (1) their utilization of friendship and kinship ties in migrating to Mexico City; (2) their geographical mobility within the metropolis; and (3) their relations with fellow Tzintzuntzeños in the capital.

Migration to Mexico City thrusts Tzintzuntzeños into a new social world. Once the initial period of dependence on their fellow migrants passes, the great categories of peasant life — "villagers" versus "outsiders" — are inverted and ultimately obliterated through participation in urban life. Kinship and friendship ties are expanded beyond the migrant group in an effort to better manipulate urban economic resources. And urban geographical separation and socioeconomic differences transform traditional attitudes toward social interaction. As the migrants cease to be encapsulated within the Tzintzuntzeño group in Mexico City, they make the shift from social ADJUSTMENT to social ADAPTATION. The expansion in their reference group is a critical phase in their urban success, because involvement with nonmigrants often brings upward mobility. Thus, despite the absence of a migrant voluntary association, Tzintzuntzeños have managed within the space of a decade to establish themselves in stable occupational and social niches in Mexico City. Tzintzuntzan migrants may lack a sense of "community" and be without a voluntary association to call their own, but as individuals they have demonstrated their ability to cope with urbanization.

REFERENCES

BRADFIELD, S.
  1963   "Migration from Huaylas: a study of brothers." Unpublished doctoral dissertation, University of Michigan, Ann Arbor.
BROWNING, HARLEY L.
  1971   "Migrant selectivity and the growth of large cities in developing societies," in *Rapid population growth: consequences and policy implications*. Edited by National Academy of Sciences, 273–314. Baltimore: Johns Hopkins Press.
BROWNING, HARLEY L., WALTRANT FEINDT
  1971   "The social and economic context of migration to Monterrey, Mexico," in *Latin American urban research*, volume one. Edited by Francine F. Rabinovitz and Felicity M. Trueblood, 45–70. Beverly Hills, California: Sage Publications.
BUTTERWORTH, DOUGLAS S.
  1962   A study of the urbanization process among Mixtec migrants from Tilantongo in Mexico City. *América Indígena* 22:257–274.
CHANCE, JOHN K.
  1971   Kinship and urban residence: household and family organization in a suburb of Oaxaca, Mexico. *Journal of the Steward Anthropological Society* 2:122–147.
COLBY, BENJAMIN N., PIERRE VAN DEN BERGHE
  1961   Ethnic relations in southeastern Mexico. *American Anthropologist* 63:772–792.
DOTSON, FLOYD
  1953   A note on participation in voluntary association in a Mexican city. *American Sociological Review* 18:380–386.
DOUGHTY, PAUL L.
  1969   La Cultura de regionalismo en la vida urbana de Lima, Perú. *América Indígena* 29:949–981.
ESCOBAR, M. GABRIEL
  1969   *The role of sports in the penetration of urban culture to the rural areas of Peru.* Kroeber Anthropological Society Papers 40 (72–81).
FOLAN, WILLIAM J.
  1962   A comment on race, class and status differences in Merida, Yucatan, Mexico. *Anthropologica* 9:43–50.

FOSTER, DONALD W.
1971 *Tequio* in urban Mexico: a case from Oaxaca City. *Journal of the Steward Anthropological Society* 2:122–147.

FOSTER, GEORGE M.
1948 *Empire's children: the people of Tzintzuntzan.* Mexico, D.F.: Smithsonian Institution, Institute of Social Anthropology, Publication 6.
1967 *Tzintzuntzan: Mexican peasants in a changing world.* Boston: Little, Brown.
1969 Godparents and social networks in Tzintzuntzan. *Southwestern Journal of Anthropology* 25:261–278.

FRANK, ANDREW G.
1970 "Urban poverty in Latin America," in *Masses in Latin America.* Edited by Irving L. Horowitz, 215–234. New York: Oxford University Press.

GERMANI, GINO
1961 "Inquiry into the social effects of urbanization in a working-class sector of Greater Buenos Aires," in *Urbanization in Latin America.* Edited by Philip M. Hauser, 159–178. New York: UNESCO.
1967 "The concept of social integration," in *The urban explosion in Latin America.* Edited by Glenn H. Beyer, 175–188. Ithaca: Cornell University Press.

GOODE, JUDITH G.
1970 Latin American urbanism and corporate groups. *Anthropological Quarterly* 43:146–167.

GULLIVER, P. H.
1971 *Neighbours and networks: the idiom of kinship in social action among the Ndendeuli of Tanzania.* Berkeley, Los Angeles, London: University of California Press.

GUTIÉRREZ DE MAC GREGOR, MARÍA TERESA
1965 *Desarrollo y distribución de la población urbana en México.* México, D.F.: Universidad Nacional Autónoma de México, Instituto de Geografía.

HERRICK, BRUCE H.
1965 *Urban migration and economic development in Chile.* Cambridge: M.I.T. Press.

KEMPER, ROBERT V.
i.p. "Tzintzuntzeños in Mexico City: the anthropologist among peasant migrants," in *Anthropologists in cities.* Edited by G. M. Foster and R. V. Kemper. Boston: Little, Brown.

KING, ARDEN R.
1967 "Urbanization and industrialization," in *Handbook of Middle American Indians.* Edited by Robert Wauchope and Manning Nash, 512–536. Austin: University of Texas Press.

LEWIS, OSCAR
1952 Urbanization without breakdown: a case study. *The Scientific Monthly* 75:31–41.
1959 *Five families.* New York: Basic Books.
1965 "Further observations on the folk-urban continuum and urbanization with special reference to Mexico City," in *The study of urbanization.*

Edited by Philip Hauser and Leo Schnore, 491–503. New York: John Wiley & Sons.

MANGIN, WILLIAM P.
1959   The role of regional associations in the adaptation of rural migrants to cities in Peru. *Sociologus* 9:23–36.

MANGIN, WILLIAM, JOHN C. TURNER
1968   The *barriada* movement. *Progressive Architecture* 49:154–162.

MILLIONES, LUIS
1970   Deporte y alienación en el Perú. El fútbol en los barrios limeños. *Estudios Andinos* 1:87–95.

ROBERTS, BRYAN
1970   "The social organization of low-income families," in *Masses in Latin America*. Edited by Irving L. Horowitz, 345–382. New York: Oxford University Press.

SIMMONS, OZZIE G., ROBERT C. HANSON, ROBERT J. POTTER
1967   "The rural migrant in the urban world of work." *Proceedings of the Ninth Inter-American Congress of Psychology.*

TOOMEY, D. M.
1970   The importance of social networks in working class areas. *Urban Studies* 7:259–270.

WOLF, ERIC
1966   "Kinship, friendship, and patron-client relations in complex societies," in *The social anthropology of complex societies*. Edited by Michael Banton, 1–22. London: Tavistock.

Ethnicity, Kinship, and Joking Among Urban Immigrants in Ghana

ENID SCHILDKROUT

This paper is concerned with the way in which a traditional ideology of social relations, the idiom of kinship, is used by first generation urban migrants in Kumasi, Ghana, to categorize and contrast intraethnic and interethnic relations. The kinship idiom, and certain prescribed behaviors that are associated with it, including ritualized joking, is used by these migrants to express status relations between ethnic groups in the urban context; to define the boundaries of ethnic communities; and to justify the assumption of kinship obligations within the ethnic community.

Most discussions of urban kinship, particularly in the African context, have ignored the way in which kinship, as a traditional ideology, can be transposed to new contexts to describe emergent patterns of intergroup relations. They have for the most part stressed either (1) the way in which kinship can be used as an adaptive mechanism to help migrants turn complex urban jungles into manageable small-scale communities, (2) the way in which migrants selectively maintain or repudiate ties with relatives in rural areas in order to either eventually return home or advance in status in town, or (3) the "breakdown" of corporate kinship groups in the urban context and the substitutes, such as voluntary associations, that have evolved to perform kinship functions.[1]

Here I am concerned with a very different aspect of kinship – the way in which kinship is used as an ideology or myth to describe something quite other than genealogically based interpersonal relations among biologically related individuals. This use of kinship can, of course, be

---

[1] For a list of references that could profitably be given here see Gutkind (1973, particularly topics 14–17).

described as "fictive;" a traditionally meaningful contrast between the categories of descent and affinity is being used metaphorically to describe and contrast relationships within and between ethnic groups, with little or no attempt to relate this usage to a genealogical map. However "fictive" is too general a term, for there are different sorts of fictions involved, and these predicate different patterns of behavior. Moreover, what is significant is not a distinction between "fictive" and "real" kinship – categories by no means always clearly distinguishable, but rather the relationship between the kinship categories of descent and affinity on the one hand, and ethnicity on the other. Whether genealogical links can be traced or not, the idiom of consanguineal kinship is used within the ethnic community to express solidarity and brotherhood and to justify the assumption of certain kinds of obligations that are associated with kinship. The contrasting idiom of affinity, and the joking behavior that this traditionally prescribes, is used to express the social distance and status relationships between different ethnic communities. Since not all affinal joking is the same, however, particularly in the degree of amity or hostility it expresses, this can be used as a sensitive symbolic gauge to express changing relations between ethnic groups.

There is nothing about this use of kinship idioms to symbolize patterns of intraethnic and interethnic relations that is necessarily urban. It is true that the subjects of this paper are first generation migrants who were born and usually raised in rural areas where kinship is the major means of conceptualizing social relations. After migrating, they apply their traditional concepts of kinship to a new situation and use these to structure part of their urban experience – to justify certain claims upon members of their own ethnic community and to express certain tensions between their own ethnic community and others. However, the same relationship between kinship idioms and ethnicity has been observed in rural areas – by this writer among migrants in rural Ghana and in Upper Volta in Mossi society. The constant features are the juxtaposition of ethnic categories in situations where cultural integration is occurring but where ethnicity continues to be used as a means of conceptualizing status differences. While the importance of the contrast between descent and affinity and the use of joking to express affinal ties may be a characteristically African cultural idiom, it is possible that other symbolic forms are transposed in similar ways in different ethnographic contexts.

THE KUMASI SETTING

Kumasi, today Ghana's second largest city, was the traditional Asante capital, and has been a center of attraction for migrants since at least the early nineteenth century, when it was the center of an extensive empire extending southwards to the Guinea Coast and northwards to what is now the Upper Region of Ghana.[2] After the British conquest of Asante in 1900, the colonial government encouraged the settlement of traders and laborers from northern Ghana and the surrounding countries of Upper Volta, Mali, Niger, Togo, Dahomey and Nigeria. As a result, today approximately half of Kumasi's population of about 250,000 is not Asante, but consists of migrants and immigrants categorized locally as strangers and, in some cases as aliens nationally.[3] About sixty percent of these strangers are categorized by the Asante, by southern Ghanaians, and sometimes by themselves, as "northerners" whether they are from northern Ghana itself or from the surrounding countries. The rest of the strangers in Kumasi are southern Ghanaians or non-West Africans – Lebanese, East Indians, or Europeans.

Despite the diversity of origins of the northerners and their urban born children, these migrants are united by their common status as strangers, their adherence to Islam, their use of Hausa as a *lingua franca*, their predominance in certain economic sectors – mainly trade, unskilled labor, and some crafts – and in many cases by common cultural traditions.

The Mossi constitute one of the largest northern groups in Kumasi. They began migrating to the town as traders and laborers around the turn of the century. Today there are well over 5000 Mossi living in Kumasi, many permanently. Approximately one third of the community was born in Ghana.[4] In many ways the urban born have lost touch with traditional Mossi culture. Like second and third generation immigrants from other northern groups, they are increasingly incorporated into a Hausa-speaking Islamic community known as the *zongo*. Among these urban born immigrants, although ethnicity is still reckoned through patrifiliation and

---

[2]   There was a settlement of northerners in Kumasi in the nineteenth century (see Wilks 1966), but for the most part the community discussed here traces its origins to the turn of the century. For details on pre-colonial Asante see also Wilks (1967).

[3]   The definition of citizenship has changed several times since Ghanaian independence in 1957, but first generation immigrants born outside Ghana and, in most periods, their Ghanaian-born children, have been defined as aliens (see Schildkrout (1970).

[4]   The figures are based on the *Ghana Census for 1960*. The 1970 census is not useful with regard to aliens since it was taken shortly after the government issued orders to aliens to leave the country or register.

is sometimes socially and politically important, it has little cultural meaning, particularly for the urban born. Among first generation immigrants, however, ethnic identity is still associated with traditional values, and cultural similarities and differences between migrant groups can be important as a basis of association and as a standard of evaluation. For this reason the type of joking described below occurs much more frequently among first generation immigrants than among their urban born children.

The Mossi are a Voltaic people, Gur speakers, with close cultural and linguistic bonds with the Dagomba, Mamprusi, Tallensi, Dagati, Grusi, and others.[5] All of these groups are well represented in Kumasi, but this paper focuses on Mossi relationships with the Dagomba and the Mamprusi. Like the Mossi, these peoples have traditions relating to the development of centralized kingdoms in their societies. In Kumasi, they often act as political allies on the basis of their shared traditions. Formerly, when their numbers were small, they were under the jurisdiction of a single immigrant headman.[6] According to the 1960 Ghana Census there are approximately 3000 Dagomba and 500 Mamprusi resident in Kumasi.

In Kumasi, because most of them are Muslims, the Mossi, Dagomba, and Mamprusi are also closely associated with the Hausa, the Yoruba, and other Muslim migrants in the *zongo* community. Social relationships across ethnic boundaries are often very close, interethnic marriage is common,[7] and ethnicity is often totally irrelevant in defining social relations. Nevertheless, in some contexts, ethnic categories are described by migrants as competitors for prestige and for economic and political advantages. This does not mean that the *zongo* can accurately be described as ethnically stratified. There is no single hierarchy or scale which would be accepted by members of all communities, and the boundaries of the ethnic communities themselves are defined differently in different contexts. Nevertheless, ethnicity is still often used as one component, among others – such as length of residence, wealth, Islamic education – in the evaluation of status. It is also, at times, a real basis for differential status, for example when members of an ethnic community obtain for

---

[5]   For ethnographic descriptions of these peoples see among others Fortes (1945, 1949), Goody (1962, 1967); Manoukian (1951), Rattray (1932), and Skinner (1964).

[6]   In Kumasi all ethnic communities with a population of approximately one thousand have appointed their own headmen. (see Schildkrout 1970a and 1970b). The Mamprusi are perhaps an exception to this demographic pattern, accounted for by their tradition of chieftaincy.

[7]   In a sample of 560 marriages among residents in eighty-nine Mossi owned houses, 24 percent of marriages were between members of different ethnic categories. Half of this sample consisted of Mossi migrants; the rest were from many different groups (Schildkrout 1969).

members of their own group resources such as jobs or advantages in particular areas of trade.

IDIOMS OF KINSHIP

Unlike urban born immigrants who have small networks of genealogically close kin, most first generation migrants come to Kumasi with kinship concepts but with few actual kin. Yet for immigrants of both generations kin are still important, and many roles continue to be defined in terms of kinship. Consequently kinship relationships among rural born immigrants, beside those formed through marriage, are often voluntarily contracted, through the metaphorical use of kinship terms and the performance of kinship roles. After a number of years, sometimes generations, kinship ties that were voluntarily created may become indistinguishable from genealogically based ties. When these bonds are first formed, however, people are aware of a distinction between "real" kinship (*dangi sosai*, in Hausa) and the metaphorical use of the kinship idiom. I refer to these two types of kinship as specific and generalized kinships.

Specific kinship relations are those in which the use of a kin term and the assumption of certain roles is justified by genealogical claims. The actual genealogical link may be "fictive," as for example in cases of adoption, but nevertheless each link in a genealogical chain can be specified, whether or not these links refer to fictive or biological ties.[8] Among immigrants in Kumasi specific kinship is almost invariably genealogically close kinship since it usually obtains between people who have, at most, a common great-grandparent. This is simply a function of the short history of the community. Specific kinship is reckoned bilaterally and networks of specific kin consist of closely related consanguines and affines who are not necessarily members of the same ethnic community.

In contrast to specific kinship ties, migrants, particularly those of the first generation, have many kinship relationships which are not backed up by genealogical claims. I refer to this usage of the kinship idiom as generalized kinship. Since the genealogies of most migrants are of short depth,[9] these generalized kin are not distant kin in a genealogical sense.

---

[8] Adoption and the difficulties in distinguishing fictive and biological kinship are discussed further in Schildkrout (1973).

[9] This does not include kin in the north. The extent to which ties are kept up with these relatives varies in different ethnic communities. Among the Mossi very few settled migrants maintain contact with kin outside Ghana.

Generalized kin may be as close as specific kin in terms of behavior. They are related, however, because kin terms have been applied and because the rights and obligations associated with kinship have been assumed. The reason for the use of a kin term is pragmatic and no genealogical justification is needed to explain the usage.

All first generation and some urban born migrants have many such generalized kin based on an extensive use of the idiom of consanguineal kinship. Certain terms, those mainly referring to kin who would traditionally be included in one's patrilineage, are used within the ethnic community with no genealogical justification other than an occasional vague claim of having a common ancestor a very long time ago, sometimes as far back as the group's historic or mythic founder. The idiom is the familiar one of brotherhood, but brotherhood clearly modelled on a concept of unilineal descent.

There are many ways in which such kin relationships are actually contracted. Co-residents in a house, co-workers in the market or on a job, or people from the same home locality, often assist one another at life-crisis ceremonies, providing bride wealth, naming each others' children, financing funerals, and so forth. Relationships of clientage between settled immigrants and newly arrived migrants often turn into such generalized kinship relationships when a patron or landlord assumes roles that the lineage head in Upper Volta traditionally would perform, such as finding a wife for the new migrant. Once such roles are assumed, the use of the kinship idiom is justified and the moral obligations may persist, as long as the rights and obligations of kinship are met, often over several generations.[10]

The particular kinship idiom which the Mossi and other northerners use within their own ethnic community in Kumasi is associated with patrilineal descent. The terms most used in a generalized sense within the ethnic community are those for father, father's brother (same as father – *sama* or *baba*), father's sister, elder and younger sibling, and child. On the other hand, the term for grandparent is used bilaterally and for this reason is rarely used metaphorically within the ethnic community. The term for mother's brother, traditionally extended to all men of one's mother's patrilineage, is never used metaphorically within the Mossi community. These terms, like terms for affines, are only used among Mossi to refer to specific kin.

The term the Mossi use to describe the ethnic community itself is *budu*. This refers to a class or category to which membership is gained

---

[10]   See Cohen's discussion (1969) of the Hausa in Ibadan for similar instances.

through descent. Among the Mossi uterine kin are not in one's *budu*, but all agnatic groups, from lineages of the smallest depth to what is frequently translated into English as "tribe" are *budu*. The Mossi also note the Asante pattern of matrilineal descent and argue that the *abusua*, or matrilineal descent group, is a *budu*.

This generalized use of certain kinship terms illustrates, then, that the concept of unilineal descent is used to define the boundaries of the urban ethnic community. This idiom symbolically identifies a large category of migrants who are potential kin, who are expected to come to one's aid if necessary and who can justifiably make certain demands on the basis of this common identity. However, in defining ethnicity it is clear that the idea of descent merges with that of provenance. For example, Mossi identity is formally conferred by patrifiliation, while all those who claim to be Mossi do so because they, their parents, or grandparents, come from a particular area of Upper Volta, where in contrast to other Voltaiques, they identified themselves as Mossi. Within Upper Voltan Mossi society, however, many people who identify themselves as Mossi in Kumasi would stress other ethnic identities – those that refer to their provenance before incorporation into Mossi society, itself ethnically complex due to processes of migration, conquest, and other forms of social and cultural incorporation. In Kumasi the most recent migration is relevant in defining ethnic categories, but it is clear that in this definition the concept of descent is not easily separable from that of provenance. Nevertheless, given this ideology, the idiom of agnatic kinship is used both to define the ethnic community and to validate the assumption of morally binding kinship obligations.

If ethnicity is conceptually linked to a notion of unilineal descent, it is not surprising that relations between ethnic categories can be integrated into this cognitive system. As was noted above, the Mossi recognize cultural and historical links with other Voltaic peoples, including the Dagomba and Mamprusi. To anticipate the discussion of joking which follows, the Mossi categorize the Dagomba and Mamprusi as affines. On the basis of marriages among the ancestors of these groups, the generalized use of the idiom of affinal kinship is justified, and this in turn elicits the ritualized joking traditionally characteristic of many affinal relationships. This pattern is not confined to Voltaic migrants; many other groups[11]

---

[11] Various Hausa groups have joking partnerships based on cultural and historical ties; the Mossi also joke with Gourma and Wala; the Beriberi, Wangara, and Fulani joke; as do the Gonja, Chokosi, and Dagomba. Zabarma joke with Grusi; Yoruba with Beriberi; and there are others. Not all of these joking relationships are identical, but a comparison of them all is beyond the scope of the present paper.

in Kumasi have similar relationships with culturally related peoples, and the pattern has been observed frequently elsewhere in Africa.[12]

The contrastive use of the idioms of kinship and affinity among migrants in Kumasi can be summarized schematically. In Table 1, if S refers to specific kinship and G to generalized kinship as I have defined these above, then the way these idioms are used to contrast interethnic and intraethnic relations can be illustrated. In Table 1, internal refers to relations within an ethnic category and external refers to interethnic relations. It must be noted, of course, that G, whether referring to kinship or affinity, subsumes S. That is, while the Mossi for example use certain agnatic kin terms in a generalized way within their own group, this does not preclude the existence of specific agnatic ties within this group. Similarly, the generalized use of the idiom of affinity does not preclude specific affinal ties on the basis of actual interethnic marriage. Note also that the same diagram could be presented simply by writing + for G and — for S to show just the presence or absence of the generalized use of these idioms.

Table 1.   Diagram of the use of kinship and affinity among migrants in Kumasi

	Kinship	Affinity
Internal	G	S
External	S	G

This states that consanguineal kinship terms, in particular in this ethnographic context, those associated with descent, are used in a generalized sense within the ethnic community. Affinal terms are only used to refer to specific kin within the ethnic community. In interethnic relations, however, kinship terms associated with consanguinity and particularly descent are used only to describe specific kin, that is, after a marriage has actually occurred. But affinal terms are used in a generalized, categorical way across ethnic boundaries. Thus the Mossi may apply terms for "mother's brother" to any Mamprusi man, or terms for "cross-cousin"

1

[2]   This is such an extensive pattern in African kinship that it is impossible to list all references to joking in the context of kinship. However authors who mention joking between ethnic categories include Goody (1959), Griaule (1948), Gulliver (1957, 1958), Hammond (1964), Labouret (1929), Mitchell (1956), Moreau (1941, 1944), Paulme (1939), Radcliffe-Brown (1940, 1949), Reynolds (1958), Rigby (1968), Smith (1959), Tait (1950), White (1957), Wilson (1957). Three sorts of explanations have been advanced: that such joking represents an extension from the domestic family (e.g. Goody 1959); that it is an aspect of cosmology (e.g. Griaule 1948); and that it reflects historical relationships between groups, (e.g. Gulliver 1957; Mitchell 1966; Reynolds 1958; Wilson 1957).

to any Dagomba. These particular usages, and the joking behavior that accompanies them, are discussed further below.

AFFINITY AND INTERETHNIC RELATIONS

Just as the notion of descent is based on a putative tie to a remote ancestor, the notion of affinity linking distinct ethnic communities is based on notions about marriages among the founders of these groups. These linkages connect ethnic categories in the traditional context, just as they do in the migrant community in Ghana. They can be compared to inter-clan joking partnerships that have been noted elsewhere in Africa (among others Colson 1962; Fortes 1949; Goody 1962; Griaule 1948; Richards 1937; Rigby 1968; Stefaniszyn 1950). Thus, Mossi society in Upper Volta is said to have been created out of intermarriages between intrusive conquerors or royals (known as Nakomce) of Mamprusi or Dagomba origin,[13] and women of autochthonous groups, known collectively as Talse but distinguished in different localities as Foulse, Bisa, Ninissi, and others. Royals and commoners (Nakomce and Talse) are conceptually opposed categories in Mossi society. They are distinct in terms of their origins and in terms of their eligibility to hold political and ritual offices. Although cultural distinctions between these categories have become blurred, they remain important structural concepts and reflect status categories which continue to have some importance in Mossi society.[14] On the basis of marriages between the ancestors of these groups, Nakomce call Talse *yeśba* (plural *yeśramba*), mother's brother or simply maternal kin (noted also in Zahan 1967). This justifies joking partnerships between members of these categories. Other myths similarly incorporate other ethnic groups, such as the Fulani and the Yarse, who have also to some extent been culturally integrated into Mossi society. The interpretation offered here is that these myths about interethnic relationships persist in the face of cultural incorporation and are acted out in joking behavior in order to stress status differences between the categories. They reflect the Mossi notion that their society is stratified and that this stratification reflects the ethnic complexity of their society.

---

[13]　From the point of view of the Mossi both the Mamprusi and the Dagomba were once part of a single category, Dagbamba. There are many versions of the origin myth which explains the creation of three separate Mole-Dagbane kingdoms.

[14]　This statement invokes the ethnographic present. In present day Voltaic society the importance of these categories is undoubtedly changing, but Mossi migrants continue to refer to them.

As Smith (1959) pointed out in reference to the Hausa, although the actual facts of stratification may be much more complicated than such a linear model implies, ethnicity provides a simple model. Among other things, such a model has a built-in way of ensuring perpetuity of the system as long as the notion of ethnicity is linked to a notion of descent.

In Kumasi a similar approach can be used. There, where the Mossi form a single ethnic category *vis à vis* other more distant groups, the traditional statuses of these sub-groupings of Mossi society are irrelevant. Thus, Mossi emphasize a different aspect of their origin myth in Kumasi and conceive of themselves as descendants of a common ancestor, Ouidraogo, the Nakomce founder of the first Mossi kingdom. Consequently within the Mossi migrant community affinal terms, including the term *yeśba*, are not used categorically, and the joking which expresses these relationships does not occur, except when specific kinship can be traced. However the pattern remains; it still expresses ethnic and status distinctions, but the relevant ethnic categories are defined differently. On the basis of the marriages between their ancestors the Mossi, Mamprusi, and Dagomba are linked as affines and maternal kin (see Figure 1). The Mossi categorically regard the Mamprusi as maternal kin since their ancestress, Nyennenga, was the daughter of a Mamprusi ruler. She ran away to Mossi country where she gave birth to Ouidraogo, the Mossi ancestor. The Mossi refer to the Mamprusi as maternal kin (*yeśba*) or as grandparents (*yabramba*, singular *yaba*). Both the mother's

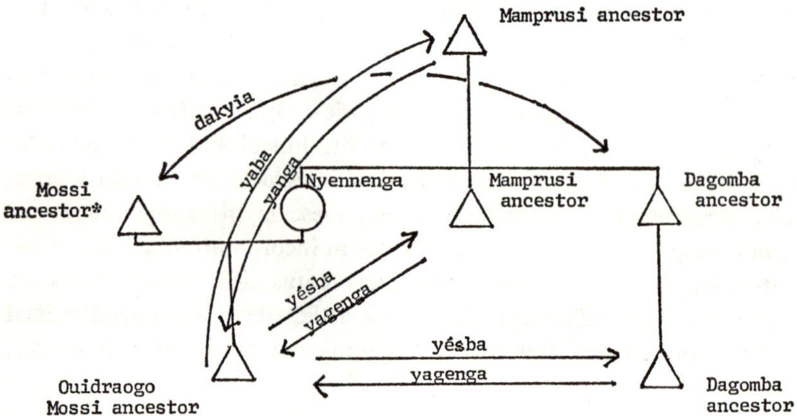

* The ethnic identity of Nyennenga's husband varies in different versions of the origin myth, probably to justify the incorporation of various autochthonous peoples into Mossi society.

Figure 1.   Putative ancestral relationships among three Mole-Dagbane communities in Kumasi, showing kin terms used to describe interethnic relationships among migrants

brother/sister's son (*yeśba/yagenga*) relationship and the grandparent/ grandchild (*yaba/yanga*) relationship justify joking. A similar myth explains the Mossi/Dagomba link. Nyennenga is said to have had a brother who founded the Dagomba kingdom. The Mossi and Dagomba thus explain their relationship in terms of a cross-cousin link, also justifying joking. The Mole term to describe joking relationships is *dakiri*, from *dakyia*, the term for wife's brother and sister's husband, but used for all affines. This term is also used to describe the cross-cousin relationship between the Mossi and Dagomba since from one point of view, the ancestors of these peoples were brothers-in-law. Nyennenga's marriage gave rise to the Mossi while her "brother's" adventures created Dagomba. The terms *yeśba* and *yagenga* however are also used to describe the Dagomba/Mossi relationship. In the context of the prevailing emphasis on unilineal descent, all non-agnatic kin may be referred to here as affines. This follows Mossi usage in describing joking relationships. In fact, whether joking behavior is explained in terms of a model of affinity or uterine kinship depends upon the generational perspective in which joking partners cast their interaction. This is a matter of choice, and as I will argue below, depends upon relative age and other factors involved in the relationship of those who joke. Since all ties are putative, the explanatory genealogical link can be voluntarily selected.

JOKING IN THE URBAN CONTEXT

Joking between the Mossi, Dagomba, and Mamprusi, as well as between members of other ethnic communities, occurs frequently in Kumasi. It occurs between individuals who do not know each other, who use joking, as Mitchell (1966) suggests as a way of placing each other in familiar categories; it also occurs repeatedly between people who are in frequent contact. It occurs in day to day interaction as well as on ritual occasions such as funerals. On the night of the Muslim new year, ʿ*Ashura*, people go from house to house seeking their joking partners to "trouble them." On this one occasion, one can observe elaborate joking between members of numerous ethnic communities as well as between people who are specific kin.[15]

---

[15] This occasion is called *zambende* by the Mossi and *jifan wuta* [throwing fire], *wowo* [play], or *daran ciki ciki* [night of the full stomach] by the Hausa. As in other joking, fire and water symbolism is important on this occasion. See Douglas (1968: 374) for a possible interpretation of this symbolism, involving the destruction and regeneration of the relationships invoked in the joke.

Characteristic of all joking is the fact that the same behavior would be inappropriate or obscene in another context (see Douglas 1968). Thus on one occasion a man claimed he was a Hausa and approached a Dagomba who had recently arrived in Kumasi. He called him *kafiri* (pagan) and told him he was shabby and dirty and should return home. The Dagomba became angry. As he was about to strike the joker, a Mossi bystander stepped in and explained that the joker was really Mossi. At this point the provocation became a joke and anger turned to amusement. Joking behavior is, then, appropriate in Kumasi between members of certain ethnic categories and not others. But what, really, is the "joke in the social structure" (Douglas 1968: 366) that makes this behavior amusing in one context and insulting in another?

Joking, as Rigby (1968) shows, says something about boundaries. In Kumasi, as well as in traditional Mossi society, interethnic joking can be viewed as a symbolic comment on the simultaneous disappearance of cultural boundaries and the persistence of structural ones, symbolized by ethnic categorization.[16] A process of cultural integration and incorporation, on the one hand, is confronted by the persistence of discreet status categories symbolized by ethnicity. As among the Gogo (Rigby 1968) this disjunction is expressed in terms of the contrast between descent and affinity. Descent represents structure and affinity represents community, in Turner's terms (1966), to which Rigby relates his discussion (1968: 152). In Kumasi, as I have shown above, the concept of descent is embodied in the concept of ethnicity, which may be regarded as an aspect of social structure. Affinity and community represent the cultural continuities which threaten and confront ethnic boundaries.[17] In all of these cases, as Douglas states (1968: 371) "a joke confronts one relevant structure by another less clearly relevant, one well-differentiated view by a less coherent one, a system of control by another independent one to which it does not apply."

The way in which cultural incorporation and ethnic differentiation operate in traditional Mossi society has been discussed sufficiently for the purposes of this paper. It is still necessary to describe the relationship between joking, culture, and ethnicity in Kumasi in more detail, and to relate this to differences in various modes of joking. Interethnic joking in Kumasi cannot be understood unless its occurrence and non-

---

[16]   For a more extensive discussion of ethnicity as a structural rather than cultural principle in Kumasi see Schildkrout (1974).

[17]   It is perhaps interesting that a draft of this paper was completed before I had consulted either Douglas (1968) or Rigby (1968). This seems to me to only reconfirm the usefulness of the approach discussed here and presented in these two papers.

occurrence at various levels is taken into account. The Mossi community, as I have explained above, conceives of itself as a corporate descent category in Kumasi. Internal status differences at this level are not related to ethnicity and are not conceptualized in terms of descent. Despite structural and cultural diversity in traditional Mossi society, in Kumasi, Mossi migrants emphasize their cultural and social solidarity. This is particularly evident in contexts where Mossi are relating to non-Mossi, but also is apparent in internal relations, as shown by the way in which Mossi employ the idiom of generalized kinship among themselves.

Among the many migrant and indigenous groups in Kumasi, some ethnic communities are closer in terms of cultural, historical, and linguistic background than others. Thus the Mossi are closer in these terms to the Mamprusi and the Dagomba than to the Hausa, Yoruba, or Asante. Permitted joking affirms this cultural solidarity in the idiom of affinity; it symbolically states that within Kumasi the Mole-Dagbane peoples are a community: not a corporate category like the Mossi, but a community integrated through affinal bonds; potential or actual allies. Joking is mainly in Gur dialects, so that linguistic solidarity *vis-à-vis* non-Gur speakers is also affirmed. Given the importance of Hausa as a *lingua franca* and of Twi as the dominant local language, this use of language to symbolize cultural and social identity is important.

However, because of its ambivalent nature, joking affirms disjunction as well as conjunction. While the fact that joking is permitted affirms the solidarity of the Gur speakers, it also affirms each one's distinct identity. This distinctiveness is structural, not cultural, however. Traditional linguistic and cultural bonds cannot really be used as a means of conferring status in Kumasi insofar as status is determined by ethnicity at all. This is because cultural categories are not ranked in Kumasi, while ethnic ones to some extent, in some contexts, are. Joking occurs precisely in this domain where cultural boundaries are blurred but where ethnicity, and the concept of descent on which it is based, can be used to express status differences.[18] Thus social and political solidarity at this level is based on an alliance, not to stretch the kinship idiom – on incest.

Although all of this interethnic joking is in the idiom of affinity, dif-

---

[18]   It might be argued that joking affirms that the Gur speakers are an ethnic category in relation to more distant ones, such as the Hausa. I formerly took this view, but no longer do. In arguing that ethnic cateogories are based on descent I am admittedly taking an emic view, but it is these emically defined categories which are used when categories are compared and ranked. Cultural ones are implicit in behavior but are not used as the basis of operative models of social structure. In some cases, of course, as in the linguistic distinction between Gur and Hausa speakers, cultural and structural distinctions coincide.

ferences in the types of joking can be observed. In Rigby's discussion of Gogo joking, variations in joking behavior between different categories of kin are described and analyzed. These variations can clearly be related to differences in the types of genealogical links involved. This is the way migrants in Kumasi describe variations in their own joking patterns. Thus the Mossi claim that the reason their joking with the Mamprusi is generally less hostile and belligerent than their joking with the Dagomba is that in the first case there is a generational difference necessitating respect, while in the second, they are dealing with cross-cousins, a more symmetrical relationship. But in Kumasi, unlike in the Gogo situation, the interethnic joking I am describing is based on generalized or meta-phorical kinship. Individuals can joke on the basis of their ethnic identity alone, whether or not they also are specific kin (which justifies the usual kinship joking). They are free to select which aspect of their genealogical link they want to stress. When a Mossi and a Mamprusi joke, if the Mamprusi is considerably older, the joking will probably be in the grand-parent/grandchild idiom. If they are closer in age, the mother's brother/ sister's son tie (*yeśba/yagenga*) may be invoked should there be any need to explain the joking. Most often, it is ethnicity rather than other markers of status such as age that determines the kind of joking involved. This, I will argue, is based on the differing economic and political relationships between ethnic categories, not on the genealogical models the Mossi use to explain their joking.

The repertory of joking includes behavior familiar in kinship joking: obstruction of ritual, particularly funerals; theft or begging; insults; or physical assault such as attempting to put pepper in the eyes of mourners at funerals or pouring water on people. When the Mossi joke with the Mamprusi they usually beg their "grandparent" (*yaba*) for money. This joking is asymmetrical and is relatively mild. Joking between the Mossi and the Dagomba is more overtly hostile. The Dagomba seem more often to be the aggressors, but I am uncertain on this point and both groups deny it, claiming that the joking is symmetrical and based on the fact that they are cross-cousins, or simply *dakyia*. Thus on one occasion a Dagomba jumped into a Mossi grave and refused to move until paid, while Dagomba women harrassed mourners at the deceased's house. These two groups claim that because they are cross-cousins, they cannot intermarry. This is "like incest" they sometimes say; on other occasions the Mossi claim they do not marry Dagomba because these women are witches and bring misfortune. In fact, however, intermarriage is common; but the level of specific kinship and affinity and the symbolic level on which interethnic joking occurs are quite distinct.

If the particular emphasis given to different joking relations is related not to genealogical relationships as the Mossi claim but to economic and political factors, then as these aspects of interethnic relations change, the quality of joking can be expected to change. However we cannot be sure that the hostility reflected in joking directly reflects social relations. Hostility in joking occurs when relations involve both competition and the recognition of community. When tension is very high, joking ceases altogether. Then, accusations of witchcraft, as in the second explanation above of why Mossi men should not marry Dagomba women, become covert accusations and are no longer considered amusing. Nevertheless, given the difficulty of positing a simple one-to-one relationship between joking symbolism and social relations, it is still the case that the more hostile Dagomba/Mossi joking is correlated with a greater degree of economic and political competition between these two groups. This is supported by an analysis of political events and economic relationships that can only be briefly referred to here. During a long dispute over succession to the Imamate of the Kumasi central mosque, the Mossi and Mamprusi were allies, while the Dagomba were opposed to both groups. Citizenship was a crucial issue in the dispute and would have justified an alliance between the Mamprusi and Dagomba. However the Mamprusi joined the Mossi in supporting the Hausa candidate rather than the Dagomba candidate for assistant Imam. Competition between the Mossi and Dagomba in the cattle and kola trade is also intense. This may be related to demographic factors. As noted earlier, there are far fewer Mamprusi traders in Kumasi than either Dagomba or Mossi ones. Moreover, Mossi traders cannot avoid passing through Tamale, a primarily Dagomba town, in carrying on long distance trade. Mamprusi territory is somewhat to the east of the major north/south trade route and has never provided competition for the Mossi.

CONCLUSION

I have discussed the use of the idiom of kinship and its application to interethnic relations in two contexts: among the Mossi in Upper Volta and among migrants in Kumasi, Ghana. In both cases the contrastive idioms of descent and affinity are used to categorize two conceptually different fields of social relations: those within corporate ethnic categories and those between these categories. In both contexts, interethnic joking in the idiom of affinity is used to express status distinctions among peoples who are not clearly differentiated culturally. In Upper Volta this reflected the process of cultural incorporation which characterized the development of Mossi society. In Kumasi this was due to the cultural, historical and linguistic similarities among Gur speakers in relation to the local Asante population and other migrant communities.

I have suggested that it is useful to look at joking in terms of a series of levels of occurrence and non-occurrence.[19] At the "lowest" level descent rather than affinity is emphasized. Status differences cannot be correlated with ethnicity and cultural variations are non-existent or denied. This level was illustrated by the Nakomce and Talse in Upper Volta, and the Mossi in Kumasi. At the next level cultural boundaries between ethnic categories are blurred or ambiguous. They are not clear markers of status differences and, in fact, cultural and linguistic solidarity may be emphasized. Ethnicity cannot be clearly expressed through cultural discontinuities, but the idiom of affinity, including joking, is used to stress the persistence of these categories. Mossi society in Upper Volta and the Mole-Dagbane community in Kumasi are representative of this level. At the "highest" level, joking again does not occur. This is illustrated by relations between Mole-Dagbane peoples and the Hausa or Asante in Kumasi. No ties of categorical kinship or affinity link these groups, and ethnic differences are correlated with clear cultural and linguistic boundaries.

Joking occurs, then, only when ethnicity persists but is not clearly related to cultural boundaries. Taking the opposition between descent and affinity as its symbolism, interethnic joking expresses the persistence of ethnic categories as status categories in situations of cultural incorporation. This kinship symbolism includes its own built-in contradiction, but this is just the point of the joking, of course. Consanguineal kin are closer than affines, but affines are still kin. I am arguing here that in the two contexts I have discussed this idiom is being used to conceptualize not simply the relationships between ethnic categories, but also the ambivalence inherent in their relationships in terms of a dichotomy between structure and culture. Affinity and joking are used here to express structural discontinuities within cultural communities.

[19]   Mary Douglas (1968: 361) suggests that "the alternatives of joking and not joking would be susceptible to the kind of structural analysis which Leach (1961: 23) has applied to controlled and uncontrolled modes of mystical power."

REFERENCES

COHEN, A.
1969 *Custom and politics in urban Africa.* London: Routledge and Kegan Paul.

COLSON, E.
1962 "Clans and the joking relationship among the Plateau Tonga of Northern Rhodesia," in *The Plateau Tonga.* Manchester: Manchester University Press.

DOUGLAS, M.
1968 The social control of cognition: some factors in joke perception. *Man* 3: 361-76.

FORTES, M.
1945 *The dynamics of clanship among the Tallensi.* London: Oxford University Press for International African Institute.
1949 *The web of kinship among the Tallensi.* London: Oxford University Press for International African Institute.

GHANA GOVERNMENT
1964 *1960 Ghana Census.* Accra: Government Printing Office.

GOODY, J. R.
1959 The mother's brother and sister's son in West Africa. *Journal of the Royal Anthropological Institute* 89:61-88.
1962 *Death, property and the ancestors.* London: Tavistock.
1967 *The social organization of the Lo-Willi* (second edition). London: Oxford University Press for International African Institute.

GRIAULE, M.
1948 L'alliance catharique. *Africa* 18:242-58.

GULLIVER, P.
1957 Joking relationships in central Africa. *Man* 57:225.
1958 Joking relationships in Africa. *Man* 58:191.

GUTKIND, P.G.
1973 "Bibliography on urban Africa," in *Urban anthropology.* Edited by A. Southall. London: Oxford University Press.

HAMMOND, P.
1964 Mossi Joking. *Ethnology* iii, 3: 259-67.

LABOURET, H.
1929 La parenté à plaisanteries en Afrique occidentale. *Africa* 2:244-54.

LEACH, E. R.
1961 *Re-thinking anthropology.* London: Athlone Press.

MANOUKIAN, M.
1951 *Tribes of the northern territories of the Gold Coast.* London: Oxford University Press for International African Institute.

MITCHELL, J. C.
1956 *The Kelela dance.* Rhodes-Livingston Paper 27. Manchester: Manchester University Press.
1966 "Theoretical orientations in African urban studies," in *The social anthropology of complex societies.* Edited by Michael Banton, 37-69. ASA Monograph 4. London: Tavistock.

MOREAU, R. E.
   1941   The joking relationship (utani) in Tanganyika. *Tanganyika notes and records* 12:1–10.
   1944   Joking relationships in Tanganyika. *Africa* 14:38-6400.
PAULME, D.
   1939   Parenté à plaisanteries et alliance par sang en Afrique occidentale. *Africa* 12:433-44.
RADCLIFFE-BROWN, A. R.
   1940   On joking relationships. *Africa* 13:195–210. (Reprinted in Radcliffe-Brown 1952)
   1949   A further note on joking relationships. *Africa* 19:133-40. (Reprinted in Radcliffe-Brown 1952.)
   1952   *Structure and function in primitive society*. London: Cohen and West.
RATTRAY, R.
   1932   *Tribes of the Ashanti hinterland* (two volumes). London.
REYNOLDS, V.
   1958   Joking relationships in Africa. *Man* 58:21.
RICHARDS, A. I.
   1937   Reciprocal clan relationships among the Bemba of North East Rhodesia. *Man* 37:188-93.
RIGBY, P.
   1968   Joking relationships, kin categories and clanship among the Gogo. *Africa* 38:133-55.
SCHILDKROUT, E.
   1969   Ethnicity, kinship and politics among Mossi immigrants in Ghana. Unpublished doctoral dissertation, Cambridge University.
   1970a Strangers and local government in Kumasi. *Journal of Modern African Studies* 8:251-69.
   1970b "Government and chiefs in Kumasi zongo," in *West African chiefs: their changing status under colonial rule and independence*. Edited by M. Crowder and O. Ikime, 370-93. Ibadan: Caxton Press.
   1973   The fostering of children in urban Ghana: problems of ethnographic analysis in a multi-cultural context. *Urban Anthropology* 2:48-73.
   1974   "Ethnicity and generational differences among urban immigrants in Ghana," in *Urban ethnicity*. Edited by A. Cohen, 187-222. ASA Monograph 12. London: Tavistock.
SKINNER, E. P.
   1964   *The Mossi of the Upper Volta*. Stanford, California: Stanford University Press.
SMITH, M. G.
   1959   The Hausa system of social status. *Africa* 29:239-53.
STEFANISZYN, B.
   1950   Funeral friendship in central Africa. *Africa* 20:290-306.
TAIT, D.
   1950   An analytical commentary on the social structure of the Dogon. *Africa* 20:175-99.
TURNER, V. W.
   1966   "The bond and the free." The Morgan Lectures delivered at the University of Rochester, 1966.

WHITE, C. M. N.
1957   Joking relationships in central Africa. *Man* 57.

WILKS, I.
1966   "The position of Muslims in metropolitan Ashanti in the early nineteenth century," in *Islam in tropical Africa*. Edited by I. M. Lewis,
318-41. London: Oxford University Press for International African
Institute.
1967   "Ashanti government," in *West African kingdoms in the nineteenth
century*. Edited by P. Kaberry and D. Forde, 206–39. London: Oxford
University Press for International African Institute.

WILSON, M.
1957   Joking relationships in central Africa. *Man* 57:140.

ZAHAN, D.
1967   "The Mossi kingdoms," in *West African kingdoms in the nineteenth
century*. Edited by P. Kaberry and D. Forde, 152–79. London: Oxford
University Press for International African Institute.

Ethnicity as a Factor in Italian Temporary Worker Migration

JANET M. SCHREIBER

The topic of migration and ethnicity can provide the opportunity to unravel one of the core problems of any theory of social organization: the process and adaptive features which regulate the admission of the individual to the group.

Ethnicity as one of the forms of social identity is a conceptual means whereby the individual places himself within a meaningful category, thus binding himself to a position in the social structure and cueing his social interaction with others. The definition of ethnicity results from complimentary sets of subjective interpretations both on the part of the individual and the society with which he interacts. Ethnicity not only has a subjective component whereby the actor negotiates the intricacies of his social position but it also requires the participation of others who share his symbolic system and its consequent membership categories.

In cultural systems the conventions which function to establish social identity begin from birth to encapsulate the individual as a member of a specific group and each society has multiple institutionalized means of initiation to membership categories (Cohen 1964). The migration experience, which usually pulls the individual away from his group and exposes him to other symbolic systems and therefore differing definitions of ethnic identity, gives us the ideal opportunity to study the adaptive functions of identity and the behavior of the individual in environments where his ethnicity is mutually redefined.

Italy provides an excellent laboratory for research on migration. At least since Roman times, migration has been an established pattern of culture. In fact, one can easily find seeds for this pattern in the Greek and Etruscan movements. In the last century a massive rural exodus has created radical changes in the population distribution and has become a major social problem. During the last decade migration has become principally a temporary movement directed towards the industrial centers of Europe.

When migrating to northern Italy or Europe, migrants from Molise, an ethnically heterogeneous agricultural region of southern Italy, are given new derogatory identities as "southerners" (*meridionali*) or "Italians" in relation to the host community. Annually approximately 20–25 per 1,000 population emigrate from Molise to European destinations (Schreiber 1973).

The research conducted from June 1971 to June 1973 was originally designed to study decision making and family interaction in the process of moving, with particular attention to selectivity, the nature of planning, and the implications for family members left behind. Among the 203 informants interviewed formally, 65 were of an Albanian ethnic minority and 23 from a Slavic-speaking minority group. All migrants were from the social groups with little access to power. Indeed, if a person is powerful he is usually not considered to be a migrant even if he does move out of the region. For example, a judge went to Milan, but people laughed at the thought that he might be considered a migrant. Migration is in itself a disparaged status. The politically noble and powerful figures from the region do not identify themselves as either migrants or ethnics.

When workers migrate to the industrial centers of Europe they are exposed to social, economic, and legal policies that make it difficult for them to participate in the local culture. Molisians as well as other southern Italian migrants frequently live in ghettos and do the most degrading, difficult, or dangerous jobs in the mines, the building industry, and factories. Switzerland has the most restrictive policies towards migrants. Swiss law prohibits immigration of family members of workers without annual residence permits. A special "foreigners' police" controls their movements.

The social position of the southern Italian migrant is not conditioned so much by the fact that he crosses a border, but by social contradictions much more profound. Going to a country with a strange language complicates problems of integration for his family and for the education of his children. But these same problems exist for migrant families in the industrial cities of northern Italy. Informants have said that they felt less hostility directed towards them in Germany or Switzerland than in Turin or Milan. "Wherever we *meridionali* go we are thought ill of," one informant said. Northerners told me I should not live in the South: "They're all Arabs, they use the water buffalo, they all carry guns and are violent."

Italy as a recent political construct encompasses linguistic, cultural, and historically diverse groups. In the 112 years since Italian unification, over 27,000,000 Italians have emigrated, a sum equal to half of Italy's present population. This combined with chaotic periods of foreign domination has created a perspective that is particularly Italian: the mix of local culture with its ties not to the nation-state but to another location historically significant for members of that community. Thus ethnographers report that the peasants in a Sicilian village feel themselves much closer to New York or Boston where their kinsmen are than to Rome, which represents an outside power (Gower 1971). *Campanilismo* (loyalty to the bell tower that symbolizes the home town) has characterized Italian history and social relations because communities have remained individualized units with their own distinct dialects, traditions, and images.

The definition of what constitutes an ethnic group is a matter of debate. Generally the principal criteria distinguished for membership inclusion include occupational groups, religion, territoriality, sociocultural patterns, or language. Yet the problem of defining ethnicity by outside characteristics is that ethnicity is by its nature a subjective concept, the symbolic definition of one's group as a unique combination of distinguishing sociocultural features.

In Molise, other than local identity markers, people divide themselves into three ethnic categories. There are four communities which identify themselves as *Albanesi,* for they are the descendants of Albanian immigrants who were encouraged to settle in the area after they had escaped from the Turkish invasion in the fifteenth century. These communities have maintained a separate identity; Albanian is spoken in everyday life, but all institutions conduct business in Italian.

With the advent of television all people in the community have become bilingual. This is also true for the three Slavic-speaking communities in the same region. They have maintained a separate language, a Serbo-Croatian dialect. Most of their cultural forms, however, including kinship organization, have evolved to the point that they are indistinguishable from southern Italian forms. The other communities of Molise form the majority social group of the area and identify themselves first as southerners and then as members of a specific community, reflecting the town-based differences in dialect and tradition.

All *Albanesi* and *Slavi* consider themselves to be "Italian." Informants were asked to specify three self-identifying labels. They responded with both the ethnic label and a general label as either Italians or southerners. In northern Italy or Europe they were identified by others as *meridional* [southerners], *terroni* [earthgrubbers], or *Morochini* [Morrocans], or other derogatory labels. However, they searched out others from *Albanesi* or *Slavi* towns and maintained the community traditions and dialect at home. The songs and folklore traditions of the Molisian *Albanesi* groups are maintained in *Albanesi* neighborhoods in Germany, Switzerland, Montreal, Washington, D. C., and Philadelphia. Migrants reported that they interacted whenever possible with members of their group, especially where they were subject to humiliation because of their migrant status or their nationality. They reported that being a migrant made them feel more a member of their home community.

Returned and visiting migrants were asked a series of questions about what made them migrate, why they went to that particular location, who had advised them, who they knew there, and how they had planned the move. Destination was dictated principally by two factors: reputed work availability and distance from home. Approximately one-half of the migrants went to Germany and one-third to Switzerland. They returned home to visit annually either at Christmas or in August.

In that only 28 of the 203 informants were single and half were female, the major kin tie activated in migration was the spouse (in 70 percent of the cases). Usually the husband went first, found work, and then the wife followed. The pattern for single young people interviewed was to go with a friend or a cousin or sibling. It was unusual for a single female to migrate unless she went with her parents.

Italian migration statistics for 1969 indicate that 66 percent of the migrants returning to Italy had stayed out of the country for one year or less (Instituto Statistico 1970:93). Only 24 percent of the migrants I interviewed had stayed away one year or less, the most common European definition of a "temporary migrant," but even though they stayed longer they defined themselves as being in the host country "temporarily." They left because they had reached a juncture in their life plans when they felt that they could maximize their social and economic benefits by working away from home (Schreiber 1973).

The migrants interviewed defined the situation in the host country as a passing state of relative unimportance compared with the benefits it would provide them when they returned to their home community. A migrant who is focused upon resolving his status position and demonstrating his personal adequacy for his significant others does not plan his goals in terms of the area to which he migrates. He is migrating to maximize his conditions and family status in the place of origin, not the place of immigration, and his actions are consequent to this interpretation.

The migrant's behavior becomes meaningful when set in the context of the social structure of his home community. There the individual's principal identity is familial. The position of his family and its reputation permeates all other social categories of which he is a member. Networks are highly "connected," to use Bott's terms (1971), so that categories of occupation, economics, influence, politics, and kin overlap. Individual relationships tend to be dyads of unequal status, patron-client relationships. Personal intermediation is the means used to obtain whatever is useful in goods, benefits, or services. Adulthood and married status are coterminous and the family's honor is dependent on the proper performance of the roles of parent and spouse.

The only option that exists outside of the local patron-client distribution system is the opportunity to leave the region and work in northern Italy or in Europe. The migratory exodus from Molise has reduced the population to less than it was at the time of the unification of Italy. Migration offers the individual not only economic benefits but another way to demonstrate personal adequacy and status, which he usually declares materially by constructing or remodeling a house in his home town, which remains a symbol of his increased social position.

The negotiation of honor and its oppositional component, shame, form the performance backdrop that gives significance to the behavior of these migrants. In their life plan, goals pertain to the maintenance of a respectable position in the home community. Economics provide a means to this end, a demonstration of personal adequacy with the house and the family symbols presented for validation by others.

In Goffman's (1959) terms the home community becomes the "front region," or the arena in which the performance is staged. The place to which one migrates is the corollary "back region," the place where the work is performed that will permit the maintenance of the image presented on stage.

In the front region the family's honor is presented, reciprocally maintained, and validated. The house and impeccable dress are paraded as demonstrations that the head of the family has done his role well and can be a respected member of the community. In the small towns of Molise during the Sunday promenade people are better dressed than on the streets of Paris. The physical presentation of one's self, *fare bella figura*, is the object of continual evaluation and gossip by the community.

In contrast, when the migrant is in Switzerland or in Germany, he and his family do not attempt this face behavior but rather concentrate on the business at hand, providing the economic means so that in the future they can make their debut at home. They are disparaged, demeaned, but they go into the migration situation with the hopes of extracting all possible monetary benefits. This is part of the significance of the proverb used as a synonym for migration, "to eat the bread of others." If one eats the bread of others he is not just nourishing himself but somehow putting something over on the other, tricking him.

A recent film, *Handsome, Honest, Migrated to Australia, Will Marry Chaste Country Woman*, with Alberto Sordi, is a humorous, devastating parody of these motives. The anti-hero is neither handsome nor honest and the chaste wife that arrives in answer to his mail order for a bride is an ex-prostitute looking for better things.

The experience of being defined as a member of a disparaged group can function to strengthen other facets of an individual's identity. *Slavi* migrants made friends with Yugoslavs, and *Albanesi* migrants tended to live together. Thus when being despised as either *meridionali* or Italians, the migrants from the two ethnic minorities in Molise tended to realign themselves to their own group, to generate a more positive identity, to become more *Albenesi* or *Slavi* than they had been in the home region. New identity-establishing cultural forms were also established in the home community.

In both the *Slavi* and *Albanesi* communities new institutions have been created following the increased migration to the industrial centers of Europe. Although no Italian language newspaper has been published in Molise since 1830, in two of the Albanian towns newspapers have been published in Albanian with Italian translation. Although they are the sporadic product of a few individuals, they represent a movement to establish specifically "Albanian" cultural forms. In the papers bilingual schools and programs to support special Albanian studies programs are promoted. In the Slavic towns no documents have been created but contacts have been established not only with individual Yugoslavs but with two towns near Zagreb, and the bishop of Zagreb came to visit and participate in the Saint George feast day festivities. This was the first time any formal contact had been made between the *Slavi* communities and Yugoslavia.

In conclusion, the growing literature in the areas of self-perception and self-portraiture by symbolic interactionists illuminates the process of "ethnogenesis" by analyzing the complex manipulations of impression management and label negotiation in everyday life. The maintenance of personal identity requires regular and sustained validation. This exchange can only be provided when the participants in the interaction share the same symbolic referents (Geertz 1966). When the membership categories, the criteria for definition, and the status referents change, as with the migrants studied, the individual must realign his personal constellation of identity to adapt to the new situation.

REFERENCES

BLUMER, GIOVANNI
   1971   *L'emigrazione Italiana in Europa.* Milan: Feltrinelli.
BOTT, ELIZABETH
   1971   *Family and social network* (second edition). London: Tavistock.
COHEN, YEHUDI A.
   1964   The establishment of identity in a social nexus. *American Anthropologist* 66:529–552.
GEERTZ, CLIFFORD
   1966   *Person, time and conduct in Bali: an essay in cultural analysis.* Southeast Asia Studies Cultural Report Series 14. New Haven: Yale University.
GOFFMAN, ERVING
   1959   *The presentation of self in everyday life.* New York: Doubleday Anchor.
GOWER, CHARLOTTE
   1971   *Milocca: A Sicilian village.* Cambridge: Schenkman.
INSTITUTO STATISTICO
   1970   *Annuario di statistica del lavoro e dell emigrazione 10.* Rome: Istituto Statistico.
SCHREIBER, JANET
   1973   "To eat the bread of others: migration in a province of southern Italy." Unpublished doctoral dissertation, University of California, Berkeley.

Forms of Ethnic Linkage Between Town and Country

AIDAN SOUTHALL

Ethnicity, though frequently given a false emphasis, remains the paramount problem of Africa. Intense feelings and contentions about its presence or absence feed into all situations, especially those of the national scene, where with a few notable exceptions more and more autocratic leaders are drifting, by a seemingly ineluctable process, in the direction of military dictatorships. They all publicly denounce what they call tribalism in the most stringent terms, while they are privately forced to foster it by giving special privileges to their own local group, on whom they come to rely more desperately for their core support and ultimate loyalty. Happy are those few who, like the late Tom Mboya, transcend ethnicity through the sheer depth and intensity of their urban occupational involvement, or who, like the presidents of Tanzania and Zambia, profess principles which transcend ethnicity and come from groups that offer them little temptation to practice it.

I feel that in the past anthropologists exacerbated this problem and that we have an obligation to contribute in however small a way to setting the matter straight. In the case of Uganda and any other country which I examined closely, I have found — as I am sure many others have — that practically all the groups which we long acquiesced in calling tribes are not in fact what they have been taken to be. Popularly and with little effective correction by anthropologists, they are assumed to be clearly distinct local and cultural groups whose origins are so primeval that their identity is virtually impossible to modify. Instead most of these identities are of recent origin, molded and defined by the exigencies of the colonial situation. The so-called tribes were either states and should be considered such, or they were essentially segmentary, not unitary, entities with multiple identities at a number of different levels, equally meaningful in different contexts. From the point of view of the primeval aura which usually invests them they are false and fabricated entities; but of course this in no way affects their current political relevance (Southall 1970, f.c.a).

A more correct understanding of their nature and origins, however, may render them a little less dangerous and tend to diffuse their influence more innocuously at a number of different levels. This assumes that ideas have some influence on action. In Kenya, the Luyia came into existence in the 1940's, the Kalenjin in the early fifties, and the Mijikenda in the late fifties. Yet most people seem to regard them as primeval tribes. The explorers of the 1860's found no Acholi tribe in Uganda; the Lugbara did not exist until so named after the small northern clan first encountered by the Arabs; the Batoro came into existence in about 1830; the Bakiga are simply "highlanders" so defined by the first colonial administrators. In Burton's day Nyamwezi and Sukuma simply meant people of the west and north, with a very variable contextual definition — and so on ad infinitum.

When it comes to the urban situation the confusion is even greater. It would not matter so much if tribalism and ethnicity were understood in their largely recent and essentially colonial sense. Even so, many aspects of urban behavior are better understood if organizations such as the Ibo or Luo unions are not regarded as tribal associations related to a falsely imagined primeval past but as ethnic associations related to a relevant contemporary category of phenomena. Obviously the activities of Poles and Italians in American cities, of the Irish in Liverpool or Flemings and Walloons in Brussels belong in various ways to the same type of phenomenon. All groups show the effects of migration and share the problem of national identity in differing degrees, as is the case throughout Africa. I have therefore expunged the term tribe from my anthropological lexicon and use instead the concept of ethnicity to denote all differentiations based on a sense of common ancestry and culture among individuals and groups at different levels. This avoids absurdities such as the current habit of calling "tribalism" both nepotism — or favoritism toward brothers or other kin — and caste differences between Tutsi and Hutu in Rwanda or Burundi. The utility of the concept of ethnicity, as Raymond Firth once remarked, consists in its covering a rather wide and varied range of phenomena, with a great deal in common but a rather indistinct boundary.

The recent antistructural emphasis on microbehavioral process has produced some excellent empirical studies but few effective generalizations. A promising generalization, though not quite adequate in its original form, is Parkin's distinction between hosts and migrants in Kampala (Parkin 1969). All such dichotomous labels are bound to embrace a number of factors of somewhat variable incidence and distribution. Labels are a matter of convenience, but here I do not think it advisable to blur either the distinction between host and migrant or that between centralized and noncentralized societies, both of which are fundamental but quite independent of one another.

Host status is significant, for example, in that a host group never forms an ethnic association as such. Innumerable examples bear this out: Ganda in Kampala, Kikuyu in Nairobi, Luyia in Kitale, Zaramo in Dar es Salaam, Yoruba in Ibadan or Lagos. But a group that is host in one town may form an ethnic association in another far away, as the Yoruba do in Niamey. In the case of the Ibo and the Luo, the ethnic associations were formed in foreign towns and generated home branches later. The combination of localized segmentary lineage organization with massive labor migration to cities generates a particular type of many-tiered ethnic association which does not appear otherwise. The Luo, Luyia and Ibo cases, though incompletely studied, are sufficiently documented to demonstrate this fact. On the strength of it I predicted that Tiv, having the same type of social structure, would generate the same type of urban ethnic association if heavily involved in migrant labor to cities (Southall f.c.b). I now have some evidence to suggest that this is indeed the case. In all these examples the host/migrant factors are combined with the localized segmentary lineage factor.

Other examples of contrast appear in the literature, such as the contrast between the Kru and Vai in Monrovia, the Temne and Mende in Freetown, and the Lokele and Babua in Kisangani, the former Stanleyville (Fraenkel 1964; Banton 1957; Pons 1969). The relevant factors and features in these latter cases are not sufficiently unscrambled to make adequate comparative analysis possible. The activities of the various branches of the Ibo Union of welfare and development in their home areas have often been described. Though on a smaller scale, the Luo Union has demonstrated a similar function, most recently in mobilizing the collection of building resources and establishing the Ramogi Institute of Advanced Technology (Parkin, personal communication).

I have mentioned this instance of a rather formal kind of generalization to suggest that generalization in the field of urban studies in Africa, as elsewhere, will require greater depth and breadth than we have yet achieved. The variety of urban situations in Africa provides an approximation to an experimental situation in which first one and then another variable can be held constant while the rest are studied in detail, by selecting appropriate cases with a clear experimental end in view. The attempt to do this with other people's data, collected with other ends in view, is inevitably limited by the lack of vital data. Nor is it feasible for one research worker alone to cover the necessary field; and there is no experience to suggest that grandiose team projects can succeed here. The project should be the cumulative unfolding of the collective efforts of individual fieldworkers directed to well-thought-out ends.

The variables involved in the host/migrant and centralized/uncentralized dichotomies are just one case in point. Their utility could be better assessed and empirical situations better understood if they could be used in sufficient depth in a larger number of cases. Centralized political structure and *laisser faire* policy towards the growth of a modern city out of a traditional capital are factors favoring the development of host characteristics, as in the case of the Ganda in Kampala, Amhara in Addis Ababa, or Yoruba in Ibadan. Does the same apply to the Mossi in Ouagadougou, or the Ashanti in Kumasi? We presume so but have no adequate data.

Such further exploration would greatly refine the categories, since the assumed familial and marital implications of these two dichotomies in Kampala might not follow in the cases of Ouagadougou and Kumasi with differing domestic and kinship institutions. The Kikuyu in Nairobi hardly had host status or feelings. The city was only on the edge of their country and, not being centralized, they had no traditional focus that would attract the grafting onto it of a city. Furthermore, they were oppressed by a settler-dominated colonial regime so that although they were the urban majority they were there on sufferance like the Xosa in East London and Cape Town or the Ndebele in Bulawayo (Mayer 1961; Wilson and Mafeje 1963). However, the increasingly effective political dominance of the Kikuyu in Nairobi during the post-independence period has given them much more of the status and attitudes of hosts.

Another instance of the general atrophy of promising hypotheses is Mayer's well known contrast between Red Xosa and School Xosa in East London. What are the effective determinants of such a situation? Is it the combination of proximity of rural and urban residence resulting in a reaction to the oppressive racial regime of South Africa? Proximity permits the Red Xosa to draw moral strength and purpose for their urban living from a persistent rural based traditionalism in a way that might otherwise be difficult. At the same time, it is hard to believe that such attitudes would persist if it were not for the harsh deterrents and bitter discouragements to participation in the Westernized sector of South African society.

Brandel-Syrier's study of a "Reeftown Elite" has shown that full participation in urban life and status produces a brain-washed condition in which respectable urban Africans, who are outcasts in relation to white society, nonetheless concentrate their efforts on a pathetic mimicry of white social ceremonial (Brandel-Syrier 1971). Are we to assume that all black elites in South Africa who shun political involvement because of its heavy risks and penalties approximate this condition? The School/Red dichotomy can be perceived in many other parts of Africa as an aspect of different degrees of urban involvement but without the persistent discontinuity between the two categories which is implied for the East London situation.

Why is the School/Red dichotomy not found in Cape Town (as one must conclude from the Langa Study)? Or is it present but unreported? If it is not present, is this due to the greater distances of the Langa Africans from their rural homes? Correspondingly, why are the "Oo-scuse me/Oo-Mac" categories of Langa not reproduced in East London? Or are they again present but unreported? Surely the determinants could be pinned down with much greater precision by comparative research in Salisbury, Bulawayo or Gwelo, with their slightly different blend of social and industrial *apartheid*, and in Lusaka or Livingstone, Luanshya or Ndola, where the results of a similar past but a changed present could be studied. Or are the answers to such questions still lying hidden in the field notes of those who have conducted research in all these and other places?

The extreme discontinuity suggested by Mayer's study seems to result from the combination of several factors. In the neighboring areas of the Ciskei from which most of these peoples come, there is already a long-standing rural distinction between pagan villages and Christian villages — such as those dominated by the Presbyterian Church. Thus, Red Xosa coming to East London from pagan villages and School Xosa coming from Christian villages simply carry over into the urban situation a dichotomy which is already present in the countryside. Furthermore, the conditions of East London facilitate this perpetuation because Red and School are able to rent houses for themselves so that they continue to live separately. Here the urban network is a direct extension of the rural. On the other hand, in the conditions of Langa in Cape Town, the Africans have to accept what accommodation they can get in the barrack rooms of the compounds. There is no possibility of maintaining such distinctions, and in any case the Red and School categories come from more locally mixed areas, not from separate village communities such as those which feed East London. However, in the two situations there are some similarities which can be traced.

The inhabitants of the barrack compounds in Cape Town do behave rather like Reds in keeping to themselves and not attending cinemas and dance halls like the more settled townsfolk of Cape Town, who in this resemble the School people of East London. Since the African population of both cities is so predominantly Xosa, ethnic differences are objectively slight and are not in fact manipulated for mobilizing support or expressing cleavages. Mayer exaggerated the division between Red and School by restricting his study to a rather narrow aspect of their lives and omitting the many occasions that bring Red and School together: at work, in labor disputes, and in reaction to common emergencies (as when being raided by the police), when linked by clanship to the same funerals and mourning ceremonies, or when assisting one another to send money home. There are also cases of intermarriage between Red and School, and both are brought together in some of the separatist sects such as the Bengo Church.

A distinction comparable to that between Red and School appears between those who do and those who do not belong to the mutual aid associations of home boys from the same neighborhood. Joining the associations are those who can trust one another and who can always trace, and bring pressure on, anyone who defaults or absconds. Although technically voluntary, one is in effect obliged to join as long as he can identify with this category, for to refuse is really to assert that he is "Town" and can bear responsibility for himself. The poor migrant cannot afford to do this; he needs his credit association and he does not sever his home boy ties (Mafeje, personal communication).

To judge from the East London and Langa studies, ethnic factors are unimportant in these African populations. Is this because ethnic differences are indeed very slight among them or because the overspanning white-black confrontation overwhelms lesser differences of identity? Studies of Sotho, Tswana, Nguni, and other ethnic identities in Johannesburg should throw light on this issue very easily, as the white-black confrontation is obviously in evidence there, while ethnicity is also the basis of some important group activities within the African population. Presumably those who select the Red Xosa type of option must stress ethnic differences, when present, within the African population.

The matter could be much further illuminated if sports activities and organizations, which have been considerably studied in South Africa, could be more fully and reliably interpreted in relation to the paramount need for escapist outlets and for the creation of satisfyingly status-giving roles in an oppressive situation of deprivation. Also to be illuminated is the inevitablility of the emergences of such activities and organizations when certain levels of education and urban involvement have been reached, as evidenced in other African countries where racist oppression is not a relevant factor. (I specify racist oppression, because of course other forms of social and political oppression also have become highly relevant determinants of the urban process.)

In the areas around Johannesburg it appears that the differences in the situation correlate quite clearly with the different factors involved, mainly the presence of distinct ethnic groups and the exploitation of these by the white authorities in the township and compound system. There are Pondo, Tswana, Sotho, Nguni, Shangaan, and Venda sections of townships. One must declare his "tribe" and is allocated accordingly to a compound of his specific group (Mafeje, personal communication). In these circumstances the Red/School type of identity distinction is unworkable and useless. The fellow ethnics compulsorily concentrated in the same compounds have their own language, perform their own rituals, and are only very tenuously linked to Johannesburg. The ethnic rivalry imposed upon them is carried into other fields, so that Nguni compete with Sotho for positions in the Johannesburg traders' associations, as Kikuyu and Luo might in Nairobi. But in South Africa they cannot move on to the next stage of opulence by investing in land and property.

In the Zambian Copperbelt, the mines provided coffins, truck transport, and graves in case of death so one of the main motivations for mutual benefit associations was thereby removed, and ethnic associations were correspondingly weak. However, certain distinctly situated ethnic groups tended to keep to themselves, especially the Nyakyusa from southwestern Tanzania, constituting 8 percent of the labor force of the mines. They concentrated particularly in certain mining towns such as Kitwe and specialized in certain kinds of hazardous work such as lashing.

Leaving their wives at home, they often lived in tight little groups, sharing the same single men's quarters, eating their own kind of food and speaking, of course, their own language which no one else understood. They participated very little in sports and leisure activities with other ethnic groups. They even came close to forming their own trade union, but finally threw in their lot with the rest (Clyde Mitchell, personal communication). Epstein's very well-known account (1958) tells how, in the labor organization of the Copperbelt, occupational interests generally triumphed over the ethnic structure favored by the mine authorities. Although strong ethnic associations were not formed, home boy groups comparable to those described for Langa were important and they provided the basic cells which were transformed into the structure of the United National Independence Party.

Elsewhere in Zambia there was greater need for ethnic associations, in places where the employment structure was less monolithic and fewer services were provided. Thus, there was a "Sons of Barotse" organization in the city of Livingstone. Other activities, which provide the strength of ethnic organizations elsewhere, were discouraged or forbidden by the colonial government. When the Mazabuka people organized to tax themselves to build more schools at home, the government prevented them from doing so and required them to support only government approved schools. Schapera described how Tswana chiefs actually ordered men to go to work in the mines and send back money for schools. Another factor partly substituted for ethnic associations in Zambia: as in Tanzania, many peoples had clan and cross-cousin joking relationships, which they were able to extend to general inter-ethnic patterns of reciprocity and mutual aid in the urban situation (Elizabeth Colson, personal communication). The host-migrant distinction was irrelevant in Zambia and in the rest of southern Africa because the urban areas were white-dominated and no African ethnic group could achieve the status of host.

The strength or weakness of the ethnic factor in African urban life is influenced also by government policy, past and present, whether colonial or independent. Thus, it would appear that in Windhoek (Namibia) ethnic organization was definitely imposed upon the African population by the early German administration. Even in the absence of such imposition, ethnic organization in some form seems to have been an inevitable product of the early urban migrant-labor situation, and to have been so regarded by both its African participators and white colonial administrators (and black administrators also, in the case of Monrovia). It was thus treated as a matter of convenience in Dar es Salaam, the Copperbelt towns, Monrovia, Freetown, and many other places.

Anglo-Saxon colonialism regarded urban ethnic organization either neutrally as a convenience, or, in the case of settler countries, more positively as a proper element maintaining and perpetuating the inferior life of Africans in the city, helping them not to be confused or spoiled by new Western institutions. Epstein's analysis demonstrated the contradictions and ultimate failure of this attitude in the Copperbelt. Was there any comparable sequence of events in the Rand? If not, how is this to be explained? An explanation is especially needed as the above attitude appears to be strong in South Africa where white companies promote ethnic dance teams as a subtle attempt to emphasize to the white world the unchanging primitive tribal culture of the happy African in the white-ruled city.

By contrast, there was an intrinsic bias against any official recognition or countenancing of ethnic differences in French colonial theory, although in practice the exigencies of local situations led to numerous variations. It would appear that this contrast of the colonial era has been reversed naturally during the period of independence, in which it is the independent governments of English-speaking Africa which have shown by far the greatest sensitivity about organizations and activities based on ethnicity, often amounting to official prohibition. The paradox is, of course, that while the potential contribution of permitted ethnic organization to political separatism is justifiably feared, there is a great yearning to return to the indigenous sources of African culture, which are felt to have been disparaged during the colonial era, and to drink fresh draughts of inspiration from them.

A different aspect of the relation between urban and rural living, which is becoming increasingly important in the independent countries of tropical Africa, is the growth of middle-class families. They live in their own houses on their own land, within reach of a town by bicycle, motor cycle, bus or car, and grow most of their own food as well as cash crops for extra income, while the husband (and, increasingly, the wife also) has a clerical or administrative job in town. This process began some decades ago in Kampala (where it has been studied by Gugler) and many other places where the situation was similarly favorable. But it could not develop in the white settler countries of southern Africa where the system of land distribution prohibited it because Africans could not usually acquire their own residential and agricultural land within easy reach of the white dominated urban areas.

The African elites of the independent countries are combining urban and rural resources in the opposite way, by living in the city where both husband and wife may have professional jobs, but acquiring farms and ranches in the countryside, even at some distance, as they can afford to maintain easy contact by car. In a formal sense this recalls the ancient practice of the urban Yoruba, who controlled their agricultural land from residences in the city.

In this case too, ethnicity remains very important, for very few people outside the local ethnic groups are prepared to risk investment in agricultural land, even if they have permanent jobs in the nearby city. However, in Kampala during the last two or three years, members of the political, administrative, professional, and business elite of all ethnic groups (though Ganda are still in the majority), attracted by the prospect of rental income, have begun very actively to buy small building plots within the urban area and to construct buildings ranging from mud-and-wattle to permanent houses and even office blocks. In fact, at the moment, the rate of return on mud-and-wattle lodging houses (capitalized at about two years' purchase) is higher than on any other form of local investment. The prevailing political climate is also an important factor because with the more frequent changes of regime, the top elite have come to feel extremely insecure in their careers, and this has acted as a very powerful stimulus to energetic entrepreneurship on the part of both men and women. The number of independent professional and business women is growing, and at the same time many wives of men in the ruling elite feel that their husbands' future careers and income are uncertain, so they wisely exploit their current income and their privileged access to loans, permits, and controlled property to make profitable investments in businesses and real estate as an insurance for the future.

What I have tried to show is that in this field of urban and ethnic social relationships and organization, the apparent diversity of different African cities and countries can be shown to vary according to quite intelligible, orderly, and consistent principles if the relevant variables are carefully sorted out. Thus, it is demonstrated that apparently unlike situations arise mainly from the same sets of factors differently combined and operating with different strength. This could be demonstrated even more convincingly, by detailed comparative studies of neighboring situations and countries of different cities and towns within the same country, studies that would illustrate how contrasting situations arise predictably from variations in the component factor combinations.

REFERENCES

BRANDEL-SYRIER, MIA
    1971   *Reeftown elite: a study of social mobility in a modern African community on the Reef.* London: Routledge and Kegan Paul.

BANTON, MICHAEL
    1957   *West African city: a study of tribal life in Freetown.* International African Institute for Oxford University Press.

EPSTEIN, A. L.
    1958   *Politics in an urban African community.* Manchester University Press.

FRAENKEL, MERRAN
    1964   *Tribe and class in Monrovia.* International African Institute for Oxford University Press.

MAYER, PHILIP
    1961   "Townsmen or tribesmen: conservatism and the process of urbanization," in *A South African city.* Cape Town: Oxford University Press.

PARKIN, DAVID
    1969   *Neighbours and nationals in an African city ward.* London: Routledge and Kegan Paul.

PONS, VALDO
1969   *Stanleyville: a study of an African urban community under Belgian administration.* International African Institute for Oxford University Press.

SOUTHALL, AIDAN
1970   The illusion of tribe. *Journal of Asian and African Studies* 5:1–2, 28–50.
f.c.a   "National integration in Uganda," in *National integration in Africa.* Edited by K. Bentsi-Enchill and D. R. Smock.
f.c.b   "From segmentary lineage to ethnic association — Luo, Luyia and others," in *Essays in honor of Lucy Mair.* Edited by Maxwell Owusu. Evanston: Northwestern University Press.

WILSON, MONICA, ARCHIE MAFEJE
1963   *Langa: a study of social groups in an African township.* Cape Town: Oxford University Press.

Comments

HANS C. BUECHLER

The papers in this conference have demonstrated anew that although the anthropological interest in the study of migration is rather recent, it is advanced enough to enable us to gain novel perspectives on such questions as the nature of "culture" and of ethnicity which go beyond the mere corroboration or even the simple reaction to popular stereotypes.

Migration provides a research opportunity somewhat akin to a laboratory experiment: changes in a migrant population can be measured against the population where the migrants originated. However, we must realize the danger of taking the latter group as a constant, for the areas from which emigration takes place are transformed by the migratory process as well, and this not just in the sense that returned migrants may stimulate change but in a more fundamental sense that both migrants and those whom they leave behind must adapt to the exigencies of the migratory process.

The initial result of the analysis of migration processes has been the refutation of the common notion that migration must necessarily alter the groups involved beyond recognition. Indeed, as Sutton has remarked in her discussion in another session in this conference, we may have become too dazzled by the mere fact of cultural and ethnic continuities that have persisted in spite of migration. We must not forget that perhaps the very reason why regularities in patterns of social interaction persist among migrants is their flexibility, or ability to adapt to new situations, in other words to INCORPORATE change. Judging from the papers in this session we may already be in the position to describe the nature of some of the ways in which these regularities operate in migratory situations.

Here I shall attempt to analyze the meanings of ethnic identification by contrasting it with its social interactional basis in each of the papers by Schreiber, González, Schildkrout, and Kemper, and relate our view to those expressed in Southall's synthetic paper.

First we must ascertain in each instance the situations of adaptation. It becomes clear from a comparison of the papers that the migrant is not necessarily adapting to a specific social entity, e.g. "the city" or "Swiss society," but to certain contingencies the migration situation imposes upon him. The southern Italians described by Schreiber are adapting to the problems posed by intermittent migration characterizing the *saisonnier* or seasonal migrant, and more specifically negative Swiss stereotypes regarding migrants of southern Italian origin. Gonzalez shows two divergent migration situations in the Dominican Republic: mixed internal and overseas migration by Serranos and mainly internal migration by lowland peasants. In addition, there are a wide range of situations Dominican migrants are exposed to even within a family. These differences may arise from differences in the degree of contact maintained with the place of origin as well as household size and sex of the migrant. The Mossi in Schildkrout's example adapted to an urban situation where they were thrown together with a number of related tribes. Finally the Tzintzuntzeños described by Kemper adapt to a situation in which on the one hand personalistic ties are crucial for achieving economic ends but where on the other geographical dispersal and lack of means of communication is the price exacted for even slight improvements in living conditions.

Having established the general conditions faced by the migrants let us now attempt to show how the process of adaptation to the respective migrant situations is facilitated by flexible preexisting patterns of interpersonal behavior and how these patterns are expressed symbolically through ethnic identification. The Italian migrants to Switzerland make use of certain linguistic continuities from their Slavic and Albanian past to reestablish links with migrants from these areas. This fact is symbolically expressed by stressing Albanian or Slavic rather than Italian or southern Italian identity. Two sharply diverging behavioral bases for migratory adaptation can be discerned in the Dominican Republic. In the case of the Sierran migrant successful migration is based on the ability to transfer a family's status in the wider society intact to the next generation. This transfer, which in migration situations takes the form of investment in education, preexists in the land inheritance patterns followed in the Sierra. In contrast, migrants from the Flatlands adjust to urban life by means of behavioral patterns (e.g. marital flexibility) developed under a slave-plantation system. On the symbolic level the Serranos express their identity by stressing the adherence to strict marital fidelity (important in the successful functioning of the land inheritance system in the Sierra), while the lowlanders profess only a negative identity in making constant excuses for their behavior. Unlike the Dominicans, the Mossi establish ties with ethnically related tribes based on the similarity of traditionally practiced trades. These ties are symbolically affirmed by extending kin terms and joking behavior to non-kin contexts. Finally the Tzintzuntzeños in Mexico City adjust to the new situation by utilizing specific narrow channels opened to them by kin who migrated before them and which vary from individual to individual. In other words they continue to some extent in a network segment previously established in their home community but become more selective in their choices of individuals they interact with. Furthermore they relate to only a very few close relatives on a continuous basis while using their other potential links in this network segment only initially or intermittently, building instead personalistic ties with "outsiders."[1] The ease with which the Tzintzuntzeños abrogate their old ties and enter new ones would seem to contradict our theory that new adaptations are based upon preexisting ones. And yet in some respects the creation of "outside" personalistic ties is not an entirely new element in the lives of migrants to Mexico City. The most direct continuity lies in the fact that patronage ties with outsiders are an important element in the lives of non-migrant Tzintzuntzeños too (cf. Foster 1967). But there are more covert continuities as well. Wilson's (1969) examples of Mexican factories show that integration is achieved in part through symmetrical and asymetrical personalistic relationships. In the former intra-generational kinship ties and *compadrazgo* ties seem to be directly equivalent; in the latter asymetrical personalistic ties are parallel to kin ties between individuals of different generations (e.g. an uncle who is a foreman and a nephew apprentice). Again it would seem that the creation of new ties is a flexible reinterpretation of preexisting principles of organization.

Let us now examine the relationship between ethnicity and its behavioral bases. It becomes immediately apparent that the nature of this relationship cannot be taken for granted but must be established empirically. In some of the cases under discussion, there is indeed a one-to-one correlation between behavior and symbolic expression. Thus the Dominican Serranos' identification entails the expression of ideals which are intimately related to the very essence of their society: the *sucesión*. The same is true for Schreibers' migrants to Switzerland; and yet in this case the correlation is already more complex. For in Italy, Albanian and Slavic identity

---

[1] Kemper does not discuss the degree to which Tzintzuntzeño migrants identify themselves conceptually and symbolically with their home community.

traditionally expressed isolation from other southern Italians. As a result of the new migration situation, this meaning has become intensified but in addition ethnic identification now also expresses the expansion of social contacts to include other Slavs and Albanians. Moreover there are different reasons for distinguishing oneself from southern Italians in Italy than in Switzerland. While in Italy it simply expresses the preponderance of social contacts within ethnic categories, in Switzerland it becomes, in addition, an attempt to avoid an ethnic identification with negative connotations. In the case of the lowland Dominicans the relationship between behavior and ideals is an inverse one, an inversion which may be considered to be forced upon these Dominicans by a dominant racist society. Finally in the Ghanan example ethnic identification has entirely new functions. In this case joking relationships become a means of expressing more complex and varied social relationships within formerly fragmented groups as well as the establishment of ties between culturally related groups which formerly had little contact.

In conclusion, if one analyzes identification, the behavioral regularities on which it is based, and the specific contexts to which it applies separately, the meanings of ethnicity become more apparent. Our analysis has borne some resemblance to that of Southall's in that we too have searched for regularities in social interaction which underly the overt forms of ethnic identification. However we doubt whether it is meaningful to correlate such manifestations of ethnic identification as voluntary associations DIRECTLY with types of situations. We would contend that we must first ascertain whether these manifestations are related to their social-interactional base in the same manner. As we have seen this relationship is complex and manifold indeed.

Furthermore it becomes clear that ethnic identity does not refer to the definition of bounded groups at a given point in time alone. Indeed rather than speaking of ethnic IDENTITY, a term which implies a discernible state, it seems more appropriate to speak of ethnic IDENTIFICATION, a process which entails the constant redefinition of social boundaries appropriate to given situations and the intensification of existing linkages, and often fulfills many additional functions such as escaping undesirable categorization and communicating the creation of entirely new social ties. Southall's contention that most tribal identities are of recent origin would lend support to this view. The study of migration thus enables us to redefine static concepts into dynamic processual ones, an essential step in the formulation of predictive models.

REFERENCES

FOSTER, G.
  1967 *Tzintzuntzan: Mexican peasants in a changing world.* Boston: Little, Brown.
WILSON, C.
  1969 "The social organization of the Mexican factory." Unpublished doctoral dissertation, Columbia University, New York.

Biographical Notes

JANET ABU-LUGHOD (1928–   ) is Professor of Sociology and Urban Affairs at Northwestern University where she directs the Comparative Urban Studies Program. She has worked, taught, and published in the fields of city planning, urban sociology, and demography both in the United States and the Middle East. In addition to numerous monographs, articles, and contributions to collections she has authored a book on American housing and written a social and ecological history of Cairo (*Cairo: 1001 years of the city victorious*). Her current research is on North African urbanism.

RICHARD N. ADAMS (1924–   ) was born in Ann Arbor, Michigan. He has been Professor of Anthropology at the University of Texas at Austin since 1962. Prior to that he held a similar post at Michigan State University. He has been an ethnologist with the Smithsonian Institution Institute of Social Anthropology and a scientist with the World Health Organization. He studied at the University of Michigan and Yale University, receiving his doctorate from the latter in 1951. His published works deal with contemporary Latin American society, especially Peru and Guatemala, and problems in the study of power in complex society.

HANS C. BUECHLER (1940–   ) was born in Switzerland and grew up in Bolivia. He studied at the University of Geneva (1962), at the Sorbonne, and at Columbia University (Ph. D. 1966) and has taught at the Université de Montréal (1966–1968) and at Syracuse University where he is presently an Associate Professor in the Department of Anthropology. His research interests include agrarian reform and rural-urban migration in the Andes and lately international migration in Europe. He is co-author of *Land reform and social revolution in Bolivia* (1969) and *The Bolivian Aymara* (1971) and author of *The masked media* (n.d.).

Ramiro G. Cardona is an architect, specializing in sociology and urban and regional planning (Facultad Latinoamericana de Ciencias Sociales and University of California at Berkeley). He has directed urban studies with particular emphasis on internal migration and squatter settlements. In 1971–1972 he directed the Office of Regional and Urban Planning of the National Planning Department of Colombia. For the academic year 1972–1973, he received the Parvin Fellowship from Princeton University, where he completed a book with Alan B. Simmons, *A general model of internal migration in Latin America*. At present, he is directing a research program on Spatial Distribution of the Population for the Corporación Centro Regional de Población, Bogotá, Colombia. He has published five books and directed two prize-winning films on urbanization. He is the co-author and editor of two books on spatial distribution of the population in Latin America and in Colombia, which will be published in the near future.

Brian M. Du Toit (1935–   ) was born in Bloemfontein, South Africa. He studied at the University of Pretoria where he received his B.A. (1957) and M.A. (1961) degrees, and at the University of Oregon where he received his Ph.D. (1963). He was a lecturer at the University of Stellenbosch and the University of Cape Town, and presently is Professor of Anthropology at the University of Florida. Recent publications include *People of the valley: life in an isolated Afrikaner community in South Africa* (1974), *Akuna: a Guinea village community* (1975), "Dagga: the history and ethnographic setting of *Cannabis sativa* in Southern Africa," in *Cannabis and culture*, edited by Vera Rubin (1975).

Nancie L. González (1929–   ) is Professor and Chairperson, Department of Anthropology, Boston University. She received her B.S. in Nutrition (1951) from the University of North Dakota and her M.A. (1955) and Ph.D. (1959) in Anthropology from the University of Michigan. She has taught at the University of California at Berkeley, the University of San Carlo in Guatemala, the University of New Mexico and the University of Iowa. She also worked for several years as Research Anthropologist at the Institute of Nutrition of Central America and Panama (INCAP). She is president of the Society for Applied Anthropology (1974–1975), a Fellow of the American Anthropological Association, and a member of the

Latin American Studies Association. Her publications include works on medical anthropology, films on anthropology, urbanization and migration Latin America, the Caribbean, Spanish-speaking peoples of the United States, and applied anthropology.

JOEL M. HALPERN (1929–   ) was born in New York City. He received his B.A. from the University of Michigan in 1950 and his Ph.D. in Anthropology from Columbia University in 1956. He has been Professor of Anthropology at the University of Massachusetts, Amherst since 1967. He has done field work in Yugoslavia, Laos, and the Arctic. His publications include *The changing village community* (1967), *A Serbian village in historical perspective* (with Barbara K. Halpern, 1972) as well as articles and monographs dealing with southeast Asia, urbanization, and peasant societies. His current research interests concern historical demography and social structure.

ROBERT V. KEMPER (1945–   ) is Assistant Professor of Anthropology at Southern Methodist University. Born in San Diego, California, he received his B.A. degrees (1966) in History and Social Sciences from the University of California (Riverside) and his M.A. (1969) and Ph.D. (1971) in Anthropology from the University of California, Berkeley. He held a Post-Doctoral Fellowship in Mexican-American Studies from the National Endowment for the Humanities during the academic year 1971–1972. His interests in urban studies, migration, culture change, and applied anthropology have been pursued through field research in Mexico, California, and Texas. He was the founding editor of *Urban Anthropology Newsletter* (1972–1974) and now is Associate Editor of *Urban Anthropology*. He co-edited (with George M. Foster) *Anthropologists in cities* (1974) and has published a number of other articles and reviews on urban studies.

ALFREDO E. LATTES (1935–   ) was born in Argentina. He studied at the University of Buenos Aires (1954–1960), Centro Latinoamericano de Demografía (Cert. 1965), University of Pennsylvania (M.A. in Demography, 1970). He has been Associated Research Director of Torcuato Di Tella Institute (1966–1973), Professor of Demography at the University of Buenos Aires (1972–1974) and is now Associate Research and Director of the Center for Population Studies (CENEP) associated with the Bariloche Foundation. His numerous publications include works on differents topics of demography, specifically internal migrations and interrelations between dynamics of population and other aspects of social and economic change. He is a member of the International Union for the Scientific Study of Population (IUSSP) and the Population Association of America (PAA).

T. G. McGee (1936–   ) was born in Cambridge, New Zealand. He received his B.A. from the University of New Zealand, and his M.A. and Ph.D. from the Victoria University of Wellington, New Zealand, He has taught at the Universities of Malaya, Hong Kong, and Wellington. He is at present Senior Fellow in the Department of Human Geography, Research School of Pacific Studies, Institute of Advanced Studies, Australian National University. He is the author of *The Southeast Asian city* (1967), *The urbanization process in the Third World* (1971), *Hawkers in Hong Kong* (1974), and numerous other publications. He is at present a member of the editorial boards of *Human Organization, Urban Anthropology,* and the *Journal of Urban History.*

Helen I. Safa (1930–   ) is Graduate Director and New Brunswick Chairperson of Anthropology at Rutgers University, the State University of New Jersey. She received her Ph.D. in Anthropology from Columbia University in 1962, on a study of a Puerto Rican shanty town which has been updated and published in 1974 as a monograph, *The urban poor of Puerto Rico: a study in development and inequality.* She has published numerous articles in the field of urbanization and development in professional anthropological and sociological journals and is presently on the Executive Council of the Latin American Studies Association. She is currently working on a comparative study of determinants of women's role and status in Latin American and American society.

Enid Schildkrout (1941–   ) is Assistant Curator of African Ethnology at the American Museum of Natural History in New York. After receiving a B.A. from Sarah Lawrence College (1963), she obtained her M.A. and Ph.D. (1969) degrees in social anthropology from the University of Cambridge. Before coming to the American Museum she taught at the University of Illinois (Assistant Professor 1970–1973, on leave 1972–1973), McGill University (Visiting Assistant Professor, 1972–1973), and Sir George Williams University (Visiting Assistant Professor, summer 1973). She has done three years of field work in Ghana and Upper Volta mainly on ethnicity, politics and kinship among urban immigrants.

Janet M. Schreiber (1941–   ) is Assistant Professor of Medical Anthropology at the University of Texas Health Science Center, Houston, School of Public Health. Her field research has focused on migration and health problems in Mexico and Italy. She received her Ph.D. in Anthropology from the University of California at Berkeley in 1973. She is currently developing a program to give health professionals applied field training.

Alan B. Simmons (1941–   ) was born in Ontario, Canada. He studied sociology at the University of British Columbia (B.A. 1963, M.A. 1965). He then continued his graduate work at Cornell University in the International Population Program where he recieved his Ph.D. (1970) with a dissertation on fertility and rural-urban migration in highlandColombia. He has taught at York University in Toronto and at the Centro Latino-americano de Demografía in Santiago, Chile (1972–1973). He is at present an Associate Director of the Population and Health Sciences Division of the International Development Research Centre of Canada.

Aidan Southall (1920–   ) is Professor of Anthropology at the University of Wisconsin, Madison. He was educated at Cambridge and London Universities and spent many years teaching and researching in East Africa, especially Uganda, where he held the positions of Professor of Sociology and Social Anthropology, Dean of the Faculty of Social Sciences, and Chairman of the East African Institute of Social Research at Makerere University, Kampala. He is author of numerous books and articles, including "Lineage formation among the Luo" (1952); "Alur society: a study in processes and types of domination" (1956); "Townsmen in the making: Kampala and its suburbs" (with P.C. Gutkind, 1957); "An operational theory of role" (1959); *Social change in modern Africa* (edited, 1961); "Population movements in East Africa" (1962); "The illusion of tribe" (1970); "Kinship, descent and residence in Madagascar" (1971); *Urban anthropology: cross-cultural studies of urbanization* (edited, 1973).

Scott Whiteford (1942–   ) studied at Beloit College, Stanford University, and the University of Texas. He has taught at the Universidad Católica de Salta in Argentina and Michigan State University, and 1975 became a Research Project Coordinator at the Centro de Investigaciones Superiores of the Instituto Nacional de Anthropología e Historia in Mexico. His special interests include urbanization and migration, social power, and economic anthropology.

Index of Names

Index of Subjects